Sikh Heritage
Ethos & Relics

Sikh Heritage
Ethos & Relics

*For Andrew and Bettina Ayre
With my best wishes
Roopinder Singh
23.4.2018*

Bhayee Sikandar Singh
Roopinder Singh

RUPA

Dedicated to

Sardar Kartar Singh Lotay
(of Kampala, Uganda, and Leicester, England)

First published in 2012 by
Rupa Publications India Pvt. Ltd.
7/16, Ansari Road, Daryaganj
New Delhi 110002

Sales centres:
Allahabad Bengaluru Chennai
Hyderabad Jaipur Kathmandu
Kolkata Mumbai

Copyright © Bhayee Sikandar Singh and Roopinder Singh 2012

All rights reserved.
No part of this publication may be reproduced, transmitted, or stored in a retrieval system, in any form or by any means, electronic, mechanical, photocopying, recording or otherwise, without the prior permission of the publisher.

ISBN: 978-81-291-1983-4

10 9 8 7 6 5 4 3 2 1

Bhayee Sikandar Singh and Roopinder Singh assert the moral right to be identified as the authors of this work.

Cover & Book Design by
Peali Dutta Gupta
pealiduttagupta@pealidezine.com

Printed in India by **Lustra Print Process Pvt. Ltd.**

This book is sold subject to the condition that it shall not, by way of trade or otherwise, be lent, resold, hired out, or otherwise circulated, without the publisher's prior consent, in any form of binding or cover other than that in which it is published.

A contemporary painting of Guru Hargobind preserved at village Bhai Rupa. Descendents of Bhai Rup Chand have a significant collection of Sikh relics.

Contents

Introduction: Perspectives on the Punjab's Most Meaningful Heirlooms
by Paul Michael Taylor VIII
Preface XII
Acknowledgements XVI

ETHOS
The Land and its People 02
Guru Nanak and His Teachings 16
The Gurus and the Spirit of Sikhi 28
Persecution Strengthens Character 62
Sikh Kingdoms: Evolution and Sovereignty 74

HERITAGE
Locating Relics *by Mohan Singh* 96
Bhai Rup Chand 100
Custodians at Bhai Rupa 108
Custodians at Bagrian 124
The Phulkian States 134
Custodians at Patiala 138
Custodians at Nabha 154
Custodians at Bilga 176
Custodians at Darauli 180
Custodians at Sursinghwala 184

Selected Bibliography 193
Appendix 194
Picture credits 196
Index 197

The Ten Gurus and Guru Gobind Singh's Four Sons (Gouache on paper, early nineteenth century.)
This painting from the Kapany Collection of Sikh Art was displayed for six months at the opening of the Smithsonian's exhibition *Sikhs: Legacy of the Punjab* (2004), and displayed a second time at the Fresno (California) venue of the exhibition (Fresno Art Museum).

Introduction
Perspectives on the Punjab's Most Meaningful Heirlooms

It is an honour for me, on behalf of the Smithsonian Institution's Sikh Heritage Project, to introduce this truly unique volume of new perspectives on the material and the intangible heritage of the Sikhs. This book's two authors have worked in a unique partnership that transcended their individual accomplishments. Bhayee Sikandar Singh is co-editor of the magazine *Nishaan*. His position within the cultural life of the Punjab gives him unprecedented access. His upbringing, training and interest give him a unique insight into the subject that he has tackled in this book.

Roopinder Singh is deputy editor of the 131-year-old daily newspaper, *The Tribune*, which is the largest circulated English newspaper in North India. A respected editor, scholar, journalist and an accomplished photographer, he is author of many books, including a critically-acclaimed volume on the founder of the Sikh religion, Guru Nanak Dev.

Together, they worked for five years and combined their different kinds of expertise to write with profound authority and eloquence. As a result of this successful teamwork the general reader—even those readers with little awareness of Sikh traditions—will surely feel the powerful appeal of being led along the very same paths trodden by the founding Gurus of Sikhism. The immediacy and presence of history is all around us as we read this book, particularly because history inheres within the Sikh 'relics' or heirloom heritage objects from throughout the Punjab and beyond, in ways that few, if any other, authors could more authentically describe.

As the authors note, many of the families who own the heirloom artefacts most directly associated with the earliest founders of the Sikh faith have made them available for publication here for the first time, for which historians and the public owe a debt of gratitude to these families, to the authors and to the many others who have helped bring this book to print.

Nishān (Khanda), Steel, contemporary.
The *Nishān*, popularly called the *khanda*, a prominent Sikh symbol, served as an iconic piece at the entrance to the Smithsonian's exhibition. The Smithsonian's annual Sikh Heritage Lectures led up to and complemented the exhibition.

Working together with the Sikh Heritage Foundation (of Weirton, West Virginia), the Smithsonian Institution, as America's national museum, was pleased to play an early role in encouraging the authors to bring together the great wealth of information that they have produced in the present book. Certainly, the topic and subject-matter of the objects described here had been a subject of interest and preliminary study within the Smithsonian's Sikh Heritage Project, founded in 2000 with the support of many donors, including those who later set up the (independent) Sikh Heritage Foundation.

In April 2003, at the third of the Smithsonian's annual Sikh Heritage Lectures (held that year in Livonia, Michigan), Dr Gurpreet K. Maini presented an informative and well-illustrated lecture on family heirloom collections of Sikh relics in the Bagrian family, to which Bhayee Sikandar Singh belongs. She called everyone's attention to their importance for art history and for understanding the broader cultural history of the region. Also participating that year from Chandigarh was the distinguished museum administrator and scholar Mohan Singh, who concurred with the importance of registering and publishing such private collections. Both these scholars were extremely helpful later when, in June 2006, the Smithsonian co-organised, with the Anandpur Sahib Foundation, in cooperation with the Indian National Trust for Art and Cultural Heritage (INTACH) and the Sikh Heritage Foundation, the international conference on 'New Technologies for Preservation, Research, Exhibition, and Publication'. Held primarily in Chandigarh, with site visits at Patiala and Anandpur Sahib, this conference was sponsored by the Indo-US Science and Technology Forum (IUSSTF) of Washington, DC, and New Delhi.

Bhayee Sikandar Singh was quite generous when I, later, (in May 2007) proposed to him that perhaps our project might be able to locate some scholars of material culture who could write a book about these previously unpublished relics within the important collection of his own family at Bagrian. After a pause he responded, 'I'd rather write it myself.' Subsequently, he got Roopinder Singh on board and they have indeed masterfully produced the present volume. Instead of confining the narrative to relics in the possession of the descendants of Bhai Rup Chand, both at Bhai Rupa and Bagrian, they have enlarged the scope of the book and included the important Phulkian families of Patiala and Nabha, whose Maharajas have significant collections (indeed the collections of the Maharaja of Patiala were among those which the Smithsonian conference participants in 2006 were allowed to visit and examine, for which we all remain extremely grateful), as

Entrance to the exhibition *Sikhs: Legacy of the Punjab,* in the Santa Barbara Museum of Natural History (Santa Barbara, California), where the exhibition opened in February 2009.

well as the families at Sursinghwala, Darauli, Bilga and other places. Roopinder Singh has taken most of the pictures of the relics.

The resulting book is a unique and very important document. It is detailed, beautifully illustrated, systematic, and intellectually rigorous—yet, not at all like a typical museum catalogue of a public or private collection. The 'systematic' nature of the book is not in the descriptions of the media that make up the objects, nor of their forms. It is, rather, in the thoroughgoing and systematic placement of each object within a historical sequence of actions by the earliest founders and developers of the Sikh tradition, as that can now expertly be deduced from the highly localised oral and written traditions of Sikh cultural studies. It is, therefore, most logical that the authors chose to begin this book on Sikh relics by summarising, in their own authoritative voice, the history and ethos of the Sikhs, with special emphasis on the ten Gurus, whose actions, teachings, and relations with individuals (and their descendants) most directly infuse the objects within family collections described in the latter part of the book.

Both the Sikh Heritage Foundation and the Smithsonian hope that this book will be the first of a series of books presenting new and previously unpublished material alongside authentic and well documented voices and interpretations of Sikh heritage. The costs towards the production of the book have generously been supported by the Sikh Heritage Foundation of Weirton, West Virginia, and especially by two of that city's households who made the book possible, Dr Amrik S. Chattha and Mrs Jaswinder Kaur Chattha, and Dr Charan Singh Nandra and Mrs Surinder Kaur Nandra. The assistance provided by Dr Gurpreet Maini, and the efforts of both this book's authors, have all been a purely unpaid work of great service to scholars and the public. Our profound thanks go out to all of them, and to all the 'Keepers of the Heritage' families who have shared their unique place in history through the pages of this book.

PAUL MICHAEL TAYLOR
Director, Asian Cultural History Program (and)
Curator of Asian, European, and Middle Eastern Ethnology,
Smithsonian Institution,
Washington, DC, USA

Another view of the exhibition *Sikhs: Legacy of the Punjab* at the Smithsonian in Washington, D.C. (2004). The label in the case called 'Sacred Book Becomes Last Guru', explains that a prop is used in the exhibition instead of the actual Guru Granth Sahib, stating that in this public museum environment we do not ask our visitors to cover their heads and behave as traditionally is proper in the presence of the actual sacred text. Millions of museum visitors have learned about Sikh traditions through this exhibition.

Preface

The Sikh religion is founded in reality. The Sikh Gurus were not mythological characters or flights of poetic imagination. They were real and walked this earth, living the life of ordinary people, fulfilling their social and familial responsibilities, even as they performed extraordinary deeds. The Gurus are exemplars for all Sikhs as their lives can, and should, be emulated.

Every time a Sikh prays, he invokes the memory of the Gurus, recounts their lives and cites them as his role models. There is a continuity of connect between the living Sikh and his heritage, extending all the way back through history to the days of the Gurus.

Some families are blessed because of their association with the Gurus, which is recalled through oral tradition and/or recorded in contemporary texts. The tangible manifestations of their heritage are the articles bestowed upon them by the Gurus, at times things the Gurus had personally used, which keep the ethos alive.

Heritage is both tangible and intangible. The Gurus' gifts are the tangible heritage and their directions and mandates are the intangible aspect. The real import of tangible elements of heritage comes alive when projected against the background of the intangible heritage, which, in a way, is the ethos of the people. Every relic, every article is a living symbol of ethos and reminder of a living heritage, which strengthens the community's will and cause.

The gifts of the Gurus, the artefacts associated with their lives and their belongings are sacred for the 'Keepers of Heritage', the families blessed by the Gurus. The reverence with which they keep them vouch for their authenticity.

These gifts have to be nourished, cherished, and generations have to be consecrated to uphold them. The Keepers have an allegiance to the way of the life taught by the Gurus and have helped keep the Sikh *maryada* (practices) pristine over centuries of hardship and glory. What they have in their possession, in remote areas or in Gurdwaras associated with Sikh history, was for a long time not exposed to exploitation or commercialisation.

It is our bounden duty to preserve these articles of heritage. We must help these custodians to preserve these artefacts. In modern-day conflicts, collections in museums and big cities become vulnerable, as was the case in Iraq and, nearer home, in the destruction of the Sikh Reference Library in Amritsar and the Gurus' relics kept at the Akal Takht. Heritage items preserved in small villages or personal collections have the advantage of being spread out widely.

In our selection of the collections, we have chosen a few families that are interlinked with Sikh history and religion and whose mutual associations date back to the Guru period.

As we shall see, one man's love and devotion (*sidak*) earned him the status of the Guru's brother, Bhai. But that man's consecrated life and utter faith bestowed honour unparalleled on generations to come and inspired his progeny to live up to the Guru's trust and serve the community for generations.

Bhai Rup Chand's family has been the central axis round which Sikhi grew in the Malwa area, and was among the first to assist the tenth Guru to rebuild the community after the exodus from Anandpur in 1705-6. The Phulkian families were the pillars of the community in this area. Thus, these families form the central scene of the presentation.

Of late, numerous items have emerged, with the owners claiming historical/ religious import. One has to be wary about such claims. The questions we posed to ourselves were: was there a historical relationship of the possessor with the Guru, or record of the Guru visiting the place on an occasion during which the articles could have been bestowed? Do the present custodians have continuity of possession? Besides other resources, we found Bhai Kahn Singh Nabha's *Gurshabad Ratnakar Mahankosh,* an encyclopaedia of Sikh religion, first published in 1930, as the most authentic source, and as such we have relied heavily on its affirmations.

Time past and time present are both present in time future. Heritage artefacts, preserved and faithfully documented history, have helped rebuild a people even after thousands of years. Every relic, every article is a live symbol of the ethos and a reminder of the living heritage, which strengthens the community's will and cause. Preservation of our past and conservation of today will help our future.

A journey into the Sikh ethos, history, theology and lore is imperative for one to understand the significance of the relics of Sikh heritage cherished and held sacred by those upon whom they were bestowed. We undertook this exploration and, having taken a path less travelled, we now feel we must share the wonders we discovered on this expedition with you, dear reader.

Sikh Gurus, Mughal Empire, and the World

	GURUS, LIFE DATES, GURU PERIOD	SIKH HISTORY: IMPORTANT EVENTS	RULERS: SULTANATE AND MUGHAL (start of reign)	CONTEMPORARY WORLD EVENTS
1	**Guru Nanak** 1469-1539 1469-1539	**1507**: Guru Nanak, the founder of Sikhism, proclaims the unity of God and universality of faith	**1450**: Bahlol Lodhi **1489**: Sikander Shah **1517**: Ibrahim Lodhi **1526**: Babur **1530**: Humayun	**1492**: Columbus lands in the Americas **1498**: Vasco da Gama reaches India **1503**: Leonardo da Vinci paints *Mona Lisa* **1516**: Sir Thomas More's *Utopia*
2	**Guru Angad Dev** 1504-1552 1539-1552	Gurmukhi script is developed	**1540**: Sher Shah Suri	**1517**: Martin Luther's 95 *Theses*, catalyst for Protestant Reforms **1524**: First German Protestant hymn book
3	**Guru Amar Das** 1479-1574 1552-1574	**1565**: Akbar visits Guru Amar Das	**1555**: Humayun **1556**: Akbar	**1534**: Henry VIII recognised as head of the Church of England **1543**: First statement of heliocentric system by Nicolaus Copernicus
4	**Guru Ram Dass** 1534-1581 1574-1581	**1577**: Ramdaspur, later Amritsar, founded on land given by Akbar		**1558**: Elizabeth I crowned Queen of England **1572**: St. Bartholomew's Day massacre of French Protestants (Huguenots) in Paris
5	**Guru Arjan Dev** 1563-1606 1581-1606	**1588**: Mian Mir lays the foundation stone of Harmandar Sahib **1598**: Akbar visits Guru Arjan Dev **1604**: Adi Granth installed		**1588**: Defeat of the Spanish Armada by England **1597**: Japan banishes Christian missionaries **1600**: East India Company incorporated **1602**: Galileo finds laws of gravitation
6	**Guru Hargobind** 1595-1644 1606-1644	**1612**: Guru Hargobind imprisoned in Gwalior Fort **1621**: The Guru establishes Akal Takht, asserts secular and spiritual authority **1627**: Kiratpur founded by the Guru	**1605**: Jahangir	**1611**: King James' version of the Bible **1623**: *First Folio* of William Shakespeare's 36 plays **1637**: Rene Descartes' *Discourse on Method*. **1644**: Ming dynasty ends, Manchu begins in China
7	**Guru Har Rai** 1630-1661 1644-1661	**1658**: Mughal prince Dara Shikoh visits Guru Har Rai	**1628**: Shah Jahan	**1649**: Charles I beheaded **1651**: *Leviathan* by Thomas Hobbes **1653**: Oliver Cromwell made Lord Protector
8	**Guru Harkrishan** 1656-1664 1661-1664	**1664**: Guru Harkrishan travels to Delhi to meet Aurangzeb	**1658**: Aurangzeb	**1661**: Louis XIV assumes absolute power in France **1664**: English acquire New York from the Dutch
9	**Guru Tegh Bahadur** 1621-1675 1665-1675	**1666**: Guru Tegh Bahadur founds the city of Anandpur **1675**: Martyrdom of Guru Tegh Bahadur		**1666**: Isaac Newton develops theory of gravitation **1670**: Hudson's Bay Company is chartered
10	**Guru Gobind Singh** 1666-1708 1675-1708	**1699**: Formation of the Khalsa **1705**: Guru Gobind Singh's sons martyred; two in battle, two bricked alive	**1707**: Bahadur Shah	**1682**: Peter I becomes Czar of Russia **1692**: Salem witchcraft trials **1704**: English defeat French at Blenheim

Acknowledgements

We undertook the task of compiling *Sikh Heritage: Ethos and Relics* five years ago. The expertise, advice, help, generosity and patience of many people came to our rescue as we undertook a journey that encompassed much more and took more time than originally envisaged.

Dr Paul Taylor, Director of the Asian Cultural History Program at the Smithsonian Institution in Washington, DC was the primary motivator of the project. The Sikh Heritage Foundation, Weirton, WV, USA, particularly Dr Amrik S. Chattha and Mrs Jaswinder Kaur Chattha; and Dr Charan Singh Nandra and Mrs Surinder Kaur Nandra, were most forthcoming, and they extended all the necessary infrastructure and support. Thus the project assumed a concrete shape. This charitable foundation undertakes projects that showcase Sikh heritage in the USA. We gratefully acknowledge the help of the foundation and its members (whose names are given in the Appendix). Without them, this book would not have been in your hands.

The Keepers of Heritage, the families that have reverentially preserved the relics given to them by the Gurus, deserve our gratitude for sharing with us what they had kept largely private for long. We are thankful to Maharaja Amarinder Singh of Patiala; Maharaja Hanuwant Singh of Nabha; Bhai Gurchet Singh and Bhai Buta Singh of Bhai Rupa; Bhai Juhjar Singh of Bagrian; and Baba Daya Singh of Sursinghwala.

Prof B. N. Goswamy, eminent art historian and Professor Emeritus, Panjab University, Chandigarh, gave both direction and guidance, which was invaluable.

Dr Gurpreet Kaur Maini played a pivotal role in anchoring the project.

Mr Mohan Singh, a former curator of museums in Punjab, shared his expertise and knowledge about the relics connected with Sikh Gurus from different parts of Punjab and elsewhere.

Mrs Inderjit Kaur, former Vice-Chancellor, Punjabi University, Patiala and former Chairman, Staff Selection Commission, New Delhi, guided this endeavour. Often, she leaned on the scholarship of her husband, the late Giani Gurdit Singh, a renowned scholar and Roopinder Singh's father.

N.P.S. Randhawa, the then Director, Government Museum and Art Gallery, Chandigarh, India, allowed us to use some images of paintings in the museum's collection. Davinder Pal Singh, of the Punjab Digital Library, also gave us some images, as did a number of generous individuals who have been acknowledged in picture credits.

Paramjit and Jaspreet provided the vital spousal support without which we could not have been successful in this endeavour. Family members play a tremendous role in projects like this and we would especially like to thank Achint Kaur, Mandhir Singh, Sunint Kaur, Amarindar Singh and Jansher Singh.

We would also like to express our gratitude to the following:

Amrik Singh (Dr), Angad Bir Singh, Anurag Singh (Prof), Anne Murphy (Dr), Baljit Singh, Balwinder Singh (Prof), Dharam Singh (Dr), Gurinder Singh Mann (Prof), the late Harnam Singh Shaan (Dr), Herman de Beer, Jaswant Singh Neki (Dr), Kirpal Singh (Dr), Kuldip Dhiman (Dr), Malkiat Singh, Manjit Singh (Prof) Montreal, Pritam Singh Kohli, Puneetinder Kaur Sidhu, Pushpinder Singh Chopra, Rajpal Singh (Prof), Ranjodh Singh, and Surinder Singh (Dr).

Ethos

A close-up showing India as a part of the 'Empire of the Grand Mogol' from a map dated 1674, which has the following legend:

'L'Asie, Distinguee en ses Principales Parties, scavoir La Turquie en Asie, l'Arabie, la Perse, l'Inde, la Chine, la Tartarie, les Isles du Iapon, des Philippines, des Moluques, de la Sonde, de Ceylan, et des Maldives

L'Asie divisee en ses Principales Regions et ou se peuvellt voirl'estendue des Empires, Monarchies, Royaumes, et Estats qui partagent presentement l'Asie.'

THE LAND AND ITS People

It was a time of a clash of civilisations, and an intermingling of cultures. It was a period when there was grave darkness of religious intolerance, but it was also when sparks of new faiths and new forms of worship were seen. And, it was a time which had roots in its past and finds a reflection in our present.

Guru Nanak Dev (1469-1539), the founder of the Sikh religion, was born in a region that was, quite literally, a battleground. Geographically, it was on the route used by invaders coming into India, and ideologically, this was where Islam and Hinduism clashed.

The great religions of India stretched back to a hoary, pre-Vedic past of thousands of years ago. While over time, there were also other faiths like Buddhism and Jainism that took root and grew, yet culturally, everyone was essentially a Hindu.

The invaders of Guru Nanak's time professed Islam, a younger faith. On the surface, the division was straightforward; the Muslims were strict monotheists whereas the Hindus were polytheists. The Muslims perceived all fellow Muslims as equals, while Hindu society was dominated by the caste system, wherein a person's caste determined the adherent's status and hierarchy.

Within Islam, too, there was the Shia-Sunni division, with the latter dominating as the ruling class. Among the Hindus, there were many more streams like Vaishnavites, Shaivites, Nath Yogis, et al., and also culturally related but independent faiths like Buddhism and Jainism. What might have seemed monochromic from a distance actually had many hues and distinctions.

In these two dominant denominations—Hinduism and Islam—religious life had become overly concerned with external symbols and rituals. Outward observance was established as an end in itself. Religion had been reduced to overt displays by the followers, and its essence was lost. Guru Nanak refers to this environment, in his writings, as the moonless night (*amavas*) of falsehood; where the moon (light) of

Guru Nanak (1469-1539): the founder of Sikhism, as envisioned by an unknown artist a century ago. No contemporary representation of him is in existence.

truth was nowhere to be seen.[1]

Historical background

Invasions from India's northwest had been a regular feature during the time of Guru Nanak, and for centuries before his advent. Mahmud of Ghazni alone had invaded seventeen times between the years 1000 and 1025.

By the year 1469, India had seen rulers of various Muslim races such as Turks, Afghans, Mongols, Arabs and Persians. Muslim invasions of India had started as early as 711-13, when the Caliphates arrived from Damascus and conquered Sindh, presently in Pakistan.

Mohammad Ghauri occupied Lahore in 1186-87 and extended the borders of his kingdom all the way to Delhi. He died in 1206. After him, Qutb-ud-din Aybak took control of Ghauri's Indian possessions and founded the empire called the Sultanate of Delhi, which constituted the various Muslim dynasties that ruled India from 1210 to 1526. Along with the invaders came the Sufi saints, who were to have a great impact on the conquered people.

The Mongols sacked Lahore in 1241, and continued to fight the Sultans of Delhi for control of Punjab through most of the thirteenth century. The Khilji[2] dynasty replaced the Mamluks[3] in 1290, and the Tughlaqs succeeded the Khiljis in 1320.

Timur bin Taraghay Barlas, commonly known as Timur-e-lang[4], was a Central Asian ruler from Samarkand. He ransacked Delhi in 1398-1399 and reduced the Sultanate to a small kingdom just around Delhi. After this, two Afghan dynasties took control of the Sultanate after the Tughlaqs; the Sayyids, from 1414 to 1451, and the Lodhis, from 1451 to 1526.

It was the Lodhi dynasty, established by the Pashtun Ghilzai tribes of Afghanistan, which ruled over the Delhi Sultanate during Guru Nanak's lifetime.

Guru Nanak was a young man when Sikandar Lodhi ascended to the throne. He ruled from 1489 to 1517. During the reign of the

Guru Nanak was in Saidpur when Babur invaded the town and his army ravaged it. The incident forms the backdrop to the compositions of Guru Nanak, popularly called *Babur Bani*, in which the brutality of the invading troops is severely chastised. Along with other survivors, Guru Nanak and his companion, Mardana, the *rabab* player, were imprisoned in Babur's prison. Shown here is a detail from a late nineteenth-century painting, in the possession of the Maharaja of Nabha.

---

1 Sri Guru Granth Sahib (SGGS) p.145: The Dark Age of Kali Yuga is the knife, and the kings are butchers; righteousness has winged away. In this dark night of falsehood, the moon of Truth is not visible anywhere.
2 This dynasty was originally Turkic, though the Khilji tribe had long been settled in modern Afghanistan.
3 Qutb-ud-din Aybak proclaimed himself Sultan of Delhi in 1206. This Mamluk dynasty lasted until 1290.
4 The name translates as Timur the Lame, a reference to his becoming lame following an injury to his leg during a battle.

Babur leading his army in the Battle of Panipat, after which he established his rule in Delhi. His invasion proved to be a scourge for the people of Punjab.

Babur with Guru Nanak. On hearing that the grinding stones were rotating to the divine singing of Guru Nanak, Babur sought his audience and perceived the Holy Spirit in the Guru at Saidpur, says the *Janamsakhi* tradition. The painting given here is from an early eighteenth-century illustrated *Janamsakhi* in Gurmukhi script.

Lodhis, religious intolerance was rampant. In *Tarikh-i-Daudi*[5], it is mentioned: 'Sikandar Lodhi was so zealous a Mussalman that he utterly destroyed many diverse places of worship of the infidels and left not a vestige of them.' Many temples were destroyed and mosques were built in their place. This tradition of tyrannical orthodoxy survived till the days of Ibrahim Lodhi, who occupied the throne in 1517. Less than a decade later, Ibrahim Lodhi was defeated by Babur in 1526 and he died fighting in the battle of Panipat.

Thus began the era of the Mughals in India. Zahir-ud-din Mohammad Babur, a Chagatai-Turkic ruler, popularly remembered by history as Babur the Tiger, ruled over India from 1526 to 1530 and laid the foundation of an empire that lasted for over two centuries. Babur came from a line of great conquerors—his mother had descended from Genghis Khan while his father was a descendent of Timur-e-lang.

Babur's invasion proved to be a scourge for the people of Punjab. His memoirs recorded: 'Advanced to Sialkot, the inhabitants of which submitted and saved their possessions. But the inhabitants of Saidpur, who resisted, were put to the sword, their wives and children taken into captivity and all their property plundered.' He collected 'masses of gold and silver' and captured 'unnumbered and endless workers of every kind'. Guru Nanak was witness to the ravage of Saidpur, which he recounts in his writings that now form part of the Sikh scripture, Sri Guru Granth Sahib.[6]

The State policy was rooted in a theocratic approach. Civil law was subordinated to the *sharia* (Islamic religious law) and was, in fact, merged with the latter. Conversion to Islam was encouraged and incentives were provided for such converts. Those who resisted were condemned as *kafirs*[7] (non-believers). All the infidels living in an

---

5 *Tarikh-i-Daudi* gives the history of the Afghan rulers, from Bahlol Lodi of Delhi to Daud Karrani, the last Afghan Sultan of Bengal.
6 SGGS pp. 722, 723: Bringing the marriage party of sin, Babur has invaded from Kabul, demanding our land as his wedding gift, O Lalo! Modesty and righteousness both have vanished, and falsehood struts around like a leader, O Lalo! Songs of death are sung, says Nanak, and blood is applied instead of saffron, O Lalo! Nanak sings the Glorious Praises of the Lord and Master in the city of corpses, and voices this account.
7 A *kafir* is a person who does not recognise God (Allah) or the prophethood of Muhammad, in other words, any non-Muslim.

Islamic state were required to pay a special protection tax called the *jaziya*[8], which signified the acceptance of the superiority of Islam.

Kafirs did not have the rights of even second-class citizens. The duty of all Muslim rulers of the time was based on the *Din Panahi*[9] propounded by the Muslim religious leader Nur-ud-din Mubarak Ghaznavi in the court of Shams-ud-din Iltutmish (the third Sultan of Delhi, who ruled from 1211 to 1236). The code prescribed, among other things, the following duty for the Sultan: 'The King should protect the religion of Islam with sincere faith. But if total uprooting of idolatry is not possible, owing to the firm roots of *kufr*[10] and the large number of *kafirs*, the king should at least strive to insult, disgrace, dishonour and defame the Hindus who are the worst enemies of Allah and the Prophet.' Rule of law was replaced by the rule of might. Hindus, no matter how exalted or lowly their status, did not even have the right to life.

Scholars now tend to say that the pre-existent Arabo-Persian traditions were changed when it became apparent that 'Islamic rulers could not command a vast country without accepting certain cultural limitations to the exercise of their power'[11].

The invaders took over the administrative positions and used the indigenous people to engage in sectors such as agriculture, commerce, industry and scavenging.

Bloodshed followed invasions. Shahab-ud-din, King of Ghazni, the virtual founder of the Muslim Empire in India (1170-1206), put Prithvi Raj, King of Ajmer and Delhi, to death in cold blood. Thousands of inhabitants of Ajmer were massacred by his soldiers. After his victory over the King of Benaras, the slaughter of Hindus and the carnage carried on until, as it has been said, 'the earth grew weary of the monotony'.

When Qutb-ud-din Aybak (1194-1210) conquered Meerut, he demolished all the temples of the city and erected mosques on their sites, massacring over one hundred thousand inhabitants and enslaving about fifty thousand more. Timur invaded India in 1398 with the belief that a war on the infidels gave him 'some claim to reward in the life to come'.

Guru Nanak travelled widely and interacted with adherents and leaders of various faiths. In this folio from the early eighteenth-century *Janamsakhi*, he is depicted in dialogue with ascetics, the reclusive *yogis*, at Sumer Parbat, now called Mount Kailash.

---

8 Head or poll tax that early Islamic rulers demanded from their non-Muslim subjects.
9 Literally, the doctrine of protection of religion.
10 Literally, disbelief.
11 Muzaffar Alam, *The Languages of Political Islam: India 1200-1800*.

Guru Nanak at the *namaz* at the mosque in his village. The folio from the eighteenth-century *Janamsakhi* depicts an episode from his early life. Guru Nanak is shown standing in the picture while others are bowing. When asked why he did not bow during the prayers like the others, he told the *qazi* that while his mouth was uttering the prayer, his mind was busy trading horses! Thus, the Guru exposed the hypocrisy of the priestly order by pointing out that the prayer should be from the heart.

The Lodhi regime fell after the battle of Panipat on 21 April 1526. Punjab had already suffered five centuries of uninterrupted Muslim rule, which had crushed the backbone of the common people. Frustrated and demoralised, they were unable to defend their fundamental rights. As a consequence thereof, people generally had become selfish, narrow-minded and cynical. Centuries of persecution had killed those moral qualities which sustain a people in adversity and open the road to regeneration.

The advent of Guru Nanak was a signal for a new awakening. The Guru, assigned the role of a Diviner of Truth, when asked by a companion why the people were suffering, replied: 'It is ordained by the Creator that before coming to a fall one is deprived of his virtue.' Guru Nanak's mission was to bring back to the fore Truth and Virtue as an essential prelude to the beginning of a new era for the Indian society.

The regeneration of a nation required a regeneration of the society, which, in turn, required that every person be reconstituted from within. This transmutation was undertaken by Guru Nanak and pursued by his successors. The result was a regenerated nation which emerged as the Khalsa in 1699, two hundred and thirty years later.

Socio-religious environment

The environment from which the Sikh faith emerged and evolved was marked by socio-religious decadence on the one hand, and interplay of movements of the Bhaktas, the Siddhas and the Sufis on the other. Guru Nanak fully perceived the prevailing plurality and diversity of religious traditions in India. Though seemingly influenced by the mystical movements of the Bhaktas and the Sufis, Guru Nanak imparted a unique rationalism and coherence to the followers of Sikhism and as such, his teachings provided a distinct religious individuality and social relevance.

The Sikh Gurus were based in North India, in the region of Punjab, literally meaning 'the land of five rivers'. Here, for a period of over three-and-a-half centuries, the ruling authorities and the social elite were

Muslims. The differences between the socio-religious traditions of Islam and Hinduism were deep and many. The religious-cultural forces of Islam represented the antithesis of Hinduism. Besides being the religion of the rulers, Islam itself was too strong and definite a religion to be submerged and absorbed by the Hindu faith, both socially and theologically.

From the eleventh century onwards, Punjab came face-to-face with this new religious force backed by military might. Both geographically and geopolitically, Punjab experienced an intense influence of Islam, and Muslim domination— military, political, religious and social.

The historical setting of Punjab in which Sikhism was born, and which moulded the nature of its evolution, was determined by the operation of the distinct religious traditions and cultural patterns of Hinduism and Islam. In the domain of religion, considerable interaction had taken place between Hinduism and Islam, especially within the two mystical movements known as Bhakti[12] and Sufism[13]. These two socio-religious movements emerged in India during the medieval period. The former largely had Hindu adherents and the latter, Muslim. Both the movements sought to do away with the orthodoxy and formal ritualistic aspects of religion. Since these traditions encompassed a definite element of protest against all forms of dogmatic rigidity, the clergy of the formal religions, that is, the Brahmins and the *mullahs*, inevitably recognised these movements as an inherent threat to their hegemony.

The Siddha tradition, which appeared

Sufi saints transcend time and space in this Guler painting, which brings them on the same page. Seen in the illustration are Khawaja Muin-ud-Din Chisti, Khawaja Qutab-ud-din, Baba Farid, Hazrat Dastgir, Abn Ali Qalandar and Khawaja Nizamuddin Aulia.

---

12 The word *bhakti* is derived from *bhakta,* meaning, to serve, honour, revere, love and adore. In the religious idiom, it is attachment or fervent devotion to God, and is defined as 'that particular affection which is generated by the knowledge of the attributes of the Adorable One'. Prof Harbans Singh, *Heritage of the Sikhs.*

13 Generally understood to be the inner, mystical dimension of Islam. A practitioner of this tradition is known as Sufi.

THE LAND AND ITS PEOPLE   09

Madho Lal Hussain was a Sufi saint who is believed to have lived from 1538-1599. Legend says that Shah Hussain incorporated the name of his spiritually accomplished Brahmin friend, Madho Lal, and thereafter called himself Madho Lal Hussain. This reflected a fusion that transcended the differences between the two dominant cultures in Punjab.

to have later evolved in south India[14], was by then essentially a movement confined to the north with a distinct mystic tradition of its own, though it cannot be ruled out that it had an all-India basis and framework. Guru Nanak's teachings reflect a greater awareness of its existence and influence than of any other sect in Punjab.

From the eleventh century onwards, Hatha Yoga[15] also became a movement of considerable importance, and by the fifteenth century, it had reached its zenith in Punjab and, with a well-knit organisation, emerged as a powerful sect.

While the Siddhas were anti-Brahminical and anti-establishment, Yoga represented a reaction against metaphysical speculation and the excess of fossilised ritualism. It challenged the very foundation of medieval Hinduism—the authority of the *shastras* (scriptures). The validity of rituals and the basis of the caste system were often questioned by the Siddhas.

The Naths, another sect of *yogis*, viewed the human body with cynical contempt and regretted that the soul had been housed in this repulsive physical structure. They laid great stress on controlling the nerve centre of the mind and body and thereby sought to achieve a state of 'everlasting bliss'. According to the Siddhas, the state of redemption—*jivan mukta*, was acquired by leading a life of seclusion. They, thus, propagated detachment from society. In the process, they cut themselves off from all social conformity, and also insisted upon the necessity of developing a detachment from 'desires for sensations'. This was made a pre-requisite for moral improvement, and a total withdrawal from society was emphasised. They even opposed any association with women, who were considered to be mortal enemies of a *yogi*, and as such, worthy of condemnation.

The yogic doctrine of renunciation, as it was practised then, had social ramifications. Instead of the *yogis* being perceived as exalted spiritual souls guiding society, they were seen as mere mendicants. In an encounter with *yogis*, Guru Nanak chastised them for their lack of

---

14 It is still practised in the southern state of Tamil Nadu.
15 There are six orthodox schools of thought in Indian philosophy: Sankhya, a dualist theoretical exposition of mind and matter; Yoga, which emphasises meditation; Nyaya or logic; Vaisheshika, an empiricist school; Mimamsa, an anti-ascetic and anti-mysticism school of orthopraxy; and Vedanta, opposing Vedic ritualism in favour of mysticism.

social responsibility. He exposed their hypocrisy. Furthermore, Hinduism in Punjab, as in other parts of the country, was characterised by various forms of religious beliefs and practices. It was not a homogeneous religion as such, but an amalgamation of different religions, cults and schools of thoughts, which included both Vedic and non-Vedic elements.

In those days, rituals and pilgrimages controlled the life of the common man, and the merits of these were recognised by practically all Hindu sects. In his compositions, Guru Nanak alludes to the sixty-eight places of pilgrimage for the Hindus and exposes the vacuousness of expecting spiritual gains by merely visiting them. He held that sacrifices, burnt offerings, charity given to acquire merit, austerities, even ritual worship at places of pilgrimage, are all worthless, since despite all this, human beings continue to endure sufferings.

Religion had become more of a commercial transaction in which lower castes were exploited by the minority upper caste, who, from tradition, acquired certain privileges and added religious sanctions to them. The learned, the *pandits*, remained occupied more with intellectual wrangling than with spreading the religious spirit among the people.

Jainism[16], too, had an impact on the people of Punjab during Guru Nanak's time. However, most of the followers of this religion seem to have been confined to the trading communities. The exemplary missionary role of Jain monks played a significant role in the faith's hold over the people.

Buddhism had all but been assimilated into Hinduism by the time of Guru Nanak, and in actual practice, it came to be regarded as a sect of Hinduism. Muslim conquests, too, had delivered serious blows to Buddhist centres in Punjab.

Notwithstanding the existence of various non-Islamic cults and sects, Islam became the dominant religion due to the establishment of Muslim rule. Its key postulates were that there is one God who is the

Guru Nanak at the house of Bhai Lalo, a poor carpenter. The Guru chose to share this man's bread, which had been earned as a result of hard work, while declining to join in a feast hosted by Malik Bhago, a local chief. Bhai Lalo's name is mentioned in the Guru's compositions.

---

16 An ancient religion that prescribes a path of non-violence for all living beings in this world. Its philosophy and practice rely mainly on self-contained effort in making the soul progress on the spiritual ladder to Divine consciousness.

Guru Nanak's western travels took him as far as the holy city of Mecca. The lore of his travels describes his visit to the holy land of Islam where he is said to have slept with his feet towards the Qaba Sharif (Holy Sepulchre). On being admonished by a cleric, Guru Nanak asked the cleric to move his feet in a direction where he believed God does not exist.

creator of the universe, and is omnipotent, benevolent and compassionate and the Prophet Mohammad is His only messenger. Those who accepted the oneness of God and worshipped Him formed a community in which there was to be no distinction of high and low, superior or inferior. For truly, in God's eyes, all are equal. The brotherhood of Islam did not stop at the boundaries of a nation, race or wealth. The Muslims of Punjab were the bearers of a well-defined and formulated faith, heirs to systematically-evolved social laws and theology.

During the three centuries of Muslim rule in Punjab prior to the time of Guru Nanak, sectarian differences, ritualism and authoritarian hegemony of the Muslim orthodoxy crept into the socio-religious life of Muslims. This socio-religious life had significantly hurt the religious sentiments of non-Muslims. A dominant martial Muslim polity exercised political power in its own interest and frequently committed excesses.

The belief in one God, and also in the unity and equality of the human race among the Muslims, became only a theological dogma. Despite being members of a professedly monotheistic and egalitarian community, they practised their own class distinctions. Royals and nobles were descendants from the conquering class, while the soldiery comprised Muslims who had come with the earlier invaders and the slaves who were converts to Islam.

Guru Nanak appeared as a religious thinker and reformer in a region that had confronted, and even to some extent accepted, the Islamic influence. He was fully aware of Islam being a potent socio-religious reality in Punjab and the impact of Muslim political domination. He observed and reacted to Islam at various levels: at the level of religious formalism; of the social behaviour of the representatives of Islam, that is, *qazis* and *maulanas*; of their failure to lead a life according to what they preached to others; and to the fact of ascendancy of Islam as a political force.

Displaying a comprehensive understanding and awareness of the beliefs and practices of contemporary Muslims and their ritualism, Guru Nanak charged the *maulanas* and *qazis* with deviating from the right path. The indictment of hypocrisy was the main point of his criticism. The *qazi* was advised to regard good conduct as his Kalimah[17] and to always adhere

---

17 The creedal statement of Islam: 'There is no god but God, Mohammad is the Messenger of God.' Affirmation of the Kalimah is the first of the five pillars of Islam.

12 Sikh Heritage: Ethos and Relics

to the five principles of conduct and worship, namely, *sach* (truth), *halal* (lawful earning), *khair* (wishing well of others), *niyat* (right intention) and *sifat* (praise of lord) as his five prayers.¹⁸

Guru Nanak and the Gurus who succeeded him, too, were critical of the *qazis* and the *maulanas*, because of their bigotry and narrow-mindedness. Like their counterpart, the Brahmins, the *qazis* were told by the Guru that 'mere talk can never lead to paradise, salvation lies in right conduct. If you add spices to unlawfully earned food, it does not become lawful. Falsehood begets only falsehood'.

During the period, the well-known Sufi orders, like the Qadiris and Naqshbandis, also entered Punjab and it became a major centre of Sufi activities. Many parts of Punjab's rural pockets and towns came under the influence of Sufi *shaikhs*.

Sufism centred round the personality of a *pir* or *shaikh*, who was considered a living vice-regent of the Prophet. The most important single Sufi saint who left a deep impression on the people of Punjab was Shaikh Farid of the Chisti order. His compositions were even incorporated into the Sikh scriptures. These Sufis had acclimatised well to their local surroundings, and even adjusted the nature of their teachings to meet the needs of the local people. Muslim Sufis in Punjab had brought with them the legacy of intellectual formulations of Central Asian Sufi thought. The metaphysics of Sufi thought rested at that time on the doctrine of *wahdat-ul-wujud* (unity of being). Sufis were normally unconcerned with conversions and their significant achievement was to set up contacts with the masses, and to bind fellow human beings in bonds of love.

Guru Nanak with his lifelong companions, Mardana, the *rabab* player, and Bala, as envisioned by a later-day artist.

---

18 SGGS, p.1048: Let mercy be your mosque, faith your prayer-mat, and honest living your Quran. Make modesty your circumcision, and good conduct your fast. In this way, you shall be a true Muslim. Let good conduct be your Kaaba, Truth your spiritual guide, and the *karma* of good deeds your prayer and chant. Let your rosary be that which is pleasing to His Will. O Nanak, God shall preserve your honour.

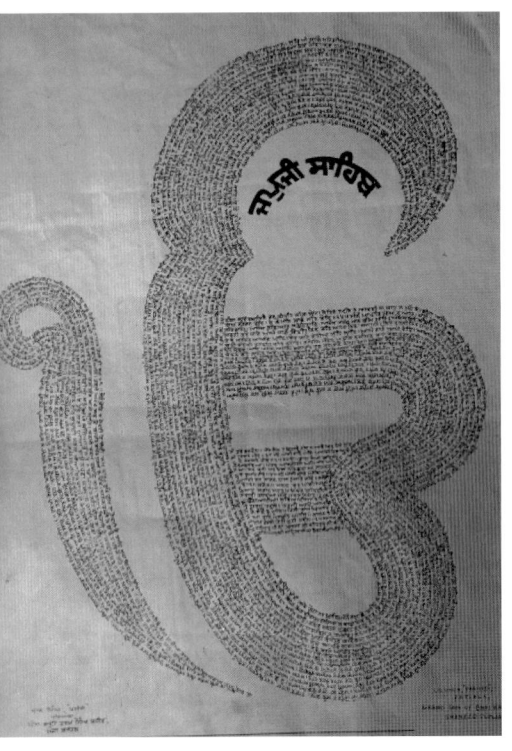

Guru Nanak's *Japji Sahib,* rendered by a calligrapher in the form of *Ekankar,* the cryptic representation of the fundamental enunciation of Sikh philosophy. The calligrapher is identified as Lal Singh 'Pardesi' of Patiala.

Punjab, thus, had become the cradle of a cosmopolitan culture. The Sufis, just like the Nath Yogis, were prominent in medieval Punjab. Among the Sufis, Guru Nanak found a message of universal love, spiritual experience of God, omnipotence and omniscience, which could be attained by supreme devotion devoid of ritualism and formalities of worship. He took note of them, and rather than borrowing from their doctrine, he sought to convince them about his own teachings and message of universal brotherhood and the necessity of translating it into the socio-economic sphere.[19] It is for this reason, it seems, that he visited various centres of religious pilgrimage, such as Multan, Baghdad, Haridwar, Benaras and Jagannath Puri.

Like the Sufi saints, Guru Nanak believed that: 'It is in the midst of work and householder's life that one is emancipated'[20]. As a herdsman, as a farmer and as a storekeeper, he himself showed the same attitude. The Guru said: 'He alone knows the way, who earns by the sweat of his brow and then shares it with others'.

Guru Nanak also believed in the organic fusion of the spiritual and worldly life, and of worship with fulfilment of social obligations. A community life based on work and sharing, a congregational mode of worship, the Sikh *sangat* was parallel to the *sama*, or musical gatherings of Sufis. Guru Nanak also attached great importance to the absolute criterion of merit by nominating Lehna (later Guru Angad Dev) as his successor, just as Sufis would do. This tradition of succession through merit was followed by all Sikh Gurus.

As the socio-religious implications of Guru Nanak's revolutionary programme became clearer, the alienation and thus the opposition of the Brahminical order, too, became marked. Sikhism took on an autonomous status as a full-fledged religion, not exhausting itself as a sect of Hinduism.

Side by side with the eclectic tendencies of spiritual movements that succeeded, in articulating the quest of the age for a new spiritual anchor, there were negative influences that corroded the socio-religious fabric. Both Hinduism and Islam had degenerated into a set of formalities and ceremonies, and according to Guru Nanak, both the communities had become oblivious to the substantial tenets of their respective religions. No wonder then, that the practice of religion lacked the kind of sustenance it ought to have given to the people.

---

19 SGGS p. 1245: Those who labour to earn, to share; they are the ones who realise the Right Path.
20 S GGS p. 522: O Nanak, meeting the True Guru, one comes to know the Perfect Way. While engaging with life—laughing, playing, dressing up and eating properly, one is redeemed.

In the words of Guru Nanak: 'Religion has taken wings and vanished. Falsity prevails like the darkness of the darkest night. The moon of truth is visible nowhere. The seed of religion has exhausted its merit with the departure of those who had sown it.' Guru Nanak's disillusionment with the prevalent religious decadence is evident. Amir Khusrau, a venerated Sufi of the time, found that the only distinguishing feature of the theologians as a class was their hypocrisy, vanity and conceit.

The *yogis* provided an easy escape to the people by not facing the responsibilities of life, and supplied them with a justification to neglect their social obligations by embracing renunciation. A *yogi* expected the social system to maintain him through the alms people gave him. Sikhism insisted upon a disciplined spirituality accompanied by a strong sense of social responsibility as an essential principle.

Sikh heritage and culture is interwoven with the places shown on this contemporary map.

Guru Nanak thus emerged as a religious leader when the environment of Punjab was soaked by religious plurality, intermingling and interaction of different beliefs and traditions. But he was equally conscious of the limitations of both Hinduism and Islam, and reacted against the negative influence of their traditions. In fact, one can envisage a Punjab deeply preoccupied with religious issues. People could find little comfort from the ministrations of the existing priestly class, and were looking for spiritual enlightenment. The moment was ripe for the emergence of a true leader who could wipe out the indignities and raise the conscience of man.

New thought alone was not enough, it had to be developed into a system and a nucleus of committed followers would be needed to help it take roots in society. Guru Nanak thus not only formulated a new religion, but in fact, laid the foundation for a community, which would act as a vehicle for the transmission of his message. Fully conscious of the time needed to effect this change, Guru Nanak passed on his mantle to his successor. It was to take over two centuries and ten Gurus to bring to fruition the revolution that Guru Nanak initiated.

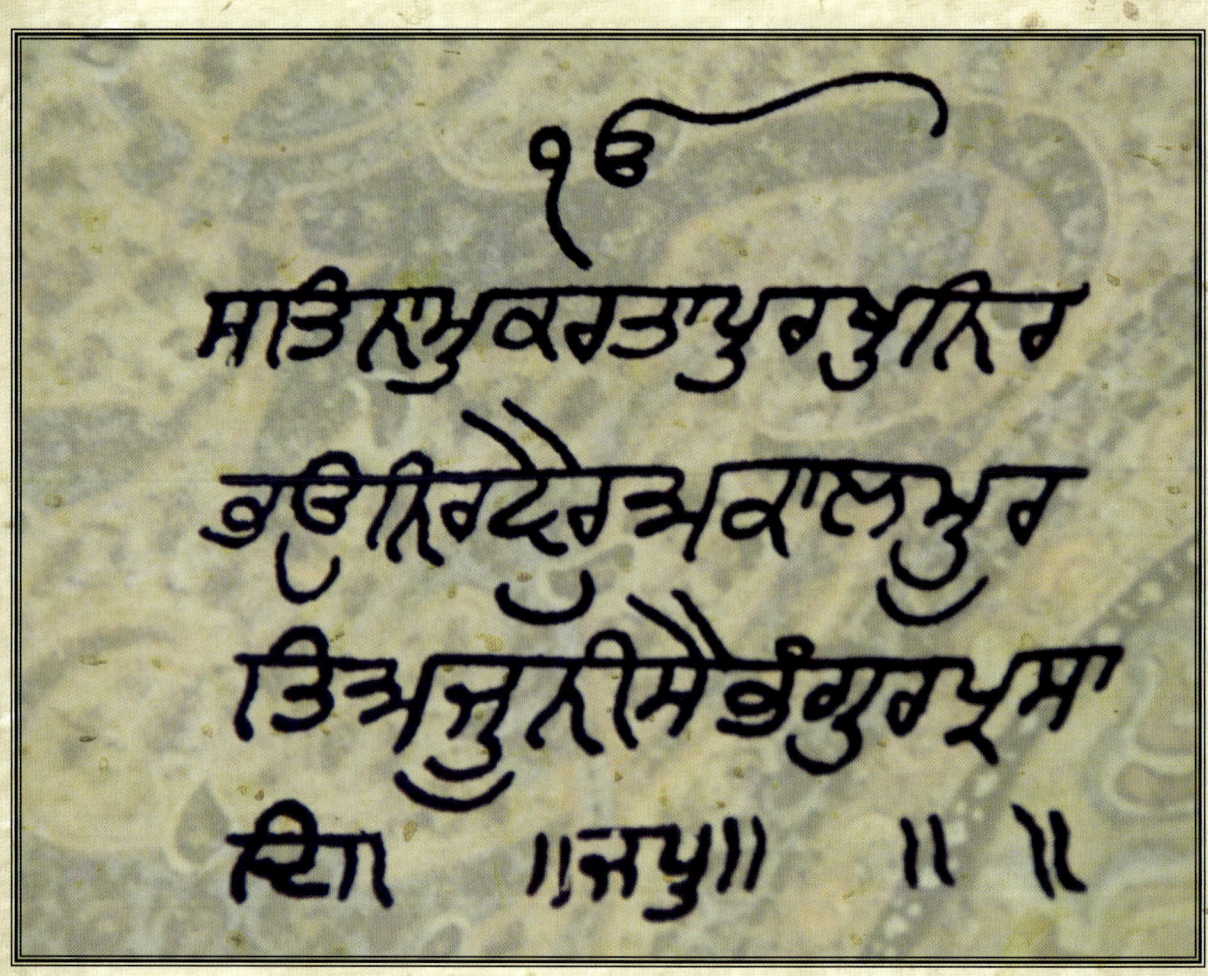

The *Mool Mantra*, handwritten by Guru Arjan Dev, from the original manuscript of the *Adi Granth* compiled in 1604. The volume is with the Sodhi family of Kartarpur. Translated, the *Mool Mantra* reads: 'Absolute Form, Truth, Name, Creator, Person. Without fear, without malafides, Timeless, Organism. Without birth, Self-subsistent, Light. Through Grace (realised).'

GURU NANAK AND HIS Teachings

'*Wahe Guru!*' the Sikhs exclaim in wonder as they endeavour to fathom the Reality of the Creator, the Ultimate Truth, the Timeless and Eternal Being.

The understanding of God, who is the Ultimate Reality, forms the core belief of any religion. Guru Nanak uses the symbol ੴ, pronounced *Ekankar*[1], to sum up the Ultimate Reality as One that permeates everything. This Reality has no name, and yet is known by innumerable names.

God is *Naam*, which means the name by which one remembers or addresses someone. In fact, He is remembered by His attributive names, names given by man according to his understanding.[2]

In Sikhism, self-realisation is the primary step to God-realisation. Through intense devotion and repetition of His name (*Naam*), the soul progresses and ascends to achieve God-consciousness and feels God's eternal presence within. Thus, *Naam* is close to what the Greeks called *Logos*.[3]

Guru Nanak affirms, 'In the beginning was the Truth. Before the beginning was the Truth, even now is the Truth. In future shall remain the Truth'—God is Absolute and makes Himself manifest in His creation. 'He is self-created, eternal and beyond time', says Sri

Kirtan, or singing of scriptures as a mode of worship, is an essential part of the Sikh practice. Bhai Mardana is regarded as the pioneer of the *rababi* tradition of *kirtan*. He was the accompanist of Guru Nanak on the *rabab*, his lifetime companion and an inseparable part of the Guru's mystic singing and travels. He was honoured by the fifth Guru who included two of his verses in Sri Guru Granth Sahib. Detail from a painting in the *Janamsakhi* series.

---

1 It is also pronounced as *Ekoankar*.
2 Guru Gobind Singh, *Dasam Granth*, p.1: Who can make an all-true proposition (*sarva naam kathe kavan*) about Thee, and the wise thus utter adjectival statements to refer to Thee (*karam naam barnat sumat*).
3 *Logos* is an ancient Greek term, originally used by Greek mystics, and frequently used in Gnostic texts. It is based on the belief that *Logos* or *Sophia* of Divine Manifestation descends on the earth through a saviour/messenger of God to redeem the sinners and mitigate the sufferings of the world. To understand *Logos* as the Divine Word, a seeker can experience it through intense internal meditation. Since Christian theology is based on Greek mysticism, the term is also frequently used in Christian context. A seventh-century monk, Maximos the Confessor (C-580-662), writes: 'Not only is the Divine *Logos* prior to the genesis of created beings, but there neither was, nor is, nor will be a principle superior to the *Logos*'. (*The Philokalia* by G. E. H. Palmer).

Guru Granth Sahib[4], the Sikh scripture, in its opening stanzas. 'There is, therefore, no sin, no virtue, no Veda or any religious book, no caste, and no gender. When God became manifest, He became what is called the *Naam* (Name) in order to realise Himself. He made Nature, wherein He has His seat and is thus diffused everywhere and in all directions in the form of "love". There is no antithesis to Him and as such the concept of evil incarnate or Satan does not exist.'

The self has always remained a favourite theme in the philosophical and religious traditions of the world, as it is considered essential, leading to the realisation of the Truth and Liberation—*moksha, mukti,* or *nirvana*.[5]

A Sikh does not aim for individual salvation or to enter a heavenly abode called paradise. He develops the best in himself, the human in the being, an element of Divinity.

As a personal God, He is capable of being loved and honoured. He has no incarnations. He Himself stands for the creative agencies. He Himself is Truth and Beauty and the Eternal yearning of the heart. In a way, the Sikh Gurus have combined the Aryan idea of immanence with the Semitic idea of transcendence, without taking away anything from the unity and the personal characteristic of God, and thus delineated a unique concept.

The universe, according to Sikh thought, is transitory, being rooted in God, who alone is Real. First, God is indivisibly one, above every other being. Second, He is the highest moral being who has inscribed all men with His *Naam* or moral presence. He is not a God belonging to any particular people; He is the dispenser of life all over the universe. He can be attained by practising His presence through the *Shabad* (Word) with intense devotion, and contemplation on *Naam* (His Name). The only way of worshipping Him is to sing His praises.[6]

The Sikh way of life believes in the upliftment of man

The opening stanza of *Jaap Sahib*, composed by Guru Gobind Singh, as seen in an illuminated folio of a manuscript of the *Dasam Granth*.

---

4 SGGS p.1: Absolute Form, Truth, Name, Creator, Person. Without fear, without malafides, Timeless, Organism. Without birth, Self-subsistent, Light. Through Grace (realised). The *Japu* begins – True, beyond the flux of Time; True, at the commencement of Time-cycles; True within the Time-flux; and True He shall also be, Nanak.

5 Essentially, the three terms refer to the liberation of the soul from the limitation of worldly existence.

6 SGGS p. 2: Sing His praises, Hear His Hymns, Have deep devotion in your heart, Banish sorrow and embrace happiness.

based on his character and deeds. It thus distinguishes itself from idle mysticism.

An ideal man, conceived for an ideal society, is not the solitary individual of yogic mysticism, but a part of society (*sagal jamaati*). The message of Sikhism is—'Abide pure amidst the impurities of the world'. There can be no worship without good actions. These actions, however, are not to be formal deeds of so-called merit for compensatory benefits, but should be motivated by an intense desire to please God and to serve one's fellowmen. Fundamental to the Gurus' thought was building man's character, based on values of truth, love and equality. It is character alone that helps in moral crises. Consequently, the Gurus did not think it sufficient only to lay down rules of conduct in a book, but built a living social organisation based on these principles.

Varanashram, and other philosophical Hindu concepts, were deeply embedded in the Indian social psyche, which they had dominated for thousands of years. The Gurus understood the strength of their challenge while asking people to adopt a new mode of living. The Gurus thus found it necessary to take in hand a whole people, through a continuous course of reorientation and schooling in wisdom and experience spread over many generations, before they were sure that the people thus trained had acquired a character of their own, and the ability to self-regulate and self-sustain.

Faced with centuries of entrenched biases, socio-religious prejudices and ritualistic redundancy, the whole value system had to be changed and it was, in fact, transmuted during this process. The spirit of man was thus raised with a belief that he was not a helpless creature in the hands of a Being with an arbitrary Will, but had the inherent Divine spark within him, which, when invoked, would enable him to uplift and redeem himself.

In Sikhism, the law of *karma*—according to which one reaps what one sows—is not inexorable. The burden of past sins, the

Guru Gobind Singh, the tenth Guru, on horseback. Detail from a Pahari miniature painting.

taint of *karma*, the weight of our past can be thrown off by delving deeper into Truth, by leading a pure and noble life and, above all, by earning the grace of God: *Gur Prasad*. Human life is an opportunity for man to rise to immortal heights, or alternatively, fall into the pit of disgrace. The scripture says, 'The Guru's word erases the blot of thousands of evil deeds of the past and the greatest sinner can become the greatest saint'[7].

Man is given a will with which he can modify the inherited and acquired tendencies of his past, and determine his future conduct. This will of man, channelled through the Guru's word, gets attuned to the Supreme Will, and acquires a force with which he can transcend his past and gain a new character altogether.[8]

The ultimate source of everything is *Akalpurakh*, the Timeless, who is also within us. Nothing exists beyond Him, not even 'evil' can function independent of God. Thus there is no antithesis to God, no Satan. Man himself is responsible for his actions, whether good or evil. One sins as long as the 'light' within remains unmanifested. Regeneration comes when one begins to subject one's tiny self to the highest Self, i.e. God, and one's own will is gradually attuned to His Supreme Will, until one feels and moves just as He wishes one to feel, and moves in sync with Him.

The problem of good and evil is only the problem of union and dis-union with God. As long as man is conscious of this, he lives and moves in union with Him. But when he is led away by the overwhelming 'sense of the self'—his *haumai* (ego)—he breaks himself away from that Unity with Him and begins to flounder in moral isolation.

Although it is difficult for man to resist evil and do good with his own power, he could acquire a transcendental capacity for the purpose if he is primed with a divine personality possessing dynamic powers. This personality is to be the Guru's; the teacher's message, the Word of the scripture, *Shabad*.[9]

The way of religion perceived for the Sikhs is not a set of views or doctrines but a way of life lived according to a definite model, based upon disciple-ship, or following a path shown by the preceptors and not just governed by a narrow framework of dos and don'ts, dictated by a clergy. The personality of the Guru is all along operative in his

Kirpan, bhagauti or sword is representative of the Divine, primal being in Sikh thought and precepts. A medium-sized *kirpan* of Guru Gobind Singh from the collection of the Maharaja of Patiala.

---

7 SGGS pp. 698-796, 97
8 SGGS p. 2: By our deeds we get our form, but Salvation comes through His Grace.
9 The message, Word, is Guru, and Guru is the Word. *Shabad* Guru is eternal, as ensconced in Sri Guru Granth Sahib.

Episodes from the lives of the Gurus were recorded later by the Sikhs and the manuscripts were titled *Gurbilas*, literally, life story. Here we see the opening pages of an illuminated manuscript of Sukha Singh's *Gurbilas-Patshahi 10* (1798) which recorded events connected to the life of Guru Gobind Singh, the tenth and last Guru.

disciple, conducting his whole being and shaping his life. Without such a personality, there would be no cohesion or direction for the moral forces in a society. There would be no force to connect man with man and then with God. Everyone would exist in moral isolation, only for himself.

When such a devoted disciple (Sikh) merges his personality into a perfect Guru, he is transformed into Khalsa, the perfect one. In this respect, Guru Gobind Singh is a role model for every Sikh. He himself describes such a perfect Sikh:

'The Khalsa is my Image special
In the Khalsa ever resides my Spirit
The Khalsa is my Beloved and Venerable Master
The Khalsa is my Divine Protector
The Khalsa is an embodiment of the True and perfect Guru.'[10]

This character was demonstrated by the Sikhs during the height of persecution and sufferings against formidable odds in the eighteenth century. The Gurus intensified their character and increased their power manifold by filling their personalities with his own, and the result was for history to take note.

The ten Gurus organised their disciples into *sangats* and infused their personality again into the Sikhs. This led to a remarkable development in the institution of 'Guru-ship', which eventually became the Guru *Panth*, thus bestowing divinity on the people.

The Sikh idea of religion was something more practical than

---
10 Guru Gobind Singh, *Sarb Loh Granth*, pp. 519-524 *Khalsa Mero Rup Hai Khas*.

Mool Mantra from the illuminated manuscript of Sri Guru Granth Sahib with the Bhai Sahib of Bagrian. The illumination is the work of nineteenth-century Kashmiri artists.

merely mystic; it was to consist of the practice of *Naam*[11] and *sewa*[12]. To practise *Naam* means to practise the presence of God by keeping Him ever in our minds, by singing His praises, and dwelling on His excellence. This is to be done not only when in solitude but also in public, where worship of this *Naam* is more effective when organised in the form of congregational recitations or singing. *Sewa*, or service, should not only be liberal, but also efficient and economical. It should do the greatest good with the least possible means.[13]

Sikhism—or this way of life whose aim is to serve and uplift mankind—necessarily requires organisation of its followers as an essential condition for its success. Moreover, where religion consists of realising God mainly through service done within the world, where people have to constantly deal with fellow people to promote each other's good, it is impossible to do so without institutionalisation.

Over the years, a new social order emerged, as also a method of administering it. The founder of this faith, Guru Nanak, had begun with two things in his religious work: the holy Word, *Shabad*, and the organised holy fellowship, *sangat*. The idea of *sangat* led to the establishment of local assemblies, headed by authorised representatives called *massands*. Every Sikh was supposed to be a member of such an organisation. The Guru was the central unifying personality, and in spite of changes in succession, the love between the Guru and the Sikh was intense. Homage paid to the Guru was made impersonal by creating a mystic unity between the Sikh and the Guru on the one hand, and the Guru and the Word enshrined in Sri Guru Granth Sahib on the other. The greatest respect began to be paid to the incorporated Word (*Shabad*), even with the Guru choosing for himself a seat lower than that of the scripture[14]. The only form of worship allowed to be practised was the meditation on the Word and singing the praises of the Creator, as inscribed in the scriptures.

---

11 *Naam Simran* is contemplative meditation, remembrance and recollection of His attributes, and hearing them within one's own consciousness. It is a journey towards inner solitude, love of the light of God within us, till the Name of God is engraved within our heart and soul, and till it becomes the ecstasy and vision of God.
12 *Sewa*: Service of mankind is service of God, and through selfless service, a person can acquire nearness to God. In Sikhism, Bhai Lehna, Baba Amar Das, and Bhai Jetha were blessed with the Guru's spirit and Guru-ship for their selfless services in the house of God. There are *Hukamnamas*, letters of the Sikh Gurus and the consorts, blessing the various *sangats* for serving the cause of the Gurus.
13 SSGS p. 26: In the midst of this world, do *sewa*, and you shall be given a place of honour in the Court of the Lord. Says Nanak, swing your arms in joy!
14 When Sri Guru Granth Sahib was first installed in Harmandar Sahib in AD 1604, Guru Arjan Dev took a seat lower than the Holy Book. This tradition was settled for all times.

The Sikh assemblies also acquired great sanctity, owing to the belief that the spirit of the Guru lived and moved among them collectively, the whole body being called the *panth*. This *panth* follows the path shown by the way the Gurus lived their lives, as also the precepts laid down by them. In turn, it is regarded as an embodiment of the Guru—*Guru Panth*.

In 1699, Guru Gobind Singh, the tenth Guru, himself received baptism from the five Sikhs he had first initiated. The *panth*, the assembly and the Guru became one. After his demise, there was no living Guru for the Sikhs. The *Shabad*, in the presence of the *sangat*, became the Guru, the guiding light and in presence of *Akalpurakh*[15], the Timeless Being.

The *panth* thus was invested with the personality of the Guru, and the incorporated Word became Gyan Guru (knowledge). This *panth*, called the Khalsa, was to be the Guru in spirit, and was authorised to work with collective responsibility, with Guru Granth Sahib as its guiding spirit. They were directed to worship none but the *Akalpurakh*[16]. The authority of the *massands* was terminated, and thus Sikhism became more of an 'ethos' than mere theology. *Amrit*—or a formal baptism—was made an integral part of this organisation[17]. All those who wanted to serve humanity through Sikhism would join it earnestly as regular members and receive baptism. This entailed and ensured that all had the same creed, which would be well-defined and not confused or corrupted with the beliefs and practices of the prevailing religions. The Guru had ordained the Khalsa to be distinct from the contemporary prevailing main religions. Such a brotherhood of the committed, the Khalsa, was to embody in itself the highest ideal of manhood as exemplified by Guru Gobind Singh's life. In this regeneration of man, the biases were terminated. This act symbolically destroyed *karma*, *kula*, *dharama* and *jaat* (deeds of the past, lineage, religion and caste).

In the ranks of the Khalsa all are equal, the lowest with the highest, in race as in creed, in political rights as in religious hopes. Women are to be baptised and to baptise others in the same way as men and enjoy the same rights.

---

15 A term often used for Godhead, an attributive name signifying His Timeless, Eternal nature.
16 The final direction to his followers by the tenth Guru was *Pooja Akaal Di, Parcha Shabad Da, Didar Khalse Da*.
17 First administered on 30 March 1699 at Anandpur. *Amrit-Khande di Pauhul* is prepared by stirring water and sugar puffs with a *khanda* or the double-edged sword, to the recitation of selected scriptures.

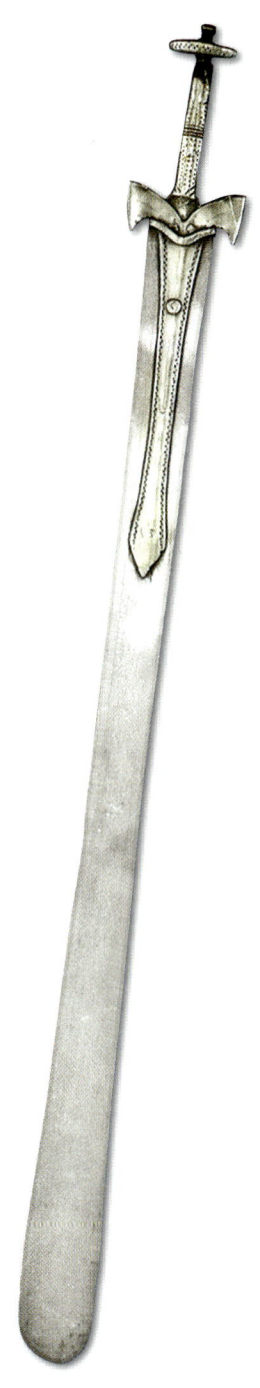

The original *khanda* used by Guru Gobind Singh for preparing *amrit* at the initiation of the Khalsa on the historic Baisakhi of 1699 at Anandpur Sahib, now preserved at Takht Keshgarh Sahib.

Being a Khalsa entails certain additional codes of discipline. The picture shows a Nihang Singh during the Hola Mahalla festival at Anandpur Sahib.

Being a Khalsa also entails certain additional codes of discipline in the shape of baptismal oaths of conduct (*rehat*). The importance of these vows cannot be understated. Religion, as taught by the Gurus, is a force that not only ennobles individuals but also binds them together to work for the service of mankind. Discipline keeps up the spirit of the individual against relaxation in times of hardship, and maintains the individual's steadfastness and loyalty to the cause.

The Sikh forms, or visible symbols, were appointed to serve as aids to the preservation of the life of the community, and anyone who likes to serve humanity through the Sikh way of life can adopt them. It is possible for a man to love God and cultivate his individual soul, which is the Sikh goal, without adopting this form. But, if he wants to work in a systematic way, not only for his own advancement, but for the welfare of all (*sarbat da bhala*) in the company of Sikhs, he must adopt this disciplinary form. This association is not with places or things but with an ever-living personality that is itself a symbol of the highest personality. As is God, so is the Guru, and as is the Guru, so must be his followers.

A baptised Sikh is thus enjoined to keep five Articles of Faith as an inalienable part of his person. These are *kesha* (unshorn hair), a *kanga* (a small comb), a *kirpan* (sword), a *kara* (an iron bangle) on his right forearm, and he should wear *kachha* (underpants which are a longer version of boxers). All starting with the Gurmukhi letter *kaka*, phonetically 'k', hence called the *kakaars*, or the 5 Ks.

The Sikh is to keep his hair uncut, which has always been associated with the ideal man and saintliness. A comb is a simple necessity for keeping the hair clean and tidy, antithetical to the ascetic with matted hair.

An iron bangle on the right arm is a sign of sternness and constraint. A sword by a Sikh's side, *kirpan*, also called *bhagauti*, represents the primal Divine energy. It is the protector of the oppressed and an emblem of power, dignity and man's sovereignty. Moreover, combined in him is the saintliness of the *rishis* of old with the sternness and strength of a knight.

The *kachha* is a symbol of continence, restraint and tolerance, and ensures briskness of movement at time of action, and comfort at times of rest. It is also symbolic of man's evolution from a state of nakedness to being civilised by covering himself.

These baptismal forms, with the accompanying commitment of purity, love and service, have aided them in keeping themselves united and their ideals unsullied even in times of the greatest of trials.

Ceremonies, among Sikhs, whether in a temple or at home, whether for birth, marriage or death, consist of nothing but praying. Constant singing of hymns from scriptures creates a frame of mind and ambience.

The Sikh is enjoined to make these five elements of forms a part of his living. This also gives him an identity that stands for commitment to the precepts mentioned above, and also makes every Sikh a living, acting, committed and unabashed epitome of the way of life given to him by his Gurus.

The Guru

The word 'Guru', a term often used in Indian religious tradition, has a special connotation in Sikh ethos. In Sikhism, the Guru is not an incarnate of God; he is not a prophet or messenger of God, in whom the light of God completely and visibly shines. He is not God and is not to be worshipped as God. The mysteries of God and His creation are known either to God or to the Guru. The true Guru is the true instrument of God's Will (*Hukam*), and is commissioned by Him to reveal His Truth to humanity.

Guru is a Sanskrit word consisting of *Gu* = darkness, and *ru* = light. Accordingly, Guru is the true enlightener of the Soul, dispeller of ignorance and spiritual guide.

A Guru is vital to man's spiritual progress, not as God Himself, but as one who shows the path and is an archetypal exemplar. It is through him that Divinity—*Akalpurakh* (the Timeless One)—instructs, and is capable of leading the believers to the highest state of spiritual enlightenment, which is experiencing the Divine presence. The Guru is a witness of God's love for His creation. He is His *Hukam* (Will) made concrete. As a guide, the Guru is Revealer of the Divine Word and message. Guru is synonymous with the Word (*Shabad*), the Divine light within, the self-revelation. He is not to be confused with the human form. The real Guru is God, for He alone is the source of all Light.

Guru Nanak and the nine Gurus along with Guru Nanak's companions. Bala is shown next to the Guru, holding a peacock-feather fly-whisk in his hand, and the *rabab* player Mardana is shown in the foreground, opposite Guru Nanak.

GURU NANAK AND HIS TEACHINGS 25

A devotee reading from an illuminated folio of an old, handwritten copy of Sri Guru Granth Sahib at Gurdwara Hathi Bhata, Ajmer, Rajasthan.

Guru Nanak says that the true Guru must be such as to unite all men. He must not be above man's capacity to emulate, as would be the case if he were a supernatural being. His humanity must be real and not feigned. He should be subject to the same laws as the ordinary human and should have attained his perfection through His Grace, which is also available to all ordinary men, and through perfect obedience to God's Will. Thus, the Guru is the central concept and theme in Sikhism. The preceptors, the ten Sikh Gurus, demonstrated this with full intensity.

This feeling of incorporation with the Guru makes the Sikh strong beyond his ordinary capacity. The transformation comes not only through close association with the Guru, something to be found in many other religions as well, but in the unique manner in which the Sikh believes that he is subsumed in the Guru.

The Sikh Gurus are revered as spiritually enlightened human beings, not worshipped as incarnations of God. In the scriptures, they declare themselves to be champions (representatives)[18] and bards[19] of God. Guru Gobind Singh declares himself to be His slave, and prohibits his Sikhs from identifying him with God.[20] Before his demise, the tenth Guru instructed the Khalsa to follow the Eternal Guru—*Shabad*, the Word—enshrined in Sri Guru Granth Sahib.

Throughout the development of Sikhism up to Guru Gobind Singh, the Guru had been assigned a place of predominance. Guru Nanak, in so many of his verses, highlights this point. As a matter of fact, in Guru Nanak's system, the Guru formed the pivot on which everything else hinged. The disciple was asked to walk on the path of the Guru, to

---

18 SGGS p. 74: I am a knight of the Lord; I met with the Guru, and I have tied a tall, plumed turban. All have gathered to watch the joust, and the Merciful Lord Himself conducts it.
19 SGGS p.150: I was a minstrel, out of work, when the Lord took me into His service. To sing His Praises day and night, He gave me His Order, right from the start.
20 Guru Gobind Singh, *Bachitar Natak*: Those who call me God, will fall into the pit of hell. Regard me as a humble servant of the Lord and have no doubt about it. I am a slave of the Supreme Being, and have come to witness the drama of the world. I say what God has said to me. I shall not remain silent on account of the fear of mortals.

remain ever-content in his Will and his Commands. But in these matters, as in everything else, the Guru was to point out the right path; he was to interpret the Will of God, and the commands of the Almighty were also to be issued through the medium of his ordinances. The Guru, therefore, was to be implicitly obeyed and his will was to be accepted.

The place of the Guru in Sikh faith and tradition is of great importance. That is why Guru Gobind Singh bestowed the pontifical office for all times to come on Sri Guru Granth Sahib and the *panth* (Khalsa *Panth*), representing the spiritual and the temporal aspects respectively. Since then, the Sikhs revere Sri Guru Granth Sahib and seek guidance from it on all crucial and not so-crucial moments in personal life. However, the reverence shown to the scripture is not to be identified with worship.

Sri Guru Granth Sahib is the ever-lasting guide and teacher. Among other things, its uniqueness lies in the fact that it is the only scripture which was compiled, edited, signed and sealed by the preceptors themselves. The integrity of this scripture is unassailable, for the simple reason that copies of the original, signed by the Gurus, are available.[21]

Many volumes of Sri Guru Granth Sahib are richly illuminated, showing the reverence with which the word Guru was treated by the Sikhs.

---

21 Old manuscripts with signatures of Guru Arjan Dev, Guru Hargobind, Guru Har Rai and Guru Gobind Singh are in existence.

Guru Nanak in a discourse with Behlol, a Muslim seer, at Baghdad, during his travel to Mecca. The legend says that so charmed was Behlol by the Guru's presence that even after he had left, Behlol sat at the same spot, saying he did not want the divine experience to be eclipsed. A Gurdwara near Baghdad Railway Station commemorated Guru Nanak's visit, where Behlol met him. The painting by an unknown artist depicts the Guru in attire that could have been of a *rabbai* of the period, although the Indian wooden toe-knob sandals (*kharawan*) are distinct.

THE GURUS AND THE
Spirit of Sikhi

The word Sikh, a derivative of the Sanskrit word *shishya*, means 'disciple'. Sikhism is best understood as a way of life, a discipline, an organised existence and not merely conceptual theology, or a set of prescribed rituals, though it does have its own unique precepts of thought.

The evolution of the Sikh movement reveals a gradual making and development of a nation of God-fearing, God-oriented humans, in the hands of ten successive leaders, the Gurus.

Guru Nanak perceived the true principles of social and religious reform and laid a foundation upon which the successive eight Gurus developed and established a society. Guru Gobind Singh, the tenth Guru, institutionalised it and established a new nation. These values fired the minds of the people with the doctrine that the lowest and highest races, castes and creeds are all equal—be it with respect to political rights, social standing or in religious hopes. The Gurus also had in their minds the duties of a state as much as the duties of an individual. This made the Sikh religion unique and distinct[1].

Indian civilisation is more than five thousand years old. Its heritage and culture, which forms the nucleus of its faith in the form of Hinduism, is over three thousand years old. Numerous schools of Indian philosophy, however different, all have one common fundamental core—the concept of *Varanashram*, a belief and precept that categorises society into four levels of social stratification. This horizontal divide straitjackets social order not by merit, achievement or talent, but by accident of birth. Over time, the idea of caste system took root and no upward or even downward mobility by deed or dispensation was allowed.

At the top of this order is the Brahminical cadre, followed by the Kshatriya and the Vaishya, with the Shudra being at the bottom-most

Harmandar Sahib at Amritsar, where Sri Guru Granth Sahib was first installed. The only form of worship here is the singing of praises of the Almighty. The four doors signify the openness and egalitarianism, essential to the Sikh ethos.

---
1 Sometimes parallels are erroneously drawn with the cults of the Bhakti movement.

rung. The category or caste into which one is born is believed to be determined by *karma* (acts of an individual in a previous birth). This *karma* theory leaves no room for shifting to another caste, however hard one strives, or whatever acts of merit one performs. This pushes the individual to extreme complacency, verging on inactivity. The individual becomes resigned to it and fatalistically accepts it as his lot.

Guru Nanak perceived this and sought to remedy the situation. For this, a concerted effort of social re-engineering was required based on a fresh value system, which was to be transmuted from the existing decadent ones.

Guru Nanak Dev, the founder

Guru Nanak Dev was born in 1469 at Rai Bhoe-ki-Talwandi, later called Nankana Sahib, now in Pakistan. His father was Mehta Kalu and his mother Mata Tripta. He was born into a decadent society, a corrupt state and a withered social structure divided by castes and creeds. At the age of seven, he was sent to the village school to study under a Hindu teacher (a Brahmin), from whom he learnt arithmetic and bookkeeping, besides reading and writing. He soon exhausted the stock of learning which the village teacher possessed, and went on to a local Muslim priest-cum-teacher (Maulavi) to learn Persian and Islamic literature.

From the very beginning he had the incisive mind of a critic and would question the established socio-religious practices. At the age of nine, when he was asked to go through the *Yajnopavitam* ceremony, prevalent among high-caste Hindus, which required him to wear a sacred thread, he refused to comply. He told the priest that he would rather have a thread that would 'neither break nor get soiled, nor be burnt or lost'[2]. This was his declaration of intent against ritualism and idle symbolism. Later, he wrote:

'Out of the action of mercy make threads of temperateness, and twisting them with righteous zeal tie in them the knot of continence. The sacred thread thus formed will be for the soul. If thou hast it, O Pandit, put it on me, it will not break; it will not get soiled.'[3]

In 1526, Guru Nanak witnessed the invasion of Babur, the Mughal, with his own eyes and was perturbed by the massacre of men, women, and children who resisted Babur's onslaught. In his compositions,

The infant Nanak is taken by his parents to Hardayal, the local *pandit,* for his naming ceremony. On the right is Pandit Hardayal.

2 SGGS p. 471: *Na eh tute na mal lage.*
3 SGGS p. 471: *Assa di Vaar.*

referred to as 'Hymns of Blood', he described the sight and protests in anguish. He rebuked the Lodhi king of Delhi for not putting up a fight to defend the country and protecting its citizens. He observed that the people were so cowed down in spirit that they mimicked the marauders' mannerisms, ate meat prepared in their fashion (kosher or *halal*), violating their own creed, and wore blue apparel in order to please the ruling class. People even adopted foreign names. This socio-political awareness, and putting the onus on the rulers to protect the people was unique, coming from a man of religious intent.

Looking at the helplessness of his countrymen, he realised that moral degradation was at the root of it all. He set out to rectify this. He called upon the people to rise and realise their inherent potential[4], and invoke the Divine strength inherent in every human. He inspired them to stand up against oppression and evil, in all forms, whether sociological or theological.

In his earliest utterances, he declared that there is no Hindu and no Mussalman (Muslim). Religion is universal. Man is merely a custodian of God's bounty. There is a universal brotherhood of man. Everyone should have freedom of belief. Equality of the sexes, castes and of social standing and ethical governance, are the right of all.

To carry his message to mankind at large, he travelled widely—from Kam Rup in the east of India to Baghdad in the west; from the heights of Kailash Mountain in the Himalayas in the north, to Sri Lanka in the south. He visited all the important places of learning and pilgrimage in India, questioning the validity of hollow rituals[5] and the blind dogmas prevailing in society, as he introduced to the world a new way of life—the Sikh way.

Guru Nanak epitomised a way of life for society in general, which is best stated in the traditional parlance as *kirt karo*, *wand chhako* and *naam japo*; that is: do honest labour, share the boons of life with all your fellow beings and always remember the Timeless, the Infinite One, who is called God, and who is the giver of it all—the essence of how the Sikh way of life is to be practised.

In the latter part of his life, Guru Nanak settled down in a place called

Guru Nanak is taken to the *padha* (the Hindu teacher) at the village school by his father to enrol at his school. A folio of the eighteenth-century *Janamsakhi*.

---
4 SGGS p. 441: *Mann to Jot sarup hai, Apna mul pachan.*
5 At Jagannath Puri, he sang his famous hymn highlighting that the Universe itself is performing the *aarti* of the Lord. SGGS p.13: Upon that cosmic plate of the sky, the sun and the moon are the lamps. The stars and their orbs are the studded pearls. The breeze is the incense, and the wind is the ceremonial whisk. All the plants of the world are the altar flowers being offered to You, O Luminous Lord. What a beautiful *aarti*, lamp-lit worship service this is! O Destroyer of Fear, this is Your Ceremony of Light.

Kartarpur[6] and established a commune that was modelled on his beliefs. This was the nucleus of the society which took complete form in the times of the tenth Guru, and was later called the Khalsa Panth. At Kartarpur, the Guru lived with his fellow Sikhs. They tilled their common land, ate in *langar* (a community kitchen)[7], without discrimination of caste, gender or creed, and together sang the glories of the Almighty in congregation.

Thus was set forth a path, a movement for the transformation of India's socio-religious scene. Guru Nanak had realised that a long and concerted effort would be required to transform the national ethos and purge the psyche of Indian society of thousands of years of prejudices and biases.

Cultures do not evolve over merely years, they take generations to grow and fructify. So deep-rooted were the decadent practices and beliefs in the minds of people that the campaign had to stretch over a few generations. The very nucleus of the social organism had to be recast, and a new society was created, in which no inimical elements of the past could verily be found or allowed to persist. This resulted in ten successive Gurus, who guided this new society from 1469 to 1708.

Guru Nanak had laid the foundation of a regenerated nation. But much had to be done before people, morally and physically degraded, could lift up their heads and come into their own again. He was not a mere reformer, but the founder of a new religion and a social order, as is obvious from the fact that he travelled abroad to countries of varied faiths and established congregations (*sangats*) and Sikh organisations at different centres. He took special care to test his followers for their integrity of commitment to the cause and, as his end approached, he appointed a successor who would continue his work after him with the same commitment. Guru Nanak chose his follower, Bhai Lehna, as his successor and spiritual heir, over his own sons, based on his merit, before passing away on 22 September 1539 at Kartarpur.

Guru Angad Dev

Born as Lehna and later anointed Guru Angad Dev (1504-1552) to carry forward the mission of Guru Nanak, he was the second Guru of the Sikhs. He gave the Sikh movement a definiteness and distinction,

Guru Angad Dev used to meet his personal expenses by selling jute yarn (*vaan*) handspun by him. This *Janamsakhi* folio depicts him (right) working at home.

---

6 Now in Pakistan, three kilometres from the Indo-Pak border.

7 Though charity kitchens were prevalent in the Sufi *khanquahs*, the Guru's *langar* was more than charity. It inculcated within the Sikhs a spirit of charity and spirituality. It became an institution for sharing and for levelling social barriers. Visitors were required to sit in a common line (*pangat*), share the same meal and then appear before the Guru. The Sikh religion's progress was based on the efficacy of such institutions.

32 Sikh Heritage: Ethos and Relics

based on the fundamentals laid down by his predecessor.

Guru Angad collected the compositions of Guru Nanak and made a compendium. Guru Nanak spoke the language of the common man, and thus brought the message within the reach of all. Guru Angad eschewed the language of clergy[8], and got the Founder's compositions written in a special script called Gurmukhi, a modified form of the ancient Bhatakshri, then prevalent in Punjab. A nucleus of the Sikh scripture was thus formed, giving a defined direction to the faith. This gave a powerful blow to the domination of the priestly class, as the Divine message now became available to the common man in his own language[9].

It was also during the time of Guru Angad that *langar*, the practice of eating together in a community kitchen, which was started at the time of his predecessor, became an essential part of Sikh practices. This made a significant contribution to the dismantling and repudiation of the caste-classified society known as *Varanashram Dharama*[10].

Guru Angad Dev, the second Guru, with Bala, Guru Nanak's lifetime companion.

The concept of *langar* broke the deep-rooted taboos and sectarian barriers of Manu's[11] theories and laid a firm foundation for a casteless society that emerged as Khalsa *Panth* in the time of the tenth Guru. Before passing away, Guru Angad appointed one of his senior disciples, Amar Das, as his successor, the third Guru continuing Guru Nanak's spirit.

Guru Amar Das

Born on 5 May 1479, at a village called Basarke, near present-day Amritsar, into a family engaged in agriculture, Amar Das was a devout and staunch Vaishnavite—a follower of the Hindu god Vishnu. Hymns of Guru Nanak recited by the daughter of Guru Angad enchanted his mind, and he sought spiritual refuge in Guru Angad. His Vaishnavite prejudices were soon removed and he became a devout follower of Guru Nanak.

Amar Das learnt from Sikh tradition that the best way to serve

---

8 At that time the texts of the two main religions, Islam and Hinduism, were written in Arabic and Sanskrit, respectively, which were not widely understood.

9 For centuries, higher learning and the Sanskrit language were confined to the higher castes. Lower castes were forbidden to learn the language, and some castes, mentions M. A. McAuliffe, were not even allowed to hear the Vedas.

10 A custom that categorised the Hindu society into four social classes (*varnas*), prescribing specific duties for each class. This, in time, led to the caste system and to social stratification and discrimination based on it.

11 Manu, the ancient Indian code-giver, enunciated the concept of caste-stratified society, established by birth and not vocation.

God was to exert oneself in the service of humanity, and he took to performing the humblest kind of work for the Guru and his Sikhs. His devotion, service and ability prepared him for the important duties of leading the Sikhs later in life. In spite of strong opposition from Guru Angad's own sons and the followers of Guru Nanak's sons, Guru Angad anointed Amar Das as the third Guru of Sikhs, in recognition of his commitment and service to Guru Nanak's mission.

Guru Amar Das emphasised the rejection of renunciation. He reiterated that the life of a householder was the only approved way of practising Guru Nanak's religion. He stressed on the necessity of believing in One Guru, One Word and only one interpretation.

During his period, the *langar* became a key institution as a leveller of people. Tradition has it that even the Mughal Emperor, Akbar, who came to visit the Guru at Goindwal, partook of *langar*[12]. People renounced their prejudices and looked up to each other as equals. The Guru impressed upon them the true value and sanctity of human life. Mankind, he said, was created in the image of God, and reiterated that it was His precious trust which had to be kept pure and strong by temperance. He banned the age-old practice of *sati*—the self-immolation of a widow on her husband's funeral pyre—among Sikhs, and was also against *purdah*, the practice of preventing women from being seen by men in public, and the requirement for women to cover themselves and conceal their form. This was another significant social reform introduced by the Sikh way of life.

The Sikh community as an organised society was established during this period. Sikh *sangats* had spread all over the country and even beyond its boundaries since the times of Guru Nanak. Guru Amar Das apportioned this spiritual domain of the house of Guru Nanak into twenty-two provinces, called *manjis*[13]. Each *manji* being under the charge of a devoted Sikh, man or woman, who was duty-bound to preach the mission of the Guru and keep the local bodies in touch with the Guru. The Gurus also drew material and other support from these far-flung congregations. This became the infrastructure upon which the edifice of the Sikh *Panth* later arose.

As for the scriptures, the Gurus' spiritual compositions had been recorded since the time of Guru Nanak in manuscripts called *pothis*. Guru Angad had passed down to Guru Amar Das his own sayings and those that Guru Nanak had given him, which were all recorded by

Guru Amar Das, as envisioned by a miniature artist

---

12 *Suraj Prakash*, also quoted by M. A. McAuliffe.
13 Literally, a small cot or a seat.

the third Guru. Added to these were Guru Amar Das' own writings, which later became the basis of the compilation of the *Adi Granth* by Guru Arjan Dev, the fifth Guru[14].

Guru Amar Das declared that the Guru's Word (*Bani*), was superior to all other scriptures. He stated the *Bani* and the Guru were one, thus the message was the Guru, the Teacher, the Enlightener. It was during his lifetime that the Sikhs became more self-contained in community matters. They evolved their own social practices for performing ceremonies like marriages and funerals with the help of the *Gurbani*.

Guru Ram Das

All successive Gurus had been anointed during the lifetime of the earlier Guru, from the times of Guru Nanak. Ram Das[15], too, was selected by his predecessor, Guru Amar Das, and consecrated as the fourth Guru in September 1574. Though son-in-law to Amar Das by relation, he became the fourth Guru on merit, for his selfless and self-effacing commitment and service to his Guru and the house of Nanak.

Centre of piety

In 1577, Guru Ram Das obtained grant of a site, along with 500 *bighas* of land, from Mughal Emperor Akbar, on payment. This is the same place where the city of Amritsar now stands. The site was originally named Ramdaspur. The Guru supervised the excavation of a *sarovar*[16] and invited men of various trades to take up residence and open their businesses in the market, which is called the Guru-ka-Bazaar[17] till date.

Over time, the city grew to become the biggest centre of trade in northern India. The social and economic relevance of the Sikh way of life was thus given a firm and living form. The concept that religion could be best practised within the secular concerns of life was established. Even people inclined to spiritualism became active in worldly affairs. This was the essence of Guru Nanak's way of life, and now it was emerging as a factual reality.

Possession of wealth is helpful in conducting human affairs[18]. For a religious man, it is not unholy to get wealthy, provided he spends

Guru Ram Das, the fourth Guru, founded Ramdaspur, as Amritsar was known earlier. He also had the *sarovar* excavated on which Harmandir Sahib is built.

---

14 The manuscript is now referred to *Goindwal Pothi*.
15 Born in Lahore on 24 September 1534.
16 An open water reservoir, in the centre of which the Harmandar was to be built. This had both spiritual and practical significance.
17 The *bazaar* was demolished in 1984-85.
18 This position marked a radical departure from the renunciant dispensations of the then-established social orders.

Guru Arjan Dev supervising the scribing of the *Adi Granth* by Bhai Gurdas, as depicted in a mural at the tower at Gurdwara Baba Atal, Amritsar. The tallest tower in the Harmandar Sahib complex is a memorial to Baba Atal Rai, the eldest son of Guru Hargobind.

his wealth in God's ways and lives in comfort, the Guru said. Skills of banking, trading in horses, embroidery and carpentry became common among the Sikhs, with Ramdaspur as the hub.

Guru Arjan Dev

Guru Ram Das breathed his last on 1 September 1581. His youngest son, Arjan Mal, who had shown his merit by devotion, bearing and proficiency in the Sikh doctrine, had been selected by Guru Ram Das to succeed him.

Guru Arjan Dev, the fifth Guru, established residence at Ramdaspur, the newly-established town, and completed the work of constructing a *sarovar* and the city. By now, the number of Sikhs had increased significantly, and Sikhs from all over the country would send their offerings to their spiritual guide, the Guru, at Ramdaspur (Amritsar). The practice of setting aside one-tenth of one's earnings (*daswand*) for the Guru's fund and sending it to Amritsar on every Baisakhi thus came into being. The Sikhs now became accustomed to their own organised society and to a government within the state, and their own financial corpus.

On 15 October 1588, Guru Arjan Dev started work on a central house of prayer, the Harmandar, or the Temple of God, often called Golden Temple[19], in the middle of the *sarovar* of Amritsar.

Sikhism's acceptance of the plurality of faiths found a major and tangible example in the fact that its foundation stone was laid by a Muslim sage, Sain Mian Mir. Its unique architecture had its doors open on all four sides, signifying that it was open to all[20]. Darbar Sahib, or the Court of the Lord, is another name commonly used for the temple in Amritsar.

The Guru emphasised the superiority of congregational worship and the merit of service (*sewa*) for the common good. He founded towns such as Tarn Taran, Kartarpur and Hargobindpur. At Tarn Taran, he even opened an asylum for lepers, another aspect of social responsibility in the emerging way of life.

Compilation of Adi Granth

An important milestone in the evolution of Sikhism was the compilation of the utterances and writings of the Gurus into a manuscript which was called the *Adi Granth*, a precursor of what is now known as Sri Guru Granth Sahib.

To preserve the integrity of the compositions of his predecessors, Guru Arjan Dev collected their writings, as well as the compositions of selected Hindu and Muslim saints that were in consonance with the Sikh ethos. To these he added his own compositions. He personally edited it and Bhai Gurdas scribed this outstanding example of secularism.

Guru Granth Sahib is the Eternal Guide and teacher of the Sikhs. It contains the pivotal thoughts, the philosophy, the purpose and intent of the Sikh faith embodied as *bani* and manifestation of Divinity in Sikh ethos. It contains the writings of the Sikh Gurus, as well as those of other men of God, all of varied faiths, from different parts of the Indian subcontinent. These compositions span the period from the twelfth to the seventeenth centuries and, as such, are a distillate of five centuries of Indian socio spiritual thought.

The subject of the Granth Sahib is man in his totality. It comprehends every aspect of life, man's beliefs and values, methods of worship, rules of conduct in society, polity, even regulation of economic activity.

Guru Arjan Dev had the Harmandar Sahib built, compilation of *Adi Granth* and became the first Sikh Guru to be martyred. Detail from a painting by R.M. Singh.

---

19 Maharaja Ranjit Singh (1780-1839) got the dome of the Harmandar Sahib plated with gold—hence the expression 'Golden Temple'.
20 In the Harmandar Sahib, it was not the Guru himself who presided; rather the honour was given to the *Shabad Guru*, the collected compositions of his predecessors and himself, as enshrined in the *Adi Granth*.

Harmandar Sahib is the most important shrine for the Sikhs. In December 1588, the great Muslim Sufi saint of Lahore, Hazrat Mian Mir, a follower of the Muslim seer Behlol and a close friend of Guru Arjan Dev, laid the foundation of Harmandar Sahib. Guru Arjan Dev installed the *Adi Granth* in the completed temple in 1604. In the mid-eighteenth century, it was destroyed more than once and was finally rebuilt in the 1760s. The gold leaf work on Harmandar Sahib was done by Maharaja Ranjit Singh. An undated, old photograph of Harmandar Sahib.

Interestingly, this book is not divided into chapters by subject. It is classified into sections under the headings of musical modes of the Indian classical musical tradition (*ragas*). Further, various hymns have references to folklore and idioms in which these must have been enunciated and intended to be sung. This emphasises the desire of the Gurus to reach the core of the common man's inner self and transform it from within.

Sikhism is essentially a religion of *Naam* (Name). In it, the most obvious religious exercise is the recitation or singing of the Guru's Word. Thus, there was a necessity to preserve the authentic Word. The Guru was responsible for organising Sikhism on a sound basis. The Guru prepared this grand volume, which, being the repository of the message, the *Shabad*, was eventually declared as the eternal Guru in 1708 by Guru Gobind Singh, the tenth and last Guru, just before his demise.

Guru Arjan, while describing the work of the organisation he had built among the Sikhs, said: 'Now the order of the Merciful has gone forth that no one shall oppress another'[21]. This was a challenge to the polity of the time.

Emperor Akbar died in 1605, and was succeeded by his son Jahangir, who was much less liberal in his views than his father. He was committed to not allowing any strong non-Islamic religious centres to be formed within his dominions. The notion of Muslims being attracted to other religions was intolerable for him. His mind was set on ending this movement of the Sikh *Panth* that was fast attracting many followers. Consequently, Guru Arjan Dev was arrested and taken to Lahore on trumped-up charges and subjected to all sorts of tortures until he died, after which his blistered body was thrown into the river Ravi on 30 May 1606.

The martyrdom of Guru Arjan marked the fulfilment of Guru Nanak's religious and ethical conjunctions. Personal piety must have a core of moral strength. A virtuous soul must also be a courageous soul. Willingness to suffer for one's convictions is a religious imperative. Convictions must be able to stand up to the utmost test, and faith in the Lord's Will must be total. It is with such a strong inner self and purity of purpose that the 'sword' had to be lifted as a last resort or physical force resorted to—so pithily stated later by the tenth Guru in his letter to Emperor Aurangzeb in 1707: 'When all measures are expended, it is but righteous to wield the sword'.

---

21 SGGS p. 74: Now, the Merciful Lord has issued His Command. Let no one oppress and harass anyone else. Let all abide in peace, under this benign rule.

Guru Hargobind

On the death of Guru Arjan Dev, his son Hargobind, born in Wadali near Amritsar on 19 June 1595, was appointed the sixth Guru. Even by the age of eleven, he had been carefully trained for this high office. Seeing the changing needs of the time, the hostility and intolerance of the established religions and the State, his father had placed him under the tutelage of Baba Budha, a veteran Sikh, who was asked by Guru Arjan to 'make a saint and a soldier' of his young son so that he would be equipped for any armed conflict, if need be.

Upon ascending onto the haloed seat as the sixth Nanak, Guru Hargobind started to don two swords on his person; one to represent the spiritual and the other the temporal interest. He sought offerings of arms and horses from his followers and strengthened the fortifications of Amritsar. In 1609, he built an edifice or a meeting place for Sikhs right in front of the Harmandar Sahib and called it the Akal Takht— Throne of the Timeless Eternal.

When Guru Nanak began his work, he was as aware of the political degradation of the people as he was of the decadence of their religion. He believed that earthly freedom was rooted in spiritual freedom. The two were inseparable.

By now the Sikhs had their own scripture, their own customs, their own religion, a temporal throne and also their own governance. This emerging power was perceived as a threat by the ruling establishment, who were heavily influenced by religious leaders, both Hindu and Muslim, in the court.

In this new society, the Brahminical order saw a threat to its exploitative hegemony and thus, it began to play on this perception by building up a bias in the mind of the rulers. The fact that this new way of life had all the elements of a free nation, including a holy book of its own, also gave an opportunity to the radical Islamists in the Mughal court to make the rulers hostile. Guru Arjan Dev had outlined the path which the community had to take, and prepared it to defend its way of life and values.

Guru Hargobind infused a remarkable martial spirit among the people, hitherto prone to passivity resulting from centuries of subjugation. Guru Nanak's mission and its message of freedom from the oppression of the rulers, from the priestly class, and from the social evils prevalent in the existing religions, was now well-entrenched among the Sikhs.

Guru Hargobind. *Gurubilas Patshahi 6,* an early account of the life and times of the Guru recorded from oral and other contemporary sources, mentions that Bhai Bidhi Chand, a close confidant and devout Sikh of the Guru, commissioned a series of paintings, including this, which is with Bhai Gurchet Singh at village Bhai Rupa. Please turn to page 115 for a larger image.

The Akal Bunga, now called the Akal Takht, at Harmandar Sahib, Amritsar, as shown in a print by William Simpson, 1864. The Akal Takht's foundation was laid by Guru Hargobind and it is considered the seat of temporal authority of the Sikhs.

Sovereign society and its capital

Guru Hargobind had established the Akal Takht as a symbol of temporal authority right in front of the seat of divinity, the Harmandar Sahib. It is no coincidence that from here he conducted the secular affairs of the community. In the open space in front of the Takht, tournaments of physical feats were held in the afternoon, and it was here that the bards would recite heroic poetry of the mundane and the spiritual.

Amritsar thus developed into a 'Capital of the Virtual State of the Sikhs'. Sikhs visited the Guru for spiritual succour and solutions to social problems, and brought him gifts of arms and horses as the Guru desired. A new spirit of moral rejuvenation and vigour emerged in Punjab, its mainspring being the spirit of faith and courage generated by the teachings of the Gurus. This virile direction that the movement took fulfilled Guru Nanak's vision for change.

Alarm bells started ringing in the court of Emperor Jahangir. Fuelled by the fanaticism of the likes of Shaikh Ahmad Sirhindi Mujaddid-i-alif-sani[22] and fanned by the Guru's jealous collaterals, Jahangir arrested the Guru and imprisoned him in the fort at Gwalior sometime between AD 1617 and 1619, along with a number of feudal chiefs from various parts of the country[23]. When at last he was going to be released, Guru Hargobind refused to leave the fort until his co-prisoners were also allowed to go. His wish was acceded to, and a number of prisoners, legend says as many as fifty-two chiefs, gained freedom along with him.

Jahangir's attitude became friendlier with time, and eventually the Guru freely preached all over Punjab and Kashmir. In Sri Hargobindpur, a town founded by the fifth Guru, a mosque was constructed, on Guru Hargobind's instructions, for the local Muslims. It is called Guru-Ki-Maseet.

The Sikh ethos of *sant-sipahi*, saint-soldier, a fusion of the

---

22 An Indian Islamic scholar (1564–1624 AD) and a prominent member of the Naqshbandi Sufi order, who gave to Islam the rigid and conservative stamp it bears today.
23 One among them was the Raja of Sirmaur, whose son Medani Parkash later hosted Guru Gobind Singh at Paonta. His son, too, was sympathetic towards the Sikhs and he harboured Banda Bahadur at Lohgarh, an act for which he was arrested and tortured to death by the Mughals.

spiritual and the valiant, was manifest in him. In his reply to a query of the Maratha saint, Samrath Ramdas (1608-1681), the Guru described himself as: 'Internally a hermit and externally a prince. Arms mean protection to the poor and destruction of tyrants. Baba Nanak had not renounced the world. He had only renounced *maya*, which is illusion and ego.' A synthesis of the heroic with the spiritual thus emerged in the process of the evolution of Sikh ethos. This was in consonance with the spirit of the teachings of Guru Nanak, and the principles determined by him and worked upon during the lives of all the succeeding Gurus.

The militarisation of the Sikhs was not a new doctrine followed by the religion; it was rooted in Guru Nanak's principles and was the foundation that led to the formation of a regenerated nation by the way of the Sikhs, which stirred up society economically and politically.

Conflict

During his tenure, even the slightest incident of confrontation became a point of conflict with the Mughal rulers. An incident involving Emperor Shah Jahan, whose favourite hawk flew into the Sikh camp, became a flashpoint. Shah Jahan sent a body of troops to arrest the Guru. The Sikhs fought back. The Mughal commander was killed and his soldiers fled. The implications of this ostensibly minor incident were far-reaching. Mughal persecution intensified and consequently, the Sikhs became more militant.

To avoid unnecessary confrontation and not to be caught unprepared for a face-off, the Guru moved out of Amritsar towards the southwest. The first halt was at Darauli, in the present-day district of Faridkot, where he stayed for an extended period of time. The Mughal troops pursued him there, and a battle ensued. The Guru had nearly 4,000 armed Sikhs with him, and the army suffered heavy losses. Lal Beg, the Mughal commander, was killed and his troops fled. The Guru had a water tank, called Gurusar, dug at the site as a memorial.

Another battle followed shortly at a place called Kartarpur. Two Mughal commanders, Mir Badhera and Paindha Khan, were killed in the fighting and the Guru's youngest son, Tyag Mal, emerged as the battle's hero. As a reward for the great valour showed by him, his name was changed to Tegh Bahadur post-battle. He was later to become the ninth Guru and is known for being an apostle of peace who sacrificed

Guru-ki-Maseet in Hargobindpur is a living monument to the egalitarian nature of the Sikh faith. It was built by Guru Hargobind for Muslims who lived in the town that he founded.

Guru Har Rai, the seventh Guru, depicted in a painting in village Bhai Rupa, probably painted there. The Guru was a great lover of nature and maintained a large constabulary at Kiratpur Sahib. Please turn to page 117 for the full picture.

his own life for the rights of others to practise their religion[24].

Guru Hargobind was still on the move after the battle when he decided to shift his headquarters to a safer haven away from Mughal dominance. He chose a place in the Shivalik foothills called Kiratpur, which then became the new centre of Sikh faith. The Guru lived there till his demise.

Guru Har Rai

Before passing away on 3 March 1644 at Kiratpur, Guru Hargobind appointed and anointed his grandson[25], Har Rai, as the seventh Guru of the Sikhs. Guru Har Rai consolidated the work of his predecessors. Even though no conflict took place with the Mughals during his time, the new Guru maintained a large constabulary of horses. He travelled widely and appointed disciples to preach the Sikh faith in different regions of the country. It was during the Guru's visit to the village of Bhai Rup Chand, whom Guru Hargobind had put in charge of the Sikh *sangat* of Brars in Malwa, that Phul, the ancestor of the families of the states of Patiala, Nabha and Jind, received his blessings. These families played significant roles in the history of Sikhs in the times to come.

Soon after Aurangzeb sat on the Mughal throne in Delhi, he summoned Guru Har Rai to Delhi to ascertain whether Sikhism and its scriptures were in any way inimical to Islam. The Guru sent his son Ram Rai instead. Bhai Gurdas, a respected Sikh from the family of Bhai Bahilo, was asked to accompany him with a copy of the Sikh scripture, the Granth Sahib. Of the many questions that he was asked, one concerned a particular line in Guru Nanak's major composition *Asa-Di-Vaar*, which says that Muslims hold that the bodies of those who are cremated go to hell, but what happens when the clay from a graveyard gets baked in a potter's kiln?

Fearing the Emperor's displeasure, Ram Rai changed the word 'Mussalman' in the original text by deliberately misreading it as '*beiman*' or faithless[26]. Though the Emperor was pleased and gave Ram Rai the Doon valley (now Dehradun) as a grant, the Guru was deeply pained at this lack of conviction and courage shown by his son by compromising the purity of the scripture. Ram Rai was banished,

---

24 *Dasam Granth*: He protected the sacred Hindu symbols, the thread and the mark on the forehead, a great feat in Kalyug. He unflinchingly sacrificed his life for the sake of their faith. He lost his life but not his commitment.
25 He was son of Baba Suraj Mal, eldest son of Guru Hargobind.
26 SGGS p. 466: The earth of the Muslim's grave becomes clay for the potter's wheel. Pots and bricks are fashioned from it, and it cries out as it burns.

and consequently his young son, Harkrishan, was selected to succeed as the eighth Guru.

Guru Harkrishan

Guru Har Rai, the seventh Guru, passed away on 6 October 1661, at Kiratpur, and his five-year-old grandson Harkrishan, son of Ram Rai, became the eighth Guru.

Ram Rai, who had been bypassed by his father, sought Emperor Aurangzeb's intervention to lay his claim to the Guru's seat. Aurangzeb summoned both the parties to Delhi. Mirza Raja Jai Singh persuaded the reluctant young Guru Harkrishan to come to Delhi and lodged him at his own house in village Raisina outside the city walls[27]. Curious about the intelligence and the maturity of the barely eight-year-old Guru, the Emperor tried to test him. Among the womenfolk of the Raja's household was the Raja's wife dressed as an ordinary maid. The child Guru had no problem in recognising her. This and some other such episodes convinced the Mughal of the merit in Guru Harkrishan's succession[28]. Ram Rai's claim was dismissed and he spent the rest of his life in Doon, conspiring against the Guru.

Guru Harkrishan, even at the tender age of eight, had a prodigious insight and ability for explaining passages from the Holy Book. He delighted the hearts of his disciples with his religious discourses and commentaries, constantly reminding them to cherish the One God alone and embrace virtues of patience, charity and love.

He died early, stricken by smallpox at the age of eight in Delhi.

Guru Harkrishan, the eighth Guru. The child Guru was summoned by Aurangzeb to explain the Sikh doctrine. The Guru was reluctant, but he was persuaded by Raja Jai Singh, who hosted him in his garden outside the Walled City of Delhi. Gurdwara Bangla Sahib in New Delhi commemorates this spot.

Guru Tegh Bahadur

As was the tradition and practice of all Sikh Gurus to appoint their successor before demise, Guru Harkrishan appointed his grandfather's youngest brother, Tegh Bahadur, son of Guru Hargobind, his successor.

Guru Tegh Bahadur was forty-four years old at the time of

---

27 The place is now commemorated as Gurdwara Bangla Sahib.
28 As George Forster, a foreign traveller, recorded later on in his 1798 book, *Journey from Bengal to England, through the Northern Part of India, Kashmire, Afghanistan, and Persia, and into Russia, by the Caspian-Sea,* this episode marked the de-facto recognition of the Sikhs' right to nominate their own 'Priest', Guru.

accession to the haloed seat of Guru Nanak as its ninth incumbent, on the Baisakhi festival day in March 1665.

The youngest of the five sons of Guru Hargobind, Tegh Bahadur was born on 1 April 1621. Brought up in true Sikh tradition, he was put under the tutelage of Bhai Budha and Bhai Gurdas. The former trained him in horsemanship and archery, and the latter taught him the classics. He grew up in an environment in which he acquired deep humility, compassion and also a firmness of mind. He held that 'Forgiveness is the austerity most meritorious. Forgiveness is the best of charities. Forgiveness is equivalent to all pilgrimages and ablutions. In forgiveness lies liberation. No other virtue parallels forgiveness. Forgiveness, then, must one learn.'[29]

However, he was no recluse. Like his predecessors, he maintained a bearing of regal dignity. With his teachings and extensive travels across the country; he infused a new element into the Sikh ethos, as reflected in his affirmation: 'He who holds no one in fear nor is afraid of anyone, acknowledge him alone as man of true wisdom.'[30]

His admirers cut across religious divides. Nawab Saifuddin Mohammad, a retired governor of Agra under Aurangzeb, lived in seclusion as Saif Khan[31] near modern-day Patiala. Having heard of the charisma of the Guru, he desired to see him, which he did, at Bahadurgarh. In November 1665, when the Guru visited Delhi, Rani Pushpa Devi of Amber played host to him.

Later, Guru Tegh Bahadur travelled to Patna. After a brief stay there, responding to the wishes of the Sikh *sangats* in remote areas of Assam and present-day Bangladesh, he moved further to the east, leaving his family behind. No other Guru had visited these areas since Guru Nanak. At Dhaka, Raja Ram Singh of Amber was leading a Mughal expedition against the local ruler, Chatardwaj Singh. The Guru stayed at a place called Dhubri and brought about a reconciliation between the Assamese and the Mughals. The locals are said to have named a hillock as Teghpur or Tegh Parbhat to commemorate the Guru's visit.

Aurangzeb, the Mughal Emperor of the time, was acting fanatically and had resorted to forcible conversions to Islam. Guru Tegh Bahadur

Guru Tegh Bahadur, the ninth Guru, remembered as the 'protector of Hind' because of offering his own life in protest to the persecution and forcible conversion of Brahmins in Kashmir. A detail from a painting in the collection of the Maharaja of Nabha.

---

29 *Sri Gur Partap Suraj Granth*, by Bhai Santokh Singh, is a classical medieval treatise on Sikh history and philosophy.
30 SGGS p.1427: One who does not frighten anyone, and who is not afraid of anyone else—says Nanak, listen, mind: call him spiritually wise.
31 He lived in a fort originally called Saifabad, which is now known as Bahadurgarh, on the outskirts of Patiala.

was approached for help by some Kashmiri Pandits, or Brahmins, who were being forced into conversion. Being a firm believer in the right to freedom of an individual to pursue a faith of his own choice, the Guru took upon himself the challenge of standing up for their rights.

The Guru told the Brahmins to convey to the Emperor that they would convert, provided Guru Tegh Bahadur did so. The Brahmins got a respite and the Guru faced the ire of the Emperor. He was arrested and taken to Delhi along with some of his companions. Bhai Sati Das and Bhai Mati Das were tortured and put to death when they refused to resile their faith. The Guru was beheaded when he refused to give up his religious beliefs.

It took the sacrifice of a man of Guru Tegh Bahadur's piety and stature to challenge this oppression. Guru Nanak's call to his followers, to come to the fold ready to 'sacrifice their heads' for the cause of human dignity and freedom of thought, came to life when his ninth successor was beheaded at Delhi's Chandni Chowk in 1675. In the words of his son, the tenth Guru, he preferred to 'give his head rather than resile from his commitment to his ideals'. This highlighted a unique aspect of universality of the Sikh faith. Guru Tegh Bahadur laid down his life for the protection of a faith not his own, but of others, even when some of their precepts and practices were inimical to his beliefs.

Martyrdom consolidates faith

Guru Tegh Bahadur was the second Guru to be martyred. He laid down his life for the sake of justice, tolerance and righteousness.

The martyrdom of two Gurus, the fifth and the ninth, marked the two defining aspects of the evolution of the Sikh ethos. Guru Arjan Dev was tortured to death after the Sikh faith had fully evolved its spiritual base, and institutionalised it into a formal scripture—the Guru Granth Sahib—and a thriving Sikh social order had been established in the Harmandar Sahib[32] at the centre of the town of Amritsar. His arrest was ostensibly for non-payment of some unjust

A painting of Guru Teg Bahadur, traditionally known as the Dhaka portrait. The watercolour was commissioned by the mother of Bhai Balaki Shah, the host of Guru Teg Bahadur, who engaged Ahsan, a royal painter of Shaistakhan, to paint a portrait of the ninth Guru during his stay in Dhaka, between 1667-68.

---

32 The honorific Sahib is normally added to the name these days, and thus it is popularly referred to as Harmandar Sahib.

Gurdwara Sis Ganj at Chandni Chowk in Delhi where Guru Tegh Bahadur was martyred, along with two other Sikhs, Bhai Mati Das and Bhai Sati Das, on the orders of Emperor Aurangzeb, in 1675.

taxes imposed by the Governor of Lahore. However, the real reason, in Jahangir's own words[33], was the magnetic appeal—spiritual and social—of this young faith, which attracted Muslims and Hindus alike. The universality of appeal of the Sikh religion, call it theology or faith or both, encompassed into one, a way of life, the Sikhi of Guru Nanak, was attracting people from all shades of society.

Guru Tegh Bahadur's sacrifice went beyond the cause of his own faith in the narrow sense. It addressed the fundamental right of every individual to choose his own path of religious practice. Guru Nanak's way of life rejects the Brahminical thought and practice. For almost two hundred years, the Sikh Gurus fought against this oppression by the upper castes in accordance with the old established religious traditions. But when the Kashmiri Brahmins were threatened with forced conversions by radical Islamists of Aurangzeb's regime, Guru Tegh Bahadur took it upon himself to oppose and challenge the move.

For doing so, he was executed. The martyrdoms of the Gurus established that the Sikh way of life stood for the universality and freedom of the human spirit, and man's freedom to profess and practice the faith of his choice.

The new faith upheld the larger issue of human rights and freedom of conscience. The State, according to the Gurus, had no authority over the individual's conscience, and any attempt to create a unitary, monolithic society by force had to be resisted. It affirmed a firm belief in a liberal and ethical social order, and a principle of acceptance of faith and freedom of its practice.

This is to be differentiated from the Islamic concept of *shahadat*, wherein you willingly sacrifice your life for propagating your religious beliefs and thus earn *jannat*, entry into heaven.

Guru Gobind Singh

The responsibility of leading Guru Nanak's mission then passed on to Gobind Rai, son of Guru Tegh Bahadur. He was born in Patna on 22 December 1666, and lived there till he was four years old. During

---

33 *Tuzak-i-Jahangiri*: A Hindu, Arjan by name, lived in the garb of a *pir* & *sheikh* and captivated the hearts of many simple-minded Hindus, and foolish and stupid Muslims by his way and means... They called him Guru and from all directions fools and fool [sic] worshippers were attracted towards him and expressed full faith in him. For three or four generations they had kept this shop warm. For years the thought had been presenting itself to me that I should either put an end to this false traffic or that he (Guru Arjan) should be brought into the fold of Islam... I fully knew his heresies. I ordered that he should be brought into my presence. Having handed over his houses, mansions and children to Murtaza Khan, and having confiscated his property. I ordered that he should be put to death with tortures.

A close-up of a painting, by Jaswant Singh, showing Bhai Jaita carrying the *sis* (head) of the ninth Guru to Anandpur Sahib. In the mêlée that followed the execution, he took the Guru's head and rushed to Anandpur Sahib, where he was received by Guru Gobind Singh. Another Sikh, Bhai Lakkhi Shah, took the Guru's torso to his hut three miles away. He cremated the body by setting his hut on fire. Gurdwara Rakabganj, in New Delhi, commemorates the spot.

this period he learnt the local language, Braj, alongside Punjabi, and also imbibed the essence of Indian literary heritage. At the age of five, he joined his father in Anandpur, where he acquired a comprehensive knowledge of Persian. His poetic genius blossomed and his deep understanding of the heritage of both the Hindu and Islamic cultures and their theology, stands out in his vast literary creations.

His father decided that he was mature enough when the Kashmiri Pandits came for help. The Guru said that it would take the sacrifice of a noble person to safeguard their right to practise their own religion. The young Gobind Rai then submitted to his father that he knew of no one nobler than Guru Tegh Bahadur. The answer pleased the Guru and he decided that his son was ready take over the mantle of the house of Guru Nanak after him.

On becoming the tenth Guru, he moved eastwards to the hill state of Sirmaur. Fascinated by the natural beauty of a spot on the bank of the river Yamuna, he founded the town of Paonta in April 1685 on a piece of land gifted by Medini Parkash, the Raja of Sirmaur. In

THE GURUS AND THE SPIRIT OF SIKHI   47

the decade he stayed at Paonta, worked out the future he envisioned for his people and the nature of socio-religious society that he would formalise as fruition of Guru Nanak's mission.

He patronised men of learning, and many poets and scholars were residents in his court. Himself an outstanding scholar and writer, he composed poetry—both, literary and spiritual—marked by sublimity of style, mystic ardour and vibrant dynamism of thought and action.

The special element in his works was the emergence of a new metaphor of the 'sword', *bhagauti*. To him, the 'sword' was symbolic of the *Akalpurakh* (Timeless Being) Himself. He described God as *Sarab Loh* (all steel).

Even when referring to God as *Sarab Loh* or Sword, Guru Gobind Singh was not oblivious of His characteristics of love and compassion[34].

The Guru presented God as the Punisher of the Evil and the Destroyer of the Tyrant, symbolically represented in weapons of war. The benevolent aspect is simultaneously and equally forcefully emphasised and He is invoked as the Fountainhead of Mercy, the Kinsman of the Poor and the Bestower of Felicity. This fusion of the devotional and the martial, of the spiritual and the heroic, emerges as the most important element of the philosophy of Guru Gobind Singh and of his career as a spiritual leader and harbinger of a socio-spiritual revolution. Quite naturally, this is reflected in the social order that he created, the Khalsa.

Poetry per se was not his aim; instead, poetry to him was a medium of revealing the Divine principle and concretising the personal vision of the Supreme Being that had been vouchsafed to him[35]. Through his poetry, he preached love, equality and a strictly ethical and moral code of conduct. He reiterated the worship of the One Supreme Being, deprecating idolatry, superstitious beliefs, and observances. The glorification of the sword itself was to secure fulfilment of God's justice. The sword was never a symbol of aggression, and it was never to be used for self-aggrandisement. It stood for righteous and brave action, for protection of truth and virtue. It was the emblem of

A miniature, depicting Guru Gobind Singh in his adolescence. The artist shows the Guru dressed in formal clothes to signify the enormous responsibility that fell on him after his father's martyrdom.

34 A couplet in his *Jap Sahib* reads:
   I bow to Thee, Lord, Who art the wielder of the sword!
   I bow to Thee, Lord, Who art the possessor of arms!
   I bow to Thee, Lord, Who knowest the ultimate secret!
   I bow to Thee, Lord, Who loves the world like a mother!
35 Guru Gobind Singh, *Bachitar Natak*: I have come into this life for Dharma, and the Lord has entrusted me with this responsibility. Wherever you spread the light of Dharma, you eliminate evil and oppression. I was born with this purpose, O Men of God, understand me well. I will propagate Dharma, protect the Good and uproot all Evil.

manliness and self-respect and was to be used only in self-defence, as a last resort[36].

During his stay at Paonta, the Guru relived the vision of his predecessors and formulated the concept and dynamics of the Khalsa society, so that what his predecessors had envisioned could be consolidated for the future. The Guru also worked out the modus for implementation and protection of such a society in the centuries-old hostile environment, entrenched theological straitjackets.

In his works, one sees the internalisation of the spiritual-mythological past of India; the heroes of mythology were depicted by him only as extraordinary humans who lost the purpose of their mission by becoming an end in themselves[37]. Characters from mythology were borrowed to infuse valour and uplift the spirit of the people to fight for their rights. Here at Paonta, the Guru prepared himself for the completion of the Divine mission.

The new metaphor of 'sword' was to ensure the success and survival of this new order; it was essential to equip the *Panth* with symbols that protect and project it. Thus, charity (*degh*) and valour (*tegh*), which were held in high esteem and practised since the times of Guru Hargobind, were now made inseparable. Added to it was their glorification as victory (*fateh*). The Sikhs acquired the slogan '*Degh Tegh Fateh*', which is often translated as 'Victory to Charity and Valour'.

In 1699, within three years of moving back to Anandpur, a formal declaration of the order of Khalsa was made. It had unique characteristics. People who wished to enrol in it were firstly asked to come prepared to sacrifice their lives for the principles and values

---

36 Guru Gobind Singh, *Zafarnama*: When all other efforts fail, wielding the sword is ethical.
37 Guru Gobind Singh, *Bachitar Natak*: Everyone made his followers recite his own name, rather than that of the transcendental Lord.

Guru Gobind Singh with his four sons at Anandpur Sahib, seated in courtly splendour. The two elder sons Ajit Singh and Jujhar Singh died fighting in the battle of Chamkaur. The two younger sons, the nine-year old Zorawar Singh and the seven-year old Fateh Singh, were captured and put to death at Fatehgarh a few days later.

THE GURUS AND THE SPIRIT OF SIKHI

Takht Sri Keshgarh Sahib marks the spot where the Khalsa was consecrated on the Baisakhi of 1699. This picture was taken during the tercentenary celebrations of the consecration of the Khalsa in 1999.

of this order, a pre-condition laid down much earlier by Guru Nanak. They were all to shed inherited prejudices of casteism and all other biases acquired over millennia. They had to work for the common good and practise ethical polity, which would liberate them from religio-economic oppression. They were to function as operatives of the Divine Will, fear no one and scare no one. Their responsibilities were first to their kin, but then they must extend equally to society beyond the Khalsa[38].

Consecration of the new order

On the Baisakhi day of 1699, the journey from Amritsar to Anandpur was complete. Sikh practices and values were reaffirmed and constitutionalised. Whatever the Sikhs were practising for over the last two centuries now became their statute. Since Guru Nanak's time, they had lived a life of utter commitment, and on this day, the Sikhs took an oath of commitment to this way of life. Now that the Khalsa had fully evolved, it was established as a definite living social entity—sovereign in itself.

In fact, 'Guru Gobind Singh was a true socialist in thought, word and deed, a proletarian of the Divine and 'Whereas Guru Nanak gave meaning to life, Guru Gobind invested death with a new purpose. Consecrated life became an objective and reality. Guru Gobind Singh, by a flash of his sword, filled the dying soul of India with life-giving light and truth, and it showed again in the life of the newborn Khalsa! The light of reality had kindled the spark of life again in the dying soul of India,' says Swami Vivekananda[39].

'Under Guru Gobind Singh's leadership, nationalism itself became a religion, and the result was the creation of a fraternity unique in character,' admits even a diehard antagonist of the Sikhs from the early twentieth century.

But, above all, 'Khalsa lived poised on sword's sharp edge, and died kissing its cold steel. Indeed iron had gone into his soul at his nativity. But it would be a mistake to associate the Khalsa with wanton wars and

---

38 The common expression for this is found in the slogan *Sarbat da Bhalaa*, proclaimed at the end of every *Ardaas* (prayer) made by a Sikh.
39 Swami Vivekananda (12 January 1863 – 4 July 1902), was the chief disciple of the nineteenth-century mystic Sri Ramakrishna Paramahamsa and the founder of the Ramakrishna Mission. He was a major force in the revival of Hinduism in the late nineteenth century, and was regarded as an antagonist of the Sikhs from the early twentieth century.

bloodshed. He took up the sword because of a crisis of conscience.'

Guru Gobind Singh had made emphatic statements to the effect that the *Akalpurakh* (the Timeless Being) can be perceived in the material world. The entire world and all sentient and non-sentient beings are, in essence, one with the Supreme Reality. This spiritualisation of the manifest social phenomena makes it relatively real, and thus worth living in.

With the creation of the Khalsa *Panth*, he gave to the world Guru Nanak's vision of the ideal human being, and an ideal microcosmic social structure. The Khalsa was required to always be in mystic communion with God by attuning himself to the Divine Will. However, this was not to say that Sikhs should turn ascetics, indifferent to the affairs of the world. Rather, this mystic communion should transform them into morally and ethically uplifted and socially awakened individuals who strive and sacrifice for the sake of justice, love, equality, righteousness, and respect of human affairs.

At that point in history, the Indian people were no strangers to religion, but never before had they felt the nationalistic feeling that Guru Gobind Singh inspired with the formation of the *Panth*. He made nationalism the religion of the Khalsa, and the Sikhs emerged as a nation.

The ideal human is a man who has the name of God on his lips and a burning desire to wage war against tyranny and oppression of all kinds[40]. During the period, the individual Sikh, too, grew from a serf to a self-respecting human being and learnt to walk erect. A just society where no one would torment the other[41] became a reality. Every individual nurtured his own free spirit and his own beliefs. He was allowed to exert and flourish socially and economically.

Significantly, from the Guru in human form, the centrality of this new faith shifted to the Guru as *Shabad* (the Word).

The dedication and spirit of the individual was at its peak. Guru Arjan Dev's martyrdom had demonstrated the highest form of acceptance of the Divine Will in the process of serving humanity. It set the first and ultimate standard for the inner strength of a man who commits himself to walk Guru Nanak's path—a path of love, dedication and service to his mankind and God.

Later, Guru Tegh Bahadur, the ninth Guru, made the supreme sacrifice. He was martyred because he stood up for the right of

---

40 Guru Gobind Singh, *Dasam Granth*, p. 570: Hail the man who lives a life of right activity and strife with the name of God on his lips.
41 SGGS p. 74: Now, the Merciful Lord has issued His Command. Let no one chase after and attack anyone else. Let all abide in peace, under this Benevolent Rule.

Nagin barcha, or serpentine war lance, used by Bhai Bachitar Singh while fighting an inebriated elephant during the Battle of Logarh, 1699. Bhai Bachittar Singh wounded the elephant, which was being used as a battering ram by the Hill Rajas attacking the forces of Guru Gobind Singh. After the animal turned around and spread panic in enemy forces, another Sikh, Uday Singh, engaged Kesri Chand, who was leading the enemy force, and killed him. The lance is kept at Takht Sri Kesgarh Sahib, Anandpur.

Guru Gobind Singh as shown in a contemporary miniature commissioned by the Raja of Mandi.

everyone, including the Kashmiri Hindus, to pursue their own faith and worship God freely.

When Guru Hargobind, at the age of twelve, was handed over the sceptre of Guru Nanak's authority, he donned two swords—symbolic of spiritual and sovereign individuality. This warrior Guru then asserted the right of the God-oriented (*Gurmukhs*) to defend themselves, their values and their society.

The two swords of Guru Hargobind and what they represented merged metaphysically, to be symbolically represented by the *khanda* or the double-edged sword in the hands of Guru Gobind Singh. To him it signified the Divine dynamism—the Divine unlimited force, synonymous with the Will of God in action. The two edges of the *khanda* had a double symbolism—the creator and protector of good and the destroyer of evil. Sikhs invoke it as a symbol of the Ultimate and are baptised by it.

Establishment strikes back

After the creation of the Khalsa, the chieftains of the small Hindu hill kingdoms around Anandpur became actively hostile towards Guru Gobind Singh and resolved to destroy this fledgling order, which they considered inimical to the existing socio-religious structure, however oppressive.

Initially, they tried to harass the Sikhs militarily. In the skirmishes that ensued, the Sikhs got the better of them and some of their chiefs were even killed. The remaining chiefs then approached the Mughal Emperor Aurangzeb and projecting the Sikh society and faith as a threat to the Mughal rule and Islam, they sought his assistance to drive the Sikhs out of Anandpur.

The hill chiefs even volunteered to bear the expenses of the imperial troops, affirming that the complaint was purely borne out of self-interest[42]. Consequently, an expedition of 10,000 troops, led by Painde Khan and Din Beg and supplemented by the forces of hill chiefs, attacked the Sikhs. They were routed by the Guru's forces on 25 June

---

42 In *Ibrat Nama*, Mohammad Qasim Lahori calls them *ishab-i-gharz*, persons who were moved by self-interest.

1700[43]. Repeated battles followed, in which the Sikhs demonstrated great courage and valour, which is immortalised in folklore.

Guru Gobind Singh withdrew from Anandgarh Fort and moved to the safety of a hillock, Nirmohgarh, a few kilometres away, near Kiratpur. In early October of the year 1700, Raja Ajmer Chand of Kehlur laid siege to Nirmohgarh, and the Governor of Sirhind sent a force under Rustam Khan to support him. In the ensuing battle, commanders Rustam Khan and his brother Nasir Khan were killed. Avoiding further confrontation, and at the invitation of Raja Salehi Chand of Basoli from across the Sutlej, the Guru, along with his forces, crossed over to his state. Later, on the intervention of Salehi Chand[44], whose wife was the younger sister of Rani Pushpa, Ajmer Chand's mother, reconciliation was effected, and the Guru returned to Anandpur.

The common man had started looking up to the Guru and his Sikhs for security and securing the redressal of grievances. When the wife of a Brahmin was kidnapped by a Mughal satrap, a force led by the Guru's son, Sahibzada Ajit Singh, rescued the lady, captured the Khan and brought him before the Guru for justice. Interestingly, now the Brahmin sought help of the Guru and not the Mughal authorities.

Even though a certain amount of reconciliation had taken place, Raja Ajmer Chand was not pacified. He personally went to the Deccan and presented a petition to Aurangzeb, pleading that the Guru had established a new religion and wanted all Hindus to embrace it and wage war against the Mughal Empire. Concerned, the Emperor ordered all troops in northern India to join the hill chieftains under the command of Wazir Khan, the Governor of Sirhind, and attack the Sikhs.

In the winter of 1704, Wazir Khan attacked Anandpur with a large force. The Sikhs were well-prepared, and both sides suffered heavy casualties. It was here that an episode took place which showed how the Guru's teachings had seeped into the followers. At the end of the day's fighting, some Sikhs complained to the Guru that a Sikh named Kanhaya was seen giving water to the wounded soldiers of the enemy. When questioned, Kanhaya admitted the fact, saying: 'I could not distinguish between the Mughal and the Sikh. All I could see was the Guru's face in every one.' Immensely pleased, the Guru commended this act. A tradition of humanitarian succour and service even on the battlefield was thus enunciated, giving a new dimension to Guru Nanak's edict of *sewa*.

A *katar* (punch-dagger) of Guru Gobind Singh, which was given to Raja Salehi Chand of Basoli, who played host to the Guru. It is now with Kanwar Sumer Singh, his descendant.

---

43 Savan Vadi 65, BK 1757
44 Salehi Chand had disagreed with the other chiefs when they broke their sacred oath earlier.

A scimitar that belonged to Guru Gobind Singh, kept at Takht Sri Keshgarh Sahib, Anandpur.

The Siege of Anandpur

On 3 May 1705[45], the Mughal forces laid siege to Anandpur, which lasted seven months till 4 December 1705[46]. It came to an end with the Mughal commanders sending a message to the Guru in the Emperor's name, expressing regret at the earlier behaviour of the imperial troops and reiterating the agreement of safe conduct if the Guru agreed to leave Anandpur. To impress their sincerity, a royal *qazi* brought an imperial letter and a verbal message from the Emperor to the Guru, giving a solemn assurance of a safe passage to the Guru and the Sikhs to Kangar in Malwa region. The assurance was cemented by an oath taken on the Holy Quran by the Mughal emissary, and on their articles of faith by the Hindu hill chiefs.

A man of God could not but have given credence to the oath of another man sworn on his Godhead. Aurangzeb was a devout Mussalman and he would have been damned if he broke his oath on the Quran, or so the Guru thought. On 5 December 1705, the Guru vacated Anandgarh fort at Anandpur, taking with him his family and a treasury of a lifetime's literary work by the cartload. He had barely gone ten miles when Mughal forces and hordes of Hindu Hill Rajas fell upon his train. The Sikhs fought valiantly but eventually, while crossing the rivulet Sirsa, which was in spate, the Guru and his family were separated, and the train washed away.

The Guru's two older sons, Sahibzada Ajit Singh and Sahibzada Jujhar Singh, along with a few chosen Sikhs accompanying the Guru, reached Chamkaur, where they took positions in the relative security of a mud fortress. The younger sons, Sahibzada Zorawar Singh and Sahibzada Fateh Singh, barely nine and seven years of age, headed towards Delhi with their grandmother in the care of a family cook, Ganga Ram Dhar. This trusted and once-faithful retainer betrayed the children and the old lady to the Mughal Governor of Sirhind[47]. Offered the choice between their faith and death, the young Singhs chose the latter and were put to death by being bricked up alive in a wall at Sirhand. Gurdwara Fatehgarh Sahib, on the outskirts of the old town of Sirhind, commemorates the spot where they were cremated.

Meanwhile, at Chamkaur, the Guru and his forty-odd companions were attacked by the Mughal army. In the fierce battle that followed on 7 December 1705, the Guru's two older sons, along with most of

---

45 5 Jeth BK 1762
46 5 Poh BK 1762
47 His family was later rewarded by Emperor Farrukh Siyar with a large estate at Andha Mughal, near present-day Mehrauli, New Delhi.

A painting by Kirpal Singh, showing Guru Gobind Singh crossing the Sirsa rivulet with his family in December 1705, after the evacuation of Anandpur. He and his forces were pursued by the Hill Rajas. The river was in spate and thus dangerous to cross. The Guru was separated from his mother and younger sons, and the Sikhs suffered many losses of men and materials, including many of the manuscripts of the literary works of the Guru's court, which had attracted many contemporary intellectuals and poets in residence.

the Sikhs, were killed while fighting, displaying unparalleled bravery and courage. Sahibzada Ajit Singh fought through the enemy lines and eventually fell at a spot about three kilometres away from the fortress.

The Sikhs then took a collective decision and resolved to request the Guru to leave Chamkaur and continue with his mission. This was perhaps the first decision of the collective, the *Panth*, called the Gurmata of the Sikh society. The Guru, honouring the decision of the collective, left Chamkaur with only two of his Sikhs. He was later helped by his Muslim admirers, who garbed him as a Muslim *pir* and took him to safety, which was provided by Rai Kalha, a neighbouring local Muslim chieftain.

The loss in Sirsa resurrected the Sikh evolution, and gave it a challenging new and heroic direction. Guru Gobind Singh moved on to the Kangar area in Malwa. The territory, barren and hostile, was home to committed Sikhs, who had been supporting the Guru's community with men and material even during the three years of siege of Anandpur[48].

---

48 A *Hukamnama* from Guru Gobind Singh is preserved at Bhai Rupa. In this the Guru summons Bhai Mehar Chand of Bhai Rupa to Anandpur and assures him of his protection.

THE GURUS AND THE SPIRIT OF SIKHI

The gate of the *kotwali* where Mata Gujari, mother of Guru Gobind Singh, and his younger sons were incarcerated in Morinda, before they were moved to Sirhand.

From the time of the sixth Guru, Sikh families in Malwa were the solid base of the community's strength and from this lot he resurrected and rebuilt the *Panth*. It was during his stay in Malwa, between 1706 and October 1707, that these powerful Sikh families were given the baptism of the double-edged sword, called *pahul*, and commissioned as the Khalsa. These Sikh leaders later helped Banda Bahadur to take on the Mughal rulers, destroy Sirhand and set forth the socio-political forces that ended up establishing the Sikh kingdom in Punjab a hundred years later. He also called upon these Sikhs to accompany him on his mission to the south[49].

Another significant task that he completed during his stay in Kangar was the preparation of the final recession of the Sikh scripture, at Damdama. Guru Gobind Singh added the compositions of his father, Guru Tegh Bahadur, to the volume earlier prepared by Guru Arjan Dev and thus, this recession left no scope for doubt about the authenticity of the pivotal thoughts of Sikh theology. It is this updated version that would later be anointed as the eternal sovereign and religious preceptor after the demise of the Guru in human form, as the eternal Guru of the Sikhs for all times, at Nanded in October, 1708, just before the tenth Guru's demise.

The final journey

From Dina, a village in present-day Bathinda district, Guru Gobind Singh wrote a letter in Persian to Aurangzeb, called *Zafarnama*, the Epistle of Victory. In it, he stressed the necessity of ethical polity in matters of public policy as well of personal conduct. Victory and defeat, he held, were to be judged by ultimate standards of morality and not by temporary material advantage. The Guru regarded means to be as important as the end. This epistle was a severe indictment of Aurangzeb, who was repeatedly berated for this breach of faith by the conduct of his satraps after the Sikhs were given assurances of safe conduct on oaths taken on the Holy Quran. The *Zafarnama* stands out as one of the most forthright essays on the centrality of truth in diplomacy, and reiterates the sovereignty of morality in

---

49 This *Hukamnama*, dated October 1706, is preserved at Bhai Rupa.

affairs of the state.⁵⁰

This letter was delivered to Aurangzeb at Ahmednagar. Deeply impressed by its contents, he immediately sent an official order, a *farmaan*, to the Deputy Governor of Lahore, to make peace with Guru Gobind Singh. He also invited the Guru for a personal meeting.

Meanwhile, the Guru decided to move southwards and called upon the Sikhs of the area of Malwa to accompany him. On 30 October 1706, Guru Gobind Singh departed from Damdama Sahib.

He was in Rajputana when, on 20 February 1707, news arrived of the death of Aurangzeb. The Emperor's death was a signal for the usual war of succession to the throne of Delhi. Prince Muazzam, the eldest son, had the reputation of being a man of liberal thought, and was also the rightful heir to the throne. On his request, Guru Gobind Singh sent a body of Sikhs to defend his right to the crown against other

A painting by Tirlok Singh depicting Mata Gujari, mother of Guru Gobind Singh, with the younger sons of the Guru, Zorawar Singh and Fateh Singh. After vacating Anandpur in November 1705, Guru Gobind Singh and his elder sons were separated from the rest of the family. The younger sons and their grandmother were betrayed by the family retainer, Ganga Ram, to the Mughals. They were eventually brought to Sirhind and imprisoned there. Later, the children were martyred while their grandmother died of grief.

---

50 In the *Zafarnama*, the Guru also warned the Mughal Emperor that if he did not come in peace, he would 'set fire under the hooves of his horses' as the people's revolution was ripe in Punjab. This revolution was later to take place after Banda Bahadur defeated the Mughal Governor of Sirhind.

THE GURUS AND THE SPIRIT OF SIKHI

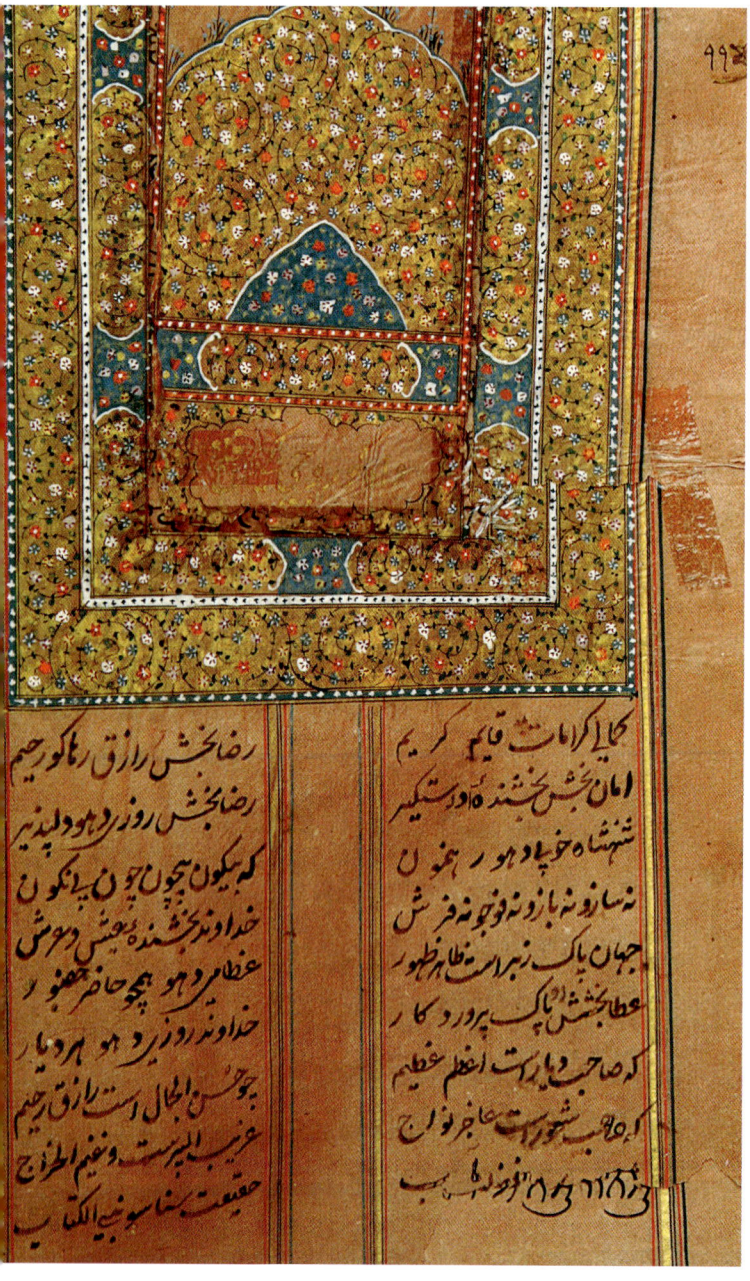

An illuminated page of a copy of *Zafarnama* written by Guru Gobind Singh, addressed to the Mughal Emperor, Aurangzeb, in which he says: 'I have lost faith in your vows and have no other option but to wield the sword'. The manuscript is kept at Gurdwara Bhai Daya Singh, at Aurangabad.

claimants. The battle of Jajau, near Agra, on 8 June 1707, proved decisive, and Prince Muazzam became Emperor of India, with the title of Bahadur Shah.

The Emperor invited Guru Gobind Singh to his court at Agra. The Guru set out with an escort of chosen Sikhs, and was received by Bahadur Shah at Agra Fort with great honour, on 23 July 1707[51]. The Emperor expressed happiness at seeing the Guru and thanked him for his visit and for the help he had given him in the battle of Jajau. Before he departed, the Emperor presented the Guru with a token of his recognition, with a *khillat*[52], which included a jewelled scarf, a *dhukh dhukhi*, and an aigrette or *kalghi*. Impressed by the spirituality of the Guru, Bahadur Shah also gave him a sword (*saif*) which belonged to Hazrat Ali, the revered son-in-law of Prophet Mohammed. This sword is now at Takhat Kesgarh Sahib at Anandpur.

The Guru's attendant, who waited outside the hall, was called in to carry the dress of honour to his camp, contrary to the Mughal practice of the recipient having to put it on in the court.

This meeting not only established cordial relations between Guru Gobind Singh and the Emperor, but also became the starting-point of parleys between the two on the question of the State's religious policy. Both of them agreed to resume these subsequently, and the Guru was hopeful that he would be able to return to Punjab at the conclusion of the dialogue that had been initiated. He sent letters to his Sikhs to this effect, which is obvious from the one addressed to the congregation of Dhaul, near Anandpur[53].

---

51 Contemporary accounts say that the Guru went fully armed to the court.
52 A formal royal gift given to honour the recipient.
53 It reads: To the *sangat* of Dhaul: You are my Khalsa. The Guru will protect you. Repeat Guru, Guru (always remember the Great Master). With all happiness, we came to the *Patshah*. A dress of honour and a jewelled *dhukh-dhukhi* worth 60,000 was presented to us. With the Guru's grace, everything else is also progressing satisfactorily. In a few days, we should also be returning. My instruction to the entire Khalsa *sangat* is to remain united; when we arrive at Kahlur, the entire Khalsa should come armed. He who comes shall be happy. Sammat 1764, dated Kartik 1/October 2, 1707. (From Dr Ganda Singh's collection of *Hukamnamas*.)

Bahadur Shah, however, had to leave suddenly for the Deccan to quell a rebellion by his brother, Kam Bakhsh. Guru Gobind Singh, instead of returning to Punjab, travelled south with him to continue the negotiations. The two camps marched together, and the Guru and the Emperor found time to have long conversations on subjects spiritual and temporal.

The escorts of the two camps often fell into mutual wrangling. Some of the Mughal soldiers had fought against the Sikhs at Anandpur in Wazir Khan's army, and they inwardly resented the friendly turn in the State's attitude towards Guru Gobind Singh.

As the Guru passed through the princely cities of Jaipur and Jodhpur, the Rajput Rajas sent their envoys to wait upon him and pay him homage. The camps crossed the Narmada into the Deccan and travelled further south to reach Nanded, on the bank of Godavari, towards the end of August 1708. Guru Gobind Singh's negotiations with Bahadur Shah remained inconclusive. He found the Emperor evasive and ostensibly helpless to take any action against fanatical satraps like Wazir Khan of Sirhind, and saw little benefit in pursuing the parleys.

On reaching Nanded, Guru Gobind Singh came upon the hermitage of a Bairagi *sadhu* (an ascetic), Madho Das, whom he baptised on 3 September 1708, with the rites and vows of the Khalsa. He was thereafter known as Banda Bahadur[54]. The Guru gave him five arrows from his own quiver and an escort, including five of his chosen Sikhs, and directed him to go to Punjab to carry on the campaign against the provincial overlords and oppressors.

Nawab Wazir Khan of Sirhind was concerned at the Emperor's preferential treatment of Guru Gobind Singh. Their travelling together to the south made him jealous, and he assigned two of his trusted men to assassinate the Guru before his closeness with the Emperor could harm the Nawab. The two Pathans—Jamshed Khan and Wasil Beg[55]—pursued the Guru secretly and met the entourage at Nanded. They frequently visited the Sikh camp and familiarised themselves with the lay of the land and the people. One evening, after *Rahiras*, the evening prayer, as the Guru was resting, one of the Pathans suddenly fell upon him and stabbed him in the left side, near the heart. Before he could attack again, Guru Gobind Singh struck him down with his sword. His other companion too fell under the swords of the Sikhs

---

54 In some documents, the baptismal name is given as Gurbax Singh. However, he is remembered as Banda Bahadur, the brave man, in Sikh lore.
55 *Guru Kian Sakhiyan*

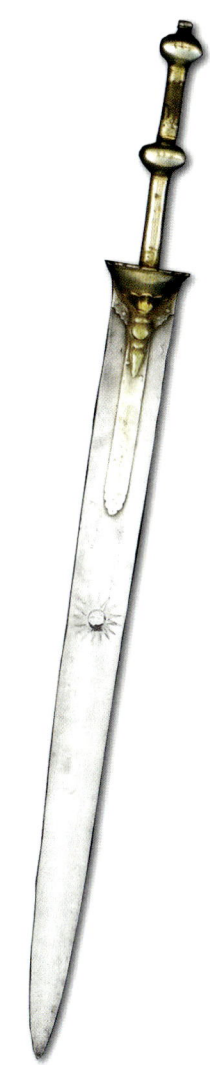

The sword (*saif*) of Hazrat Ali, the revered son-in-law of Prophet Mohammed. Sikh scribes record that the sword was entrusted to Guru Gobind Singh by Emperor Bahadur Shah when they met in Agra.

A painting depicting Guru Gobind Singh at *Takht* Sri Hazoor Sahib, Nanded. One of the five *takhts* of the Sikhs, Nanded is located on the banks of Godavari river in Maharashtra.

who had rushed in on hearing the noise.

As the news reached Emperor Bahadur Shah's camp, he sent expert surgeons, including an Englishman, to attend on Guru Gobind Singh, and his injury was healed. But not long after, as he drew the string of a powerful bow, the wound split open again and bled profusely. This weakened beyond recovery the physical frame which had withstood many stormy battles.

On 6 October 1708, Guru Gobind Singh called a gathering of his disciples and reminded them how *Akalpurakh's* Will had to be cheerfully accepted under all conditions and at all times. He asked for the Sacred Volume of the Holy Book to be brought forth. To quote the *Bhatt*[56] *Vahi Talauda Parganah Jind*[57]:

'Guru Gobind Singh, the Tenth Master, son of Guru Tegh Bahadur ... asked Bhai Daya Singh, on Wednesday, 6 October, 1708, to fetch the Revered Granth Sahib. In obedience to his orders, Daya Singh brought the Granth Sahib. The Guru placed five paise and a coconut before it and bowed his head. He said to the sangat: "It is my commandment: Accept Revered Granth Sahib in my place. He who so acknowledges it will obtain His reward. The Guru will protect him. Know this as the truth"[58].'

Another contemporary document, which authenticates the fact of Guru Granth Sahib having been vested with the final authority, is a letter issued by Guru Gobind Singh's widow, Mata Sundari. The original is now in the possession of Bhai Gurchet Singh, of the village of Bhai Rupa, to whose ancestors it was addressed. In unequivocal terms, it established the Supremacy Sovereignty and Dignity of *Guru-Shabad*. It also clearly warns against looking up to any one in human form as a Guru.

The missive, or *Hukamnama* states: 'Waheguru's Khalsa must always be alert, be possessed of discriminating wisdom. The Khalsa must believe in none other than the Timeless One. There have been only 10 masters in human form. To believe in 11th and 12th (Banda Bahadur, or Ajit Singh, adopted son of Mata Sundari), etc., is a mortal

---

56 The Bhatts were Brahmin medieval ballad singers who were the repositories of oral histories of prominent people of the time.

57 Literally, 'The Diary of the Purohit of Talauda in Jind Pargana'.

58 Giani Garja Singh, who discovered this entry, maintains that the writer, Narbud Singh Bhatt, son of Kesho Singh Bhatt, was with Guru Gobind Singh at Nanded at that time. Written according to the traditional format of the time, it reads: '*Guru Gobind Singhji, mahila dasman, beta Guru Tegh Bahadurji ka, para Guru Hargobindji ka, parpota Guru Arjunji ka, bans Guru Ram Dasji ki, surajbansi Gosal gotra, Sodhi Khatri, basi Anandpur, parganah Kahlur, muqam Nander tat Godavari, des dakkan, sammat safran sai painsath Kartik mas ki chauth, sukla pakkhe, budhvar ke dihun, Bhai Daya Singh se bachan hoya, Sri Granth Sahib lai aD, bachan pai Daya Singh Sri Granth Sahib lai aye. Guruji ne panch paise narial age bheta rakha, matha teka, sarbatt sangat se kaha mera hukam hai meri jagah Sri Granthji ko janana, jo Sikh janegatis ki ghal thaen paegi Guru tis ki bahuri karega, satt kar manana*'.

[Punjabi manuscript image]

crime. While even every other misdemeanour can be condoned by repeating the Guru's name, those who commit the crime of believing in human Gurus (after Guru Granth Sahib) will not ever be forgiven ... Khalsa ji, you must believe in no other than the Timeless One. Go only to the ten Gurus in search of the Word... The Guru resides in Shabad. The Lord hath merged his own self in the Guru through whom he hath revealed His Word. The Word is His life, of all life, for through it, one experiences God.'

A folio from a manuscript describing the last days of Guru Gobind Singh in Nanded. The account is by Mangal Singh who was present at the time of the Guru's demise. The manuscript was recovered by the late Dr Tirlochan Singh in a village near Laxmipur in Bihar.

Banda Bahadur arrived in Punjab and called upon the Sikhs to join him in fulfilling the Guru's mandate. The seal of Banda Bahadur, shown above, is on his letter addressed to Bhai Dharam Singh and Bhai Param Singh, sons of Bhai Rup Chand. The letter has been preserved by their descendants at village Bhai Rupa.
The seal reads:

> 'Degh-Tegh-Fateh o Nusrat i Bedirang,
> Yaft uz Nanak Guru Gobind Singh'

The inscription symbolically refers to a vessel, *Degh*, to provide food for all and the sword or *Tegh*, to protect the weak, helpless and the good, invoking the victory acquired by boundless patronage from Nanak to Guru Gobind Singh. It later became a statement of the ethos of Sikh sovereignty.

PERSECUTION STRENGTHENS Character

The eighteenth century was a period of great political upheaval and turmoil in Punjab. It witnessed repeated foreign invasions and also internal conflicts. But order gradually evolved out of the chaotic situation, with the process taking a whole century to work itself out. After Aurangzeb's death in 1707, Mughal authority in Punjab began to weaken. The Mughals faced a great setback because of Banda Bahadur's victory over the Nawab of Sirhind. The military success and the socio-economic upheaval that he engineered led to perplexity and uncertainty for quite a while.

Banda Bahadur

After the death of Guru Gobind Singh, Banda Bahadur, whom the Guru had initiated into his faith and baptised as a Sikh, began the task assigned to him by his Guru in right earnest.

The Guru had sent him to Punjab to continue the struggle against the oppression of the Mughal rulers. He had given him a drum and a banner as symbols of sovereignty and had bestowed on him five arrows from his own quiver as a sign of authority.

Banda proceeded to the north, and from the neighbourhood of Sehri and Khanda (southwestern Punjab, near Panipat)[1], he dispatched *Hukamnamas* conveying the message of Guru Gobind Singh to prominent Sikhs in Punjab, calling upon them to join him[2]. The Sikhs flocked to his banner from all quarters. Bhai Fateh Singh, a descendant of Bhai Bhagtu; Bhai Karam Singh and Bhai Dharam Singh, sons of Bhai Rup Chand; Naghia Singh; and Chuhar Singh were among the first who joined him with men and arms.

The Chaudhrys, Ram Singh and Talok Singh[3], liberally

The surviving of the four watchtowers built by Banda Bahadur at Sadhoura, now in Yamunanagar district of Haryana, to observe enemy movement from a distance.

---
1 The village is now called Khanda Kharkhauda and falls in the Sonepat district of Haryana.
2 Banda's *Hukamnama*, preserved at Bhai Rupa.
3 Sons of Baba Phul, they were ancestors of the present Phulkian family.

contributed to Banda's cause. Within a few months, the peasantry was up in arms against the oppression of the Governor of Sirhind.

On 26 November 1709, early in the morning, Banda Bahadur attacked Samana, a prosperous town inhabited by radicals and also the native place of Jala-ud-Din, who had been employed to execute Guru Tegh Bahadur. He next turned his attention to Sadhaura, which was another centre of Mughal oppression. The Hindus of this place were not even allowed to cremate their dead or to perform any other religious ceremony. Its ruler, Usman Khan, was hated by the Sikhs because he had tortured to death the great Muslim saint, Sayed Badrud Din Shah, popularly known in Sikh lore as Pir Budhu Shah, for his having helped Guru Gobind Singh in the battle of Bhangani against the Hindu Rajas. Sadhaura fell, and the Sikhs took possession of a small fortress in the neighbouring forests known as Mukhlisgarh. They renamed it Lohgarh.

The conquest of Sirhind

A centre of Mughal authority and an important city of Mughal administration between Delhi and Lahore, Sirhind represented everything that was abominable to the Sikhs. It was the place where the younger sons of Guru Gobind Singh had been put to death on the orders of its Governor, Wazir Khan. He was the man who had been harassing the Guru at Anandpur, had attacked him at Chamkaur, where the Guru's elder sons were killed, and had pursued the Guru up to the battle of Muktsar in Malwa. And it was Wazir Khan's agents who had assassinated the Guru at Nanded.

People of all social classes joined Banda Bahadur in this campaign. Firstly, there were families from Malwa, like those of Bhai Fateh Singh, Bhai Dharam Singh and Karam Singh of Bhai Rup Chand's clan, who had been blessed by the Gurus. Then there were the Khalsa of Guru Gobind Singh, which now rallied around Banda in a spirit of devotion and self-sacrifice to continue the struggle against the enemies of their country and religion. There were others too: Sikh leaders such as Baba Ram Singh and Baba Talok Singh of the Phul family supported the cause. The third group consisted of the discontented masses, victims of persecutions and harsh rule. This included both the Hindus and Muslims. The Sikhs of the Majha region also rushed to join them, but the battle was over by the time they caught up with the Khalsa forces.

Banda had no artillery, no elephants, and not even a sufficient number of horses for all his men. Wazir Khan was well-equipped with all the resources of the Mughal Empire to meet the advancing Sikhs. He was supported by forces from Hissar, Lahore, Eminabad, and other places,

A Gurdwara marks the spot at Chappar Cheri, also spelt Jhiri, in the foothills of Shivaliks, where Mughal forces clashed with the Sikhs under the command of Banda Bahadur. The Governor of Sirhind, Wazir Khan, was killed in this battle.

whereas Banda's army comprised inspired Sikhs and the oppressed peasantry, burning with a desire for justice.

The battle was fought on the plain of Chappar-Chiri[4] on 12 May 1710. The Sikhs, says the author of the *Ahwal-i-Salatin-i-Hind*[5], came face-to-face with the Mughals, rapidly discharged their muskets and quickly reduced the battle to a hand-to-hand fight. After a bitter battle, the Mughal army was decimated. Wazir Khan was accosted by Baj Singh. Wazir Khan rushed upon him with a lance. Baj Singh snatched the weapon from him, struck it on the head of his horse and wounded it. After a while, Wazir Khan thrust an arrow in Baj Singh's arm and drew his sword to strike the fatal blow. Fateh Singh, who was standing nearby, struck Wazir Khan with his sword which cut through his shoulder down to his waist and his head fell to the ground. The Mughal army fled the field in total disarray.

'Not a man of the army of Islam,' says Khafi Khan in *Muntakhib-ul-Lubab*, 'escaped with more than his life and the clothes he stood in. Horsemen and footmen fell under the swords of the infidels (Sikhs), who pursued as far as Sirhind.'

The town of Sirhind, which was near the scene of the battle, was captured two days later, on 14 May 1710, after a short, but sharp struggle, in which 500 Sikhs lost their lives.

Striking a coin

Banda established his authority and struck coins in the name of the Gurus. The Persian inscription in a version of his coins has been translated as:

'Coin has been struck in both the worlds herein and hereafter, under the guarantee of Guru Nanak's double edged sword, the victory of Guru Gobind Singh, King of Kings, has been achieved with the grace of Sacha Sahib. Minted at a place of peace, a picture perfect, beautiful city, where the illustrious throne of the Khalsa is to be located.'[6]

Banda Bahadur's rule was short-lived. Its consequences, however, were far-reaching. With his rule, Mughal authority and the feudal system of

A replica of a coin struck by Banda Bahadur after the conquest of Sirhind.

OBVERSE: *Sikka Zad Bar Har Do Alam Tegh-i-Nanak Wahib Ast, Fateh Gobind Shah-Shahan Fazal Sachcha Sahib Ast*

It states: 'The coin has been struck in both the worlds— here and hereafter, guaranteed by Guru Nanak under the strength of his sword. The victory of Guru Gobind Singh, King of Kings, has been achieved with the grace of Sacha Sahib, the God Almighty.'

REVERSE: *Zarb Ba-Aman-ul-Dahar Masawarat Shahr Zinat-al-Takht Khalsa Mubarak Bakht*

It states: 'Coined in the refuge of the world, the most protected place, safe and peaceful, where the auspicious throne of the Khalsa is located.'

---

4 A barren field with a pond (*chappar*) and some bush (*chheri* or *jheri*) around it, about 20 km west of present-day Chandigarh.
5 Literally, 'Account of the Sultanate of India'.
6 Singh, Surinder. *Sikh Coinage: A Symbol of Sikh Sovereignty*, New Delhi: Manohar, 2004.

society began to crumble. He was fully aware of the woes of the peasantry of the north, groaning under the oppression of exploitative landlords who were primarily agents of the rulers. Banda Bahadur immediately abolished the *zamindari* system, and made the tillers masters of the land by conferring upon them proprietary rights. This marked a revolutionary change in the social order in Punjab, and led to the emergence of peasants as a potent force in the political life of the country.

This measure had a huge impact on the agrarian structure and fiscal policies of Punjab. The *zamindars* or landlords, who were government officials responsible for payment of fixed land revenue of the villages entrusted to them, had come to assume the position of absolute proprietors. In all the *parganas*[7] occupied by the Sikhs, the reversal of the previous customs was striking and complete. 'A low scavenger or leather dresser, the lowest of the low in Indian estimation, had only to leave home and join the Guru (meaning Banda), when, in a short time, he would return to his birthplace as its ruler with his order of appointment in hand.'[8]

Such was Banda Bahadur's fearsome reputation that apprehensive of Sikhs smuggling themselves into the royal camp disguised as Hindus, Emperor Bahadur Shah ordered all Hindus employed in the imperial offices to shave off their beards. His order, issued on 10 December 1710, was a general warrant for the *faujdars* (commanders) to kill the worshippers of Nanak, that is Sikhs, wherever found (*Nanak prastan ra har jakih bayaband ba qatl rasanand*). Even in the face of this edict for a complete annihilation of the Sikhs, Banda Bahadur did not resile from the principles of his faith and maintained an attitude of tolerance towards the Muslims as a whole[9]. The mausoleum of Sheikh Ahmed Mujaddid Alif Sani, the magnificent shrine revered by the Muslims, which still stands at Sirhind as it did before the battle, is proof thereof.

The Sikhs now commanded complete power in the area, and

A picture, taken in 1936, of a Gurdwara in the Jammu Hills called Dera Baba Banda Singh Bahadur. Banda Bahadur married Sahib Kaur from Wazirabad during his stay in the area.

---

7 *Pargana*, a word of Persian origin, was a revenue unit, consisting of several *mouzas*, the smallest revenue units, comprising one or more villages and the surrounding countryside. The concept was introduced by the Delhi Sultanate and was widely used during the Mughal rule over India.

8 Irvine, William. *Later Mughals* (Reprint), New Delhi: Oriental Books, 1971.

9 As reported to Emperor Bahadur Shah on 28 April 1711 (*Akhbarat-i-Darbar-i-Mualla*): 'The wretched Nanak-worshipper (Banda Singh) has his camp in the town of Kalanaur up to the 19th instant. During this period he has promised and proclaimed: "I do not oppress the Muslims." Accordingly, for any Muslim, who approaches him, he fixes a daily allowance and wages, and looks after him. He has permitted them to recite *Khutba* and *namaz*. As such, 5,000 Muslims have gathered round him. Having entered into his friendship, they are free to shout their call—*azaan* and make their devotions, *namaz*—in the army of the wretched (Sikhs).' In doing so, he followed the tradition of the sixth Guru, who had built a mosque for his Muslim followers at Sri Hargobindpur.

were fired with a strong zeal to root out the tyranny perpetrated by Mughals[10]. The people looked upon them as their defenders. Receiving complaints from the area, Banda Bahadur led an expeditionary force across the Yamuna river and occupied Saharanpur and its neighbouring areas. Meanwhile, the Sikhs of the Jalandhar-Doaba area rose as one to throw off the yoke of the Mughals. Sayyad Aslam Khan, the Governor of Lahore, was now alarmed. He called for a religious *jihad* by the Muslim population and raised the Haidri flag for *jihad* against the Sikhs. But the Sikhs inflicted a heavy defeat on his forces at Bheelowal. They were now the masters of Punjab, east of Lahore. According to Iradat Khan[11], there was no nobleman daring enough to march against them from Delhi. 'If Bahadur Shah had not quit the Deccan, which he did in 1710, there is every reason to think that the whole of Hindustan would have been subdued by these invaders (the Sikhs),' says Sir John F. Malcolm[12].

A fledgling community of the Sikhs could not match the might of the great Mughal Empire, with its inexhaustible resources. Emperor Bahadur Shah moved against them with a mammoth army. They had to retire from Sirhind and Thanesar to their fort of Lohgarh. This forest hideout of Banda Bahadur's forces was surrounded by over sixty thousand soldiers from the imperial army, on horse and on foot, including the troops of the Rajput Princes. But on the night of 30 November 1710, Banda and his men slipped out of the fortress and vanished into the hills of the neighbouring Nahan State.

Within a fortnight thereafter, Banda and the Sikhs resurfaced. A missive was issued by him on 12 December 1710, calling upon Sikhs from all directions to join him at Kiratpur. He then led an expedition against some of the Hill Rajas, who had harassed the tenth Guru, and reduced them into submission without much opposition. The Governor of Jammu was defeated on 25 May 1711. Kalanaur and Batala also fell to the Sikhs. But being constantly pursued by the Imperial generals, once again, he had to withdraw into the hills.

Emperor Bahadur Shah died on 18 February 1712. In the

After Sirhind's Governor, Wazir Khan, was killed and the city captured, the Sikhs under the leadership of Banda Bahadur demolished the entire city, except for the *dargah* which was the headquarters of the orthodox Muslim theologian Sheikh Ahmad Shah Sirhindi of the Naqshbandi sect. These radical theologians had been hostile to the Gurus, and their opinions led to the martyrdom of Guru Arjan, Guru Tegh Bahadur and the younger sons of Guru Gobind Singh. Yet, the mausoleum was left untouched by the forces of Banda Bahadur.

---

10 'The authority of that deluded sect (of the Sikhs) has reached such extremes,' wrote Aminud Daula in June 1710, 'that many Hindus and Muslims, finding no alternative to obedience and submission adopted their faith and ritual. Their chief (Banda Bahadur) captivated the hearts of all towards his inclinations and, whether a Hindu or a Muslim, whoever came in contact with him.'
11 Mir Mubaraku-llah Iradat Khan Waza, author of *Twareekh-Iradat Khan* (1741), held high offices under Mughal emperors. In the reign of Bahadur Shah, he was Governor of the Doab. He was also a great poet.
12 A Scottish soldier whose books include *Sketch of the Sikh* (1812), *A History of Persia* (1815), *Memoir of Central India* (1823), *Political History of India from 1784 to 1823* (1826), and *Life of Lord Clive* (1836).

A Gurdwara marks the place at Gurdas Nangal, where Banda Bahadur and his forces were besieged by the Mughal army for eight month in a mud fortress. Eventually, they surrendered and were taken to Delhi as prisoners.

uncertainty that followed, the Sikhs took the opportunity to reassert themselves in the plains of Punjab. Lohgarh once again became the headquarters for Banda.

Farrukh Siyar, who succeeded Bahadur Shah to the throne of Delhi, came down heavily upon the Sikhs, and they were again driven into hiding in the hills. In the beginning of the year 1715, faced with heavy odds and chased by the might of the Mughal army, Banda and his Sikhs were besieged in the village of Gurdas Nangal.[13] The last few years of fighting had created such a terror of the Sikhs and their chief among the Mughal army, says Iradat Khan, that the commanders of the Imperial army prayed that God might so ordain that Banda Bahadur should seek his safety in flight from the siege, so that they did not have to fight him.

However, food and supplies ran short and the situation worsened. Sikhs lived off their own slaughtered animals and ate the flesh raw. 'When all the grass was gone they gathered leaves from trees. When these were consumed,' says Irvine, 'they stripped the bark (of the trees) and broke off the small shoots, dried them, ground them down and consumed them instead of flour, thus keeping body and soul together. They also collected the bones of animals and used them in the same way.'

In spite of the hardships, they withstood the might of the Mughal Empire for eight months before falling into the enemy's hands. Made prisoners, they were taken to Delhi and executed, one hundred every day. The carnage began on 5 March 1716 and continued for a week.

When offered the choice of Islam against death, not a single Sikh reneged on his faith[14]. Banda was the last to be executed on 9 June 1716. Blinded, decapitated, his flesh torn out by red-hot pincers, he remained calm and serene till the very end: 'In having been raised by God to be the scourge of the inequities and oppressions of the age,' says Elphinstone[15].

Banda had established a rule based upon a tradition that dated back to the early days of the Sikh Gurus—a benign, humanistic state. It may be noted, five weeks after his historic victory at Sirhind, on 23 June 1710, he told Jan Muhammad of Buriya (Gulab Nagar): 'I have forgiven your crime and appoint you *zamindar* of the whole *pargana*. You should proceed with your men and bring in Sardar Khan of Chundla. Then you will accompany me for the chastisement of Jalal Khan.' There was no change in his policy of fairness to people of all faiths, even after the royal Mughal edict of 10

---

13 The village is near the present-day town of Gurdaspur, Punjab.
14 Note from the East India Company observers John Surman and Edward Stephenson, in a letter dated 10 March 1716.
15 Elphinstone, Mountstuart. *The History of India*, 1841.

December, which decreed an indiscriminate killing of the Sikhs—men, women and children—wherever found. Although he was being hounded from place to place, he did not let his struggle assume the shape of communal strife.

Banda Bahadur's success may seem transitory if looked at only in terms of time, but it effected a revolution in the minds of people, of which history seldom takes notice. A will was created in the ordinary masses to resist tyranny and stand up for the national cause. The idea of a Nation-State, long dead, once again became a living aspiration. Its seed was sown and, although suppressed for some time by relentless persecution, it went on festering underground like a smouldering volcano, which erupted some forty years later with a fuller effulgence, never to be suppressed again.

Persecution

After the death of Banda Bahadur, every measure was taken by the State to destroy the power of the Sikhs and to exterminate the religion as such. The edict of Emperor Bahadur Shah, ordering a general massacre of the Sikhs, was followed up and intensified by Emperor Farrukh Siyar, who ruled between 1713 and 1719. Monetary rewards

Banda Bahadur was captured from Gurdas Nangal by the Mughal forces, after a protracted siege. Over seven hundred Sikhs were then taken to Delhi as prisoners. A painting by Kirpal Singh depicts how Banda Bahadur was paraded in the streets of Delhi in a cage mounted on an elephant. For seven days, a hundred Sikhs were killed daily. Finally, Banda Bahadur's son was killed in front of him. Banda Bahadur was then tortured and decapitated.

A part of the old gate at Mehrauli, New Delhi, near the mausoleum of the Mughal Emperor Bahadur Shah (1643-1712), where the body of Banda Bahadur was hung after the execution.

were offered for every head of a Sikh brought to Lahore, dead or alive.

The respite that the Sikhs got with the death of Emperor Farrukh Siyar, in September 1719, was short-lived. When Zakariya Khan became the Governor of Lahore in 1726, he, too, demonstrated his determination to exterminate the Sikhs in totality. Columns of his army were sent out in all directions to hunt them down.

Inspired by their earlier success, the persecutors unleashed unabashed terror. Hundreds of Sikhs were brought in from their villages and executed. These were testing times. Consequently, the resolute and committed Sikhs had to once again take shelter in the hills and forests and, for some time, were not seen around the countryside of Punjab.

This was a time of grim trial and supreme moral exaltation for them. They suffered continual oppression and there were moments when their persecutors thought they had extirpated the entire sect.

The Sikhs, however, matched the situation with a rare endurance and resilience. They sanctified this period of their history with deeds of unparalleled sacrifice and courage, and the Khalsa character manifested its truest aspect in this time of extreme suffering. The strife that was forced upon them forged their spirit. In the midst of the struggle, they did not go back on their high-minded religious ideals, nor did they foreswear their spirit of magnanimity[16].

Contemporary literature, even though written by their enemies, pays tribute to them, sometimes backhanded: 'Do not call them "dogs" (a contemptuous term for Sikhs), for they are lions, and are courageous like lions in the field of battle. How can a hero, who roars like a lion in the field of battle, be called a dog? If you wish to learn the art of war, come face-to-face with them in the field. They will demonstrate it to you in such a way that one and all will praise them for it. If you wish to learn the science of war, swordsmanship, learn from them how to face their enemy like a hero and to get safely out of an action. Singh is a title (a form of address for them). It is not just to call them dogs. If you do not know the Hindustani language, (I shall tell you that) the word Singh means a lion. Truly, they are like lions in battle and, in times of peace, they surpass Hatem[17] (in generosity)...

'Leaving aside their mode of fighting, hear ye another point in

---

16 Harbans Singh. *Heritage of the Sikhs*, second edition, 1994.
17 Hatem ibn Abdellah ibn Sa'ad at-Ta'iy Al-Najdi, a famous pre-Islamic (Jahiliyyah) Arabian chief, renowned for his eloquence, courage, generosity of spirit and passionate loyalty. His name has become synonymous with generosity in Arabic culture.

which they excel all other fighting people. In no case would they slay a coward, nor would they put an obstacle in the way of a fugitive. They do not plunder the wealth and ornaments of a woman, be she a well-to-do lady or a maidservant. There is no adultery among these "dogs"; they do not make friends with adulterers and housebreakers….'[18]

The intensity of persecution withered as Abdul Samad Khan, the Mughal Governor of Lahore, grew old and could not pursue the Sikhs with his usual ruthlessness. The enforcement of earlier edicts, too, weakened and these were now confined to those who were suspected of having taken active part in Banda's campaign.

Sikhs now started moving about more freely, visiting Harmandar Sahib more regularly. They started assembling in Amritsar on the festivals of Diwali[19] and Baisakhi[20] in large numbers, a practice, which became a custom that continues till date.

Guru Gobind Singh, having abolished Guruship in human form, had vested it in the Holy Granth, to be administered by the Khalsa. The Khalsa authority had yet to take the shape of the *Panth*. In the meantime, the Sikhs, who were fighting for their very existence, had no time to establish themselves and organise themselves on the lines laid down by the Guru.

Factious elements had emerged in the community, and matters came to a head when different parties tried to assert themselves by force.

When Mata Sundri, the tenth Guru's wife, who was overseeing the Sikh affairs from Delhi, came to know of the fissures, she sent Bhai Mani Singh[21] to restore peace, appointing him as the *Granthi* (head priest) of the Darbar Sahib. He was also entrusted the task of managing the affairs of the shrine at Amritsar.

In 1733, finding that extreme measures of persecution had failed to persuade the Sikhs to compromise on their basic doctrines and attitudes, the Mughals offered to concede to the Sikhs the status of sub-nation, and autonomous political status with a *jagir* or grant of

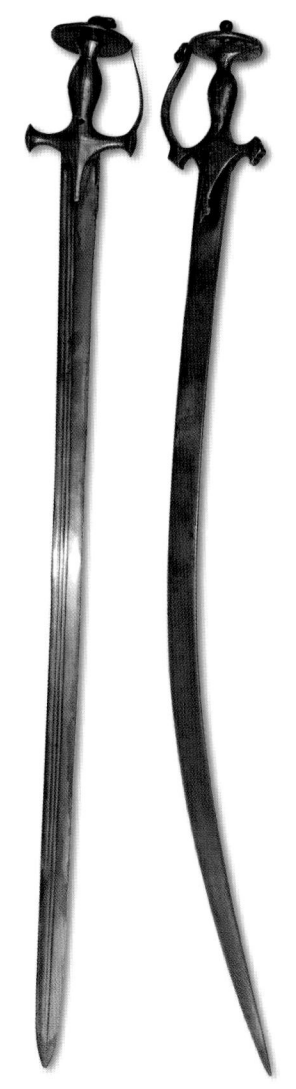

Mata Sundri oversaw the affairs of the *Panth* during the curtail period after Banda Bahadur's execution. Guru Gobind Singh had sent the sacred weapons of this grandfather, Guru Hargobind, with Mata Sahib Devan from Naded to Delhi. They are now kept at Gurdwara Mata Sundri ji in New Delhi.

---

18 History records a high and unusual tribute to the Sikh's qualities of courage and integrity during this period of harrowing oppression. The attester is their sworn enemy, Qazi Nur Muhammad, who came to India with the army of Ahmad Shah Durrani at the time of his seventh invasion of the country (1764-65).
19 The Sikhs celebrate Diwali as the day when Guru Hargobind returned to Amritsar after his release from the Gwalior fort.
20 It was on Baisakhi day in 1699 that Guru Gobind Singh founded the Khalsa.
21 Bhai Mani Singh was an eighteenth-century scholar and warrior who grew up with Guru Gobind Singh. A devoted Sikh and a courageous leader, he was the scribe of the final recension of Sri Guru Granth Sahib and was appointed *Granthi* of Harmandar Sahib by Mata Sundri. He was arrested and later hacked, joint by joint, by the Mughal authorities in Lahore on 15 November 1737.

land, comprising the *parganas* (administrative units) of Dipalpur, Kanganwal and Jhabal, of which the total income then was about a hundred thousand rupees. The Sikhs rejected it, contending that sovereignty was their divine right and could not be accepted in barter[22].

Driven out by Zakariya Khan from their homes and hearth in the plains, Sikhs had taken shelter in the hills. In the summer of 1739, Nadir Shah, the Persian invader, after plundering Delhi, was returning homewards through the Shivaliks, laden with the riches of the Mughal Empire. This was an attractive chance for the Sikhs to replenish their resources.

They came out of their hideouts, fell upon Nadir Shah's rear and relieved him of much of his booty. They also rescued a large number of Hindu girls who were being taken away by his army as spoils of war. These women were then escorted by the Sikhs and restored to their respective families.

Astonished at this, Nadir Shah called a halt at Lahore and enquired about the whereabouts of the people who had dared to rob the great robber of Delhi. 'Who are these mischief-makers?' he asked.

'They are group of *fakirs* who visit their Guru's Tank (in Amritsar) twice a year, and after bathing in it, disappear,' replied Zakariya Khan.

'But where do they live?' asked Nadir Shah.

'Their homes are their saddles,' was the reply.

'Take care then,' Nadir Shah warned, 'the day is not distant when these rebels will take possession of the country.'

Upon hearing this remark, Zakariya Khan resolved to launch an all-out campaign against the Sikhs. The previous orders were now repeated with greater emphasis and rewards were offered for the capture and destruction of Sikhs.

In 1740, Mir Musalul Khan, better known as Massa Ranghar, raided Amritsar and took over Harmandar Sahib. He desecrated the building. Two Sikhs, Mehtab Singh and Sukha Singh, infiltrated the Mughal camp, killed Massa Ranghar right in the sanctum of the Harmandar Sahib, and escaped.

With the more daring Sikhs being out of the reach of the government, its wrath fell on the ordinary Sikhs from the villages. They were brought to Lahore in hundreds and were offered the choice of Islam or death. There were no exceptions made. Saints and scholars, peasants and tradesmen, women and children, anyone who had unshorn hair

Bhai Mehtab Singh and Bhai Sukha Singh on their way to kill Massa Ranghar for desecrating Harmandar Sahib. Detail from a painting in the collection of the Maharaja of Nabha.

---

22 As it says in *Prachin Panth Prakash* by Rattan Singh Bhangu, pp. 197-200:
'What is a Nawabship to us, who have been promised a kingdom by the Guru? The word of the Guru must be fulfilled. The Khalsa was meant to rule freely. It cannot accept a subordinate position'. At last it was suggested that it should be given to someone noted for service. Kapur Singh Faizulpuria, who was then waving a big fan over the assembly, was selected for the honour. He accepted it, but not before it had been sanctified by the touch of the five Khalsas' feet.

and followed the path of Sikhism, was condemned to the same fate. The situation for the Sikhs became worse during the governorship of Yahiya Khan, the son and successor of Zakariya Khan, who took over after his father died on 1 July 1745. Governor Yahiya Khan now issued a proclamation for a general massacre of all Sikhs, wherever they could be found. Thousands were put to death daily, and their heads brought before the Subedar of Lahore for reward[23]. It was during his time that all Sikhs living in Lahore were arrested and executed on 10 March 1746.

The internal quarrels between Yahiya and his brother Shah Nawaz, followed by the invasion of Ahmed Shah Durrani of Afghanistan, gave the Sikhs a chance to emerge from their hideouts. Under the leadership of Jassa Singh Ahluwalia, they brushed aside the opposition of Adina Beg Khan, Commander of Jalandhar, and took possession of Amritsar.

They thus established themselves in the rural parts of Rachna, Bari and the Jalandhar Doabas. The new Governor of Lahore, Moin-ul-Mulk, popularly known as Mir Manu (appointed on 11 April 1748), tried to placate them. Through Diwan Kaura Mall, he procured their assistance to fight against the Afghan Governor of Multan, Zahid Khan, whom Durrani had left in charge. Having achieved his purpose and secured his seat as Governor, both of Lahore and Multan, his attitude towards the Sikhs changed. Adina Beg Khan, in the Jalandhar and Bari Doabs, was ordered to destroy the Sikhs. Often, Mir Manu himself rode out for the 'hunts' and brought in large 'bags' of Sikh scalps. As the number of male Sikhs in habitations depleted, their women and children were seized and taken to Lahore. The dark and narrow dungeons, where babies were cut to pieces and placed in the lap of their mothers, survive till date. Gurdwara Shahidganj in Landa Bazaar, Lahore, Pakistan, stands there now.

On the death of Mir Manu in November 1748, a period of chaos and confusion followed. The Sikhs availed themselves of the situation by once again establishing themselves in various parts of Punjab—now with greater strength and power.

A nation was thus forged in the crucible of time, with trials, tribulation, suffering and an all-abiding faith in *Akalpurakh*. The end product was an independent, dynamic, sovereign empire to be established by Ranjit Singh only a few decades later.

Gurdwara Shaheed Ganj Singh Singhnian at Naulakha Bazaar, Lahore. This historical site is located opposite Shaheed Ganj of Gurdwara Bhai Taru Singh. This is where Sikh women and children were martyred at the behest of Mir Manu, the then Governor of Lahore.

---

23 Syed Mohammad Latif. *A History of the Punjab from the Remote Antiquity to the Present Times*, Calcutta: The Calcutta Central Press Company Ltd, 1889.

The title of the map, dated 1849, states: 'To the Rt Hon Sir Henry Hardinge Leiut Gen G.C.B. Governor General of India, this Map of the Routes through the Punjaub (sic) and adjoining states.' Published by James Wyld, Charing Cross, London. The areas with boxed reference points are of importance to the period of Banda Bahadur.

SIKH KINGDOMS:
Evolution and Sovereignty

The large-scale persecution of the Sikhs reached its height under the Lahore Governor Mir Manu. His death resulted in a period of flux, and Sikhs took advantage of it to establish their bands and bring various areas under their influence. However, from time to time the satraps of the Mughal Empire did strike back, inflicting heavy casualties and damage.

Between 1757 and 1761, the Bhangi, Sukarchakia and Ahluwalia chieftains were able to expand and strengthen their power in the region north of the Satluj. Baba Aala Singh of the Phulkian family had carved out a principality for himself in the south. The Sikh Sardars continued their successful campaigns by triumphantly entering the city of Lahore and proclaiming Sardar Jassa Singh Ahluwalia as the King of Lahore, with the title of Sultan-ul-Qaum.

On 27 October 1761, the day of Diwali, the Sikhs decided to liquidate the Indian allies and supporters of Ahmed Shah in Punjab, since they were a hindrance to the release of the country from the yoke of the Afghan invader. A national resolution, known as *Gurmata*, was passed by the community in a general assembly of the Khalsa at Amritsar.

In January 1762, on hearing that Ahmad Shah Abdali was coming down from Afghanistan with a huge army, the Sikhs withdrew and crossed the rivers Beas and Satluj to arrange for the safety of their families in the hills of Anandpur, before returning unencumbered to take on the Shah.

As soon as Ahmad Shah learnt about the presence of the Sikhs in the area, he rushed from Lahore and took them unawares on the morning of 5 February 1762, at a place called Kup. They were attacked from all sides by the Afghans and the forces of Sirhind and Malerkotla. Thousands of people, mostly women, children and old men, were killed in the fight. This terrible carnage is remembered as the *Wada Ghalughara*, or the great holocaust, by the Sikhs[1].

Power and peace brought out the courtly style of the leaders, who were virtually the rulers. Sardar Jai Singh Kanhaiya, head of the Kanahiya Misal, with courtiers. The picture in the Pahari Sikh Kangra style, 1780.

---

1 It is to be distinguished from the first *Ghalughara* of 1746.

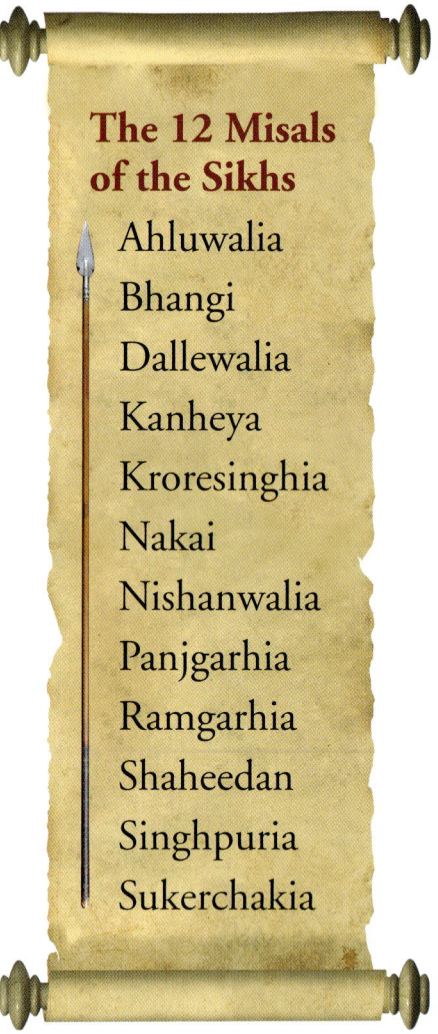

The 12 Misals of the Sikhs

Ahluwalia
Bhangi
Dallewalia
Kanheya
Kroresinghia
Nakai
Nishanwalia
Panjgarhia
Ramgarhia
Shaheedan
Singhpuria
Sukerchakia

On 10 April, in the same year, a day before the Baisakhi festival, Ahmed Shah attacked Amritsar, and blew up Harmandar Sahib. The sacred tank was desecrated with the blood and bones of men and animals, and filled up with the debris of demolished edifices.

Instead of acting as a deterrent, this fuelled the fervour of the Sikhs. Within three months, while Ahmed Shah was still at Lahore, they once again rose up in arms against Zain Khan of Sirhind and defeated him (April-May 1762). On 16 October 1762, a day before Diwali, the Shah himself suffered defeat at their hands in a pitched battle at Amritsar.

After the defeat, Ahmed Shah had to withdraw to Afghanistan. The Sikhs took advantage of his retreat. Lead by Sardar Jassa Singh Ahluwalia, they went about the country establishing Sikh *thanas* or outposts. Another young leader, Sardar Charhat Singh Sukarchakia, established himself at Amritsar and undertook the cleaning of the holy tank, and the reconstruction and restoration of the destroyed Harmandar Sahib.

In early 1764, led by Jassa Singh Ahluwalia, the Sikhs crossed the river Sutlej, besieged Bhikhan Khan of Malerkotla, and then pushed on to Sirhind. The Afghan Governor of Sirhind, Zain Khan, was killed in battle. The town was captured, and the spot where the tenth Guru's younger sons were cremated, was marked out. Gurdwara Fatehgarh Sahib, named after the youngest son, which also means 'the fort of victory' was built there. With this victory, the entire province of Sirhind—from the Sutlej in the north to the areas around Karnal and Rohtak in the south, and from the boundary of Bahawalpur state in the west to the Yamuna in the east—came into the possession of the Sikhs.

The Sikhs now had a free run of the country. They crossed the Yamuna and captured the town of Saharanpur, and went on to Delhi itself. Between 1765 and 1787, they raided Delhi fifteen times[2]. On 11 March 1783, the Sikhs entered the Red Fort and installed Sardar Jassa Singh Ahluwalia on the Mughal throne in the Diwan-e-Aam. The Emperor made peace with him and allowed Sardar Baghel Singh, who had accompanied the Ahluwalia Sardar, to build the seven historical Gurdwaras in Delhi[3]. Sikh agents were appointed in Delhi to collect protection money (*raakhi*) and octroi.

Hearing of the Sikhs' eruptions in Punjab and the failure of his generals and Governor to resist them, Ahmed Shah Abdali, once again,

---

2 Gupta, Hari Ram. *History of the Sikhs*. New Delhi: Munshiram Manoharlal Publishers. Landmarks like Pul Mathai, Mori Gate and Tees Hazari are associated with Sikh excursions.
3 Sis Ganj, Rakab Ganj, Bangla Sahib, Moti Bagh, Damdama Sahib, Majnu ka Tilla and Nanak Piao.

rushed down upon them in the winter of 1764-65 with a combined army of over 30,000 Afghans and Baluchis. But the Sikhs were now strong enough to successfully dodge and harass him. Consequently, he had to return home disappointed at the end of March 1765. Punjab was then parcelled out among the various Sikh confederacies called *misals*.

In a historic decision taken by the collective of the Sikhs (*Gurmata*) on the Baisakhi day of Samvat 1822 Bikrami (10 April 1765), the Sikhs decided at Amritsar to take possession of Lahore. All opposition was brushed aside. Within a week, on the morning of 17 April 1765, they were the masters of the capital city.

The Sikhs had by now been divided into twelve *misals*. These *misals* were republican in character. Each *misal* elected its own supreme chief and sub-chief, and every horseman in it had his right and a share in the common conquests. The combined *misals* formed the Khalsa or the Sikh commonwealth. However, over a period these *misals* and the minor chiefs acquired a hereditary character, like the dukes and barons of Europe, and consequently also fell into a pattern of infighting and decadence that diluted their character and strength.

Eventually the trans-Sutlej *misals* were integrated into the sovereign state of Punjab by Ranjit Singh. Born heir to one of these confederacies, he had the foresight to visualise a united Sikh kingdom.

Maharaja Ranjit Singh

With his superior political acumen and military genius, Ranjit Singh succeeded in consolidating the people of Punjab into one strong nation. Ranjit Singh, the only son of Sardar Mahan Singh of Sukarchakia Misal, was born of Bibi Raj Kaur, also known as Mai Malwain, on 13 November 1780. She was the daughter of Raja Gajpat Singh of Badrukhan, of the Phulkian family. Ranjit Singh was only ten years old when his father died. He showed an uncommon ability and tact in administering the affairs of his small principality and quickly won the confidence of his followers by his wisdom and courage.

A real opportunity came Ranjit Singh's way when the leading citizens of Lahore—Hindus, Muslims and Sikhs—tired of the Bhangi Sardars, and dreading an attack from their neighbour, Nizam-ud-Din of Kasur, requested him to come and occupy the city. He marched into Lahore on 7 July 1799 with his army and took it over without much resistance. This marked the beginning of a just and peaceful rule after decades of unrest and chaos.

Once in possession of the capital, Ranjit Singh started expanding the limits of his dominion. He conquered the powerful provinces of Multan, Kashmir and Peshawar, eventually carrying the battle to the

An exquisite eighteenth-century portrait of an unidentified Sikh chief.

A scene from the Lahore bazaar at the time of Maharaja Ranjit Singh. Lahore was a significant centre of trade and commerce, a magnet that attracted traders from all over because of its riches.

home of the invaders in the Northwest who had incessantly come down upon India to plunder. His name thus occupies an honoured place in the nation's history, for he stemmed forever the tide of invasions from the Northwest, across the Hindukush mountains, and taught his countrymen how to fight for a patriotic cause.

Ranjit Singh's rule was marked by a sound and enlightened system of administration. His government, called Sarkar Khalsa, recognised no distinction of religion or creed when making appointments to offices of the state. Even though the Sikhs had just passed through a period of ruthless religious persecution in the near past, he appointed a Muslim, Faqir Aziz-ud-Din, as his prime minister. His personal physician was Faqir Nur-ud-Din, and Diwan Dina Nath, a Hindu, was another minister in the Sikh court. General Ilahi Baksh was in charge of the artillery, and Imam-ud-Din looked after the fort of Gobind Garh at Amritsar. There were Dogras, Gorkhas and Muslims in his army, besides foreigners, including French, Italians, Americans and Russians. Throughout his career of war and conquest, Ranjit Singh was not known to have ravaged a city, desecrated a place of religious worship or shown harshness to a vanquished enemy.

It is said that if the historian is to fix the time in the history of Punjab during which the people—Hindus, Muslims, Sikhs and others—were most happy and prosperous, he would, with the least hesitation, name the Khalsa Raj, reign of the Sikh Lion of Punjab, Maharaja Ranjit Singh (1799-1839).

Maharaja Ranjit Singh's domain extended well beyond the boundaries of present-day Pakistan in the north. He is said to have raided far into Ghazni, from where he brought back the doors of the temple of Jagannatha, which Mohammad Ghazni had taken away. Tradition holds that these doors now stand at the Darshani Deodi of Harmandar Sahib. For centuries, invaders from the Northwest had rampaged through Punjab. For the first time in history, this direction was reversed, never to happen again.

On the eastern boundaries, Ranjit Singh was contained by the expanding influence of the British East India Company, and he had to be content with Sutlej as his eastern boundary.

Ranjit Singh ruled as an unvanquished and powerful monarch. Ironically, during his rule, Sikhism received a rude shock even in the ranks of the Khalsa, where it had been preserved more or less in its pristine purity over the decades since the Gurus. Hindu influences began to work their way into the religion. This was also to be noticed in court ceremonies where strict regard to the spirit and form of Sikhism was not observed, and extraneous 'courtly' customs were introduced.

From 1765 onwards, the Sikh *misal* (confederacy) was on the ascendance. The threat of the Mughal, Afghan and Durrani oppression and invasion had diminished. The Sikh chiefs, over the course of time, were losing the true spirit of the community, and dynastic aspirations of individual chieftains overcame the system of succession by merit. Most of them started nursing ambitions of establishing their own principalities of sorts. Ranjit Singh epitomised this process. From dynastic family aspirations emerged expansionist tendencies. Ranjit Singh's rise to power was a product of this process.

He had either overpowered or absorbed most of the *misals* west of the Sutlej, and made aggressive forays in the territories east of the river. Many a small chieftain was annexed. However the major Cis-Sutlej principalities of the Phulkian family, that is, Patiala, Nabha and Jind, were not easy prey. Fearing Ranjit Singh's aggressive designs, they sought protection under the umbrella of the British, and entered into treaties with the East India Company. What may have looked like a betrayal of the Khalsa Darbar, was, in fact, an act of sheer survival on the part of these chieftains. Ranjit Singh's expansion and attempt at establishing a dynastic rule was against the true fundamentals of the Khalsa.

While establishing his regime, Ranjit Singh had set up a benign and secular rule. But, in his administration, he avoided inducting Sikhs in key posts of trust. His confidants were either the Dogras or the soldiers of fortune from Awadh (now in Uttar Pradesh), who adopted Sikh names and garb (grew hair and took surnames of Singh).

Ranjit Singh seems to have had a burning desire to establish a dynasty. The few Sikhs of stature who disagreed with him in this respect were sidelined and brushed aside. Having come into power he, too, gave into the indulgences of wine, women and song, as was the wont of most Indian rulers. In the process, his sons also took to the extravagant pleasures of life.

Ranjit Singh is said to have been a devout Sikh. Before every major decision, he would seek guidance from Sri Guru Granth Sahib. Many a popular folktale has been told about him performing the *Ardaas* before leading his army into the waters of the river Jhelum. He got the Harmandar Sahib gold-plated. Yet, he also had a shrine at Nanded built, even though it was against the expressed wish of the tenth Guru.

It is paradoxical that as his end came near, he slid into practices contrary to what is expected of a good Sikk. Scared of death, he began performing *sankalps*[4], offering gifts to Brahmins to pray for his

Maharaja Ranjit Singh was a secular ruler who succeeded in consolidating the people of Punjab into a strong nation.

---
4 Performing prerequisites before *puja* or rituals.

Detail of a mural in Pothi Mala building at Guru Harsahai showing a well-attired Sikh *chobdar*, or attendant.

good health. Somehow, his commitment to Sikhism became acutely diluted. One reason could be that his personal life of indulgence, and his ambition to establish a dynastic rule, had led him astray from his roots. He had distanced himself from his Sikh advisers like Akali Phula Singh, who could have kept him on the true path of Sikhism by reminding him of the Divine Will (*Bhana*), and the willing acceptance of it, especially when his end was so near.

His closest confidants were loyal neither to him, nor to his people. The Dogras and soldiers of fortune from Awadh had no love lost for the Panth or the Sikh ethos. They betrayed their benefactor the moment he breathed his last, murdered his kin, looted his treasury and allied themselves to the British.

Death of Ranjit Singh and the Anglo-Sikh Wars

After Ranjit Singh's death there was a free-for-all, with rampant fratricide and multiple assassinations in the struggle for succession. The Sikh state, so powerful and formidable at one time, suddenly became easy prey for the British, who had watched Ranjit Singh and studied the situation for almost twenty years.

Eventually, as lamented by the popular bard Shah Mohammad, the Sikh army, which gave the British the toughest fight ever since Robert Clive established his rule in India, had to face defeat for lack of leadership. But it was not before they displayed the true spirit of the Khalsa, which even the British chroniclers had to accept and respect.

After the Sikh Wars of the 1840s, Ranjit Singh's erstwhile empire lay in ruins, betrayed by his confidants, the trusted Dogras, and the opportunistic converts. Only two elements stood tall as champions of the Sikh ethos. It was the Sikh soldier and the indomitable Sardar Sham Singh Attariwala who, in his old age, came out of retirement to lead the Sikhs and died fighting the British army during the battle of Sabhraon on 10 February 1846.

J. D. Cunningham, an officer of the East India Company who fought the Sikh soldiers, wrote: 'Although assailed on either side by squads of horse and battalions on foot, no Sikh offered to submit and no disciple of Gobind asked for quarter. They everywhere showed a front to the victors and stalked slowly and sullenly away, while many rushed singly forth to meet assured death by contending with a multitude.'[5]

---

5 Cunningham, J. D. *History of the Sikhs*,1849. The book was first proscribed by the British. Later, an edited version was published. It is now available in an unexpurgated version.

A defiant soldier of the Sikh army faces the British contingent during the Battle of Mudki on 18 December 1849. A detail from a painting by H. Martins published in London.

With guile, craft, cunning, and diplomacy the British took full control of Punjab. All vestiges of Ranjit Singh's administration and power were erased, and loyalists were removed. His seven-year-old son, Dalip Singh, a Maharaja only in name, was blamed for a revolt that took place, though he was ruling under the regency of East India Company. He was exiled, separated from his mother and handed over to a missionary couple, who were mandated to remove any semblance of his association with his faith, family and people from his mind.

Many in Sikh society fell back into the Brahminical practices inimical to the Sikh faith. Mahants took over the Harmandar Sahib and installed idols and deities in the *prakarama*[6]. Sikh practices were replaced with *havans*[7] and *aartis*[8]. It is said that a large number of Sikhs slipped back into the same socio-religious morass from which the Gurus had dug them out.

It was the common people who still retained some semblance of the

---

6 The walkway around the sacred pool (*sarovar*) that surrounds Harmandar Sahib, sometimes spelt as *parikrama*.
7 Ceremony involving sacrificial fire worship.
8 A religious ceremony generally practised in Hindu temples.

SIKH KINGDOMS: EVOLUTION AND SOVEREIGNTY

An etching of a Nihang warrior of the Khalsa army during the period of Maharaja Ranjit Singh.

old spirit. However, they, too, with the changes overcoming their places of worship, along with the shock they had received in the battlefield, having been let down by their leaders against the East India Company, felt paralysed for some time. The common Sikhs, thus, declined in numbers too.

British colonial rule

By the time Delhi faced the Sepoy Mutiny of 1857, Punjab was firmly under control of the British. Soldiers from Punjab formed a major part of the forces that helped the British to quell the rebellion. Sikh soldiers had no love lost for these rebels, because this very lot, from the areas of Awadh and Delhi, had earlier fought against them as mercenaries of the British. The only army constituted of all the communities of Hindustan—Hindus, Muslims, and Sikhs—which fought the British, was that of the Lahore Durbar. The British understood the character and values of Punjabis in general and Sikhs in particular rather well, and gave due recognition to it.

On coming into power, the English had seemed to quickly forget their enmity towards the Sikhs. They had admired their noble bravery and tried to befriend them. This friendship had put some heart into the Sikhs. They enlisted in the British army, where they were encouraged to keep their baptismal forms intact. However, in other ways, the Sikhs fell back to the same old superstitious practices from which their Gurus had so heroically worked to extricate them.

In their army, the British would encourage the Sikhs to preserve and practise their way of life. From the inner belief of loyalty to the Guru, they transferred their integrity to their new masters. These masters, in turn, demanded of them a life in accordance with the edicts of their Gurus. They held that one would be loyal to the master, if he had learnt loyalty to his faith. Unshorn hair, well-kept turbans, obeisance to Sri Guru Granth Sahib, regimental *granthis* and Gurdwaras became the norm. In turn, the Sikhs gave them a loyal soldiery which earned laurels as their best soldiers. This was noticeable till the end of World War II.

The Sikhs were, however, not oblivious of the socio-political upsurge against the foreign rule in their country. The inherent spirit of accepting no earthly master brought them to the forefront of the freedom movement that was emerging in the nation. Consequently, beginning with the massacre in Jallianwala Bagh in 1919 right up to the Partition of India in 1947, they were the flag-bearers of the freedom movement. In doing so, they paid a heavy price for India's independence, both in men and material, which was far greater in proportion to their being less than two per cent of India's population. With Partition, the most prosperous part of Punjab was left to Pakistan, and the Sikhs bore the brunt of massacres, forced migration and displacement.

The British had won the loyalty of the Sikhs by respecting their faith and helping them preserve their identity. But in the independent Indian nation that was formed in 1947, the very same, distinct identity that the Sikhs had carved for themselves was not welcomed by some influential elements among the majority, who felt that Sikhism was merely a branch of Hinduism. A community and faith that had stood throughout its short history for the freedom of every individual to choose his form of worship and beliefs, now found its identity threatened.

Reactions to this situation had started since Ranjit Singh's rule. The Nirankari and the Namdhari movements sought to once again build on the basis of Guru Nanak's concepts of *Nirankar* and absolutism, but did not get much traction because of their restricted scope and the schismatic character they acquired.

A movement that followed them, the Singh Sabha, however, had a deeper and broader impact. It influenced the entire community and reoriented its outlook and spirit. Since the days of the Gurus, nothing so vital had transpired to awaken the consciousness of the Sikhs.

Singh Sabha movement

The Singh Sabha movement that emerged towards the end of the nineteenth century focused on studying the original sources of Sikhism, purging the religion of extraneous influences and customs, and restoring it to its pristine purity. Those who undertook this task found that much of the true teachings of Sikhism had, by now, been overlaid with Hindu beliefs and practices, and that the work of restoration would require Sikh society to purge itself of these completely.

By leavening the intellectual and cultural processes, it brought a new dimension to the inner life of the community and enlarged its heritage. Started in the 1870s, it marked a turning-point in Sikh history. It regenerated Sikhism and made it a living force once again. The stimulus it provided has shaped the Sikhs' attitude and aspiration since then.

The main motivation of the Singh Sabha was rediscovering the Sikh identity and its self-assertion. Under this impulse, new powers of regeneration came into effect, Sikhism was reclaimed from a state of ossification and utter inertia and its moral force and dynamic vitality were restored. The Sikh mind was stirred by a process of liberation and it began to look upon its history and tradition with a clear, self-discerning eye. The purity of Sikh precept and practice was sought to be restored. Rites and customs consistent with Sikh doctrine and tradition were once again defined and established.

With the reform of Sikh ceremonial observances, came the

A painting by R. M. Singh, which depicts a Sikh soldier of the British army. The Sikhs became the backbone of the British Indian army.

SIKH KINGDOMS: EVOLUTION AND SOVEREIGNTY

Designed by architect Bhai Ram Singh of Lahore, the Khalsa College, Amritsar was established on 5 March 1892. It was both an architectural and an educational landmark of the united Punjab. The college is a living monument to the achievement of the reform movement of the time, which involved the Chief Khalsa Diwan, the Singh Sabha, as well as many tall individuals who contributed towards establishing, running and staffing this institution.

reformation of Sikh shrines which, again, was achieved by an impressive demonstration of communal upsurge, and by eventual legislative sanction secured from the government of the day. This period of fecundation of the spirit and of development also witnessed the emergence of new cultural and political aspirations. Literary and educational processes were renovated.

The main objectives identified by the Singh Sabha were the spread of modern (Western) education among the Sikhs, promotion of the study of Sikh literature, improvement of Sikh educational institutions, opening of new educational institutions, furthering the cause of female education among the Sikhs, and promotion of technical and agricultural education.

The Singh Sabha movement was a mass upsurge. Besides awareness of decadence in the practice of Sikhism, the other motivating factors at work were a reaction to what was happening in the other Indian religious traditions, and the offensive of Christian proselytisation.

The fall in the numbers of Sikhs supported dismal predictions about the final eclipse of the Sikh faith. A demographical detail was worked out by the British in 1855 in respect of the Lahore division. It found only about 200,000 Sikhs in an aggregate population of about three million in the Majha region, hitherto known as the central home of the Sikhs[9].

Now that the Sikh commonwealth had broken up, the faith's attraction for those who joined it for material gains diminished. Added to this were a series of carping lectures in Amritsar on the Sikh faith, and the narration of Guru Nanak's life in a deliberately garbled manner by Shardha Ram Phillauri, who had been engaged by the British to write a history of the Sikhs with this agenda.

To study and understand these matters, a gathering of Sikh stalwarts was convened in Amritsar[10].

An association called the Sri Guru Singh Sabha came into being

---

9 The comment on this point is from Punjab Administration Report for 1855-56.
10 Prominent among them was Thakur Singh Sandhanwalia (1837-87), a man of learning, who possessed the rare accomplishment of having mastered the two classical languages of the East, Sanskrit and Arabic. He had been a member of the Golden Temple management board appointed by the British before he turned a rebel. He had seen from close how Sikh custom and ritual had become corrupted, and felt concerned about the general state of the Sikh community and its resiling from its traditions. Other luminaries at the meeting were Baba Sir Khem Singh Bedi (1832-1905), a descendant of Guru Nanak; Kanwar Bikram Singh (1838-87) of Kapurthala; and Giani Gian Singh (1824-84).

on 1 October 1873. Local Singh Sabhas sprang up in all parts of Punjab. Those at Amritsar, Lahore, Rawalpindi, Jalandhar, Ludhiana, Ferozepore, Patiala, Nabha, Faridkot, Bagrian, Bhasaur, Kapurthala, and Shimla being notably active. To coordinate the work of the Amritsar Singh Sabha and the Lahore Singh Sabha[11], a joint board called the General Sabha was formed, which was subsequently replaced by the Khalsa Diwan, which was set up in Amritsar in 1883. This Khalsa Diwan became the affiliating centre for all the Singh Sabhas. However, differences between the Amritsar and the Lahore Singh Sabhas led to the formation of a separate body called Khalsa Diwan at Lahore in 1886.

The Khalsa Diwan was endorsed by a large gathering of Sikhs at the Malwai Bunga at Amritsar on 12 April 1900, when it was unanimously decided to establish a body, which was to be supreme in the affairs of the community. A constitution was then prepared by the committee and approved by the various Singh Sabhas and eminent Sikhs from different walks of life. It was discussed at a meeting in Burj Gianian in Amritsar on 9 November 1901.

On 19 August 1902, a main council of the Sikh Panth, called the Chief Khalsa Diwan, was constituted, and a Parbandhak[12] Committee was nominated. The first session of the Chief Khalsa Diwan was held in the Malwai Bunga on 30 October 1902. Bhai Arjan Singh of Bagrian was elected president and Sardar Sundar Singh Majithia the secretary, with Sodhi Sujan Singh of Patiala as additional secretary. Twenty-nine Singh Sabhas, including those of Amritsar, Rawalpindi, Agra, Kairon, Chhajjalvaddi, Boparai, Dakha and Badbar, a small village in Nabha state, were affiliated to the Chief Khalsa Diwan at its first session.

The Chief Khalsa Diwan now became the principal voice of the Sikh community and the medium of channelising its religious and cultural resurgence.

Until the advent of the British, the educational system in Punjab had been essentially religion-based. The Punjab, under Maharaja Ranjit Singh, was a power-locked, insular state. He introduced a Punjabi primer in schools and laid stress on educating the girl child. The Maharaja did admit into his service many foreigners, but they had to restrict themselves wholly to their professional duties. He would not let them intervene in the social and religious life of the people in any manner. It was, nevertheless, one of Ranjit Singh's ambitions to have a school, with a curriculum based on the English system, established in

Giani Ditt Singh (1853-1901), one of the founders of the Singh Sabha reform movement, was a scholar, who also edited the Punjabi newspaper *Khalsa Akhbar*.

---

11 Established by Bhai Gurmukh Singh in 1877.
12 Literally, management.

Bhai Kahn Singh of Nabha (1861-1938), who distinguished himself as a diplomat and a scholar. He was the author of the first encyclopaedia of Sikh religion, the *Gurshabad Ratnakar Mahan Kosh*.

his capital Lahore, and he spoke about it to several visiting padres. But negotiations had fallen through every time, owing to Ranjit Singh's refusal to let the Bible be taught in the proposed school.

Along with its revivalist impulse, the Sikh leaders at this time were looking to the future as well. It accepted the principle of change and exhibited sensitivity to contemporary needs. The Sikhs emerged with a strong sense of self-preservation, as well as with a will to move with the times. One of the more concretely formulated urges was for Western-style education so that they might refurbish their own religious and literary conventions and be able to compete with other communities for government employment and have their share in the power which was then available to Indians. This they did with remarkable success.

To have a college of their own for imparting instruction in English and in Western sciences and for promoting Punjabi and Sikh studies became an article of faith with them. Sikh leaders worked assiduously to realise this dream. The government, too, favoured the proposal and, in 1890, the Khalsa College Establishment Committee was set up[13]. Khalsa College was established in Amritsar on 5 March 1892. The Singh Sabha movement also established many other colleges and Khalsa schools, thus promoting large-scale education. The *Khalsa Akhbar* became the first Punjabi newspaper. *Khalsa Samachar*[14], edited by Bhai Vir Singh[15], was a prominent voice of the Sikhs and a platform for many new ideas.

Many books were written, prominent among them being Giani Gyan Singh's *Panth Prakash* and *Tawarikh Guru Khalsa*, and Bhai Kahan Singh's *encyclopaedia of Sikh religion, Guru Shabad Ratnakar Mahan Kosh*[16]. A new generation of scholars, prominent among

---

13 Lt Colonel W. R. M. Holroyd, Director of Public Instruction, Punjab, as president, and W. Bell, Principal of Government College, Lahore, as secretary. Frederick Pincott, an eminent Orientalist of London, undertook to help the college in England. Among the Sikh constituents of this 121-member committee were Sir Attar Singh, Gurdial Singh Maan of Nabha, Diwan Gurmukh Singh of Patiala, Bhai Kahn Singh, tutor to the heir apparent of Nabha state, Prof. Gurmukh Singh and Bhai Jawahar Singh (1859-1910)..

14 Founded in 1899.

15 Bhai Vir Singh (5 December 1872 -10 June 1957) was a poet, scholar and mystic. He was a man of letters who helped to revive Punjabi literary tradition and had great influence on Punjabi culture and Sikh religious interpretation.

16 Bhai Kahn Singh Nabha (30 August 1861- 24 November 1938) was a Sikh scholar and encyclopaedist. He was a court official in Patiala and Nabha states where he distinguished himself as an administrator and a diplomat. He was also the tutor of Maharaja Ripudaman Singh of Nabha. His magnum opus is *Guru Shabad Ratankar Mahankosh* (1930) a Sikh encyclopaedia. He is also the author of other treatises, including *Gurmat Martand* (1938), *Gurmat Prabhakar* (1898) and *Gurmat Sudhakar* (1899). He was a part of the team of Sikh scholars consulted by Max Arthur Macauliffe, who wrote *The Sikh Religion*.

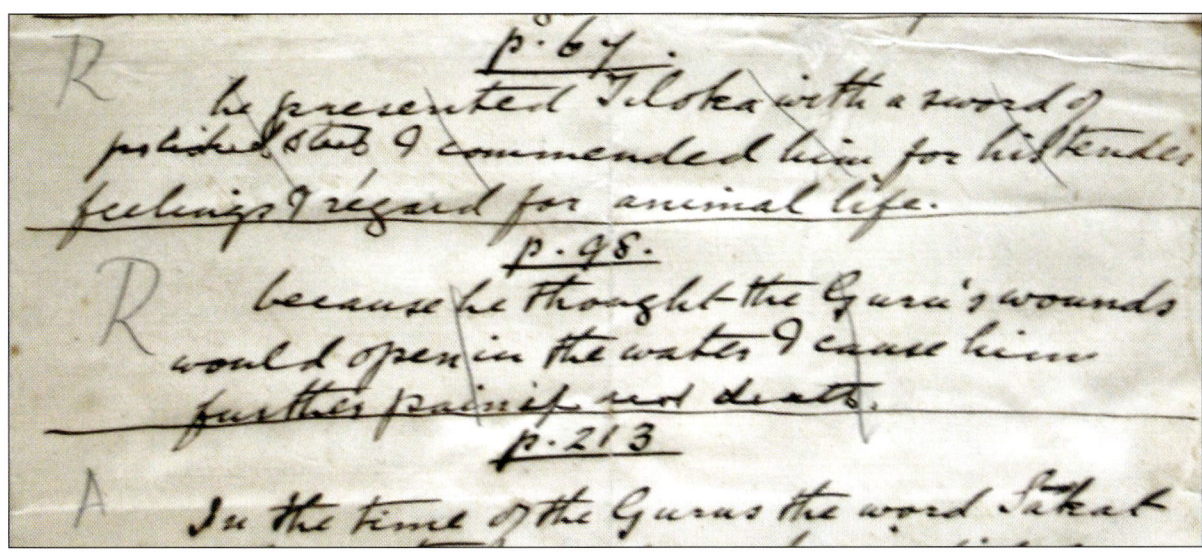

them Max Arthur Macauliffe[17], Bhai Vir Singh, Bhai Jodh Singh and Prof Teja Singh, contributed significantly towards enhancing literature on Sikhism.

Freedom fighters

The Sikhs formed a substantial part of the British army, fighting in Europe, Turkey and Africa, and making a name for their gallantry. But when they returned home, they faced a failed harvest and an epidemic of influenza in 1918 that killed an estimated 100,000 Punjabis. Discontent became widespread, and the British administration responded with restrictive laws that culminated in the Jallianwala Bagh massacre in Amritsar on 13 April 1919, in which Brigadier General R. E. H. Dyer and his men killed 379 and wounded over 2,000 unarmed and peaceful protesters[18].

A popular Gurdwara Reform Movement, spearheaded by the Singh Sabha, fought against hereditary management of important Sikh shrines, dominated by *mahants* (hereditary priests) who had brought in various Brahminical practices and rituals antithetical to Sikhism.

On 20 February 1921, at Nankana Sahib, Sikhs protested against Narain Das, a hereditary *mahant* (head priest) of the Gurdwara

A page from the original manuscript of Max Arthur Macauliffe's magnum opus, *The Sikh Religion*, first published by Oxford University Press in 1909. It was the first major account in English that paid adequate attention to traditional accounts about the Sikh Gurus and their writings.

A rare portrait of a turban-wearing M. A. Macauliffe (1837-1930), an Irishman who resigned from the British Civil Service and became a devoted scholar of Sikh history and scriptures.

---

17 Max Arthur Macauliffe (10 September 1841-15 March 1913), is renowned for his book, *The Sikh Religion*. He was a senior British administrator, prolific scholar and author. He left the British Civil Service to devote his time to studying the Sikhs and their scriptures with the help of prominent Sikh scholars, including Bhai Kahn Singh Nabha.

18 An estimated 1,200 people were killed and 3,600 wounded in the seven weeks that Punjab was administered under martial law.

Sikh luminaries of the early twentieth century. From left: Bhai Arjan Singh of Bagrian, Sir Jogindra Singh, Sardar Umrao Singh Sher-Gil, Sardar Gurdial Singh Mann, Bhai Kahan Singh, and Sir Sunder Singh Majithia in Shimla.

that marked the birthplace of Guru Nanak. The *mahant's* henchmen burnt 130 Sikhs, an action that sparked off widespread condemnation and indignation.

In another incident, Sundar Das Udasi, the *mahant* of Guru-ka-Bagh Gurdwara near Amritsar, engineered police action against reformist Sikhs. An agitation followed, in which five unarmed protesters courted arrest daily and were brutally beaten up by the police. As more and more people were arrested, the number of protesters grew.

So intense was the repression, and so peaceful the protest, that the English missionary and educationist Rev. C. F. Andrews (1871-1940) said that he saw, on 12 September 1922, 'hundreds of Christs being crucified'. Andrews describes the scene thus: '... There were four Akali Sikhs with their black turbans facing a band of about a dozen policemen, including two English officers. They had walked slowly up to the line of the police just before I had arrived and they were standing silently in front of them at about a yard's distance. They were perfectly still and did not move further forward. Their hands were placed together in prayer, and it was clear that they were praying. Then, without the slightest provocation on their part, an Englishman lunged forward the head of his *lathi* (staff) which was bound with brass. He lunged it forward in such a way that his fist which held the staff struck the Akali Sikh, who was praying, just at the collar-bone with great force. It looked the most cowardly blow as I saw it struck...'

Charles Freer Andrews was a close friend and associate of Mahatma Gandhi. He also taught Philosophy at St Stephen's College, Delhi.

The utterly peaceful and totally non-violent protest at Guru-ka-Bagh became a paradigm for the rest of the country in continuing protests against British colonialism. Non-violence as a tool of protest and revolution was thereafter adopted as a hallmark of India's fight for freedom by the nationalist leaders.

This agitation about reforms in the management of Gurdwaras increasingly brought the Sikhs in conflict with the British authorities. The Shiromani Gurdwara Parbandhak Committee's support for Maharaja Ripudaman Singh of Nabha, who had been deposed by the British authorities, resulted in it being declared an unlawful organisation on 13 October 1923.

A desire for independence resurfaced, and the Sikhs started working for the overthrow of British rule in India, playing a significant role in it. More Sikhs were jailed as political prisoners, and more Sikh freedom fighters were sentenced to death, as compared to any other community.

The British had won over the loyalty and respect of the Sikhs by respecting their faith, and helping them preserve and maintain their identity. The expression of this very distinct identity later created difficulties for the Sikhs in the newly-formed nation of India, wherein petty politics and greed for power became rampant, and the nation sacrificed value-based polity, putting aside ethics and commitments made earlier.

Within years of the Partition of India, all linguistic groups were given recognition, but Punjabi was denied its fair due. The Sikhs felt that Punjabi was being ignored only because of its association with them and their scriptures. The message that the community seemed to be getting was of denial of its own identity.

Notwithstanding all of the above, the Sikh community in Punjab led the agricultural revolution of independent India. Even though the Sikhs arrived as destitute refugees from Pakistan, they quickly rebuilt the community in Delhi and Punjab, and never seemed to be as badly off as the refugees from East Pakistan (now Bangladesh) were. The barren lands of East Punjab were transformed into the granary of India by their hard work and sweat, and Delhi was transformed with their flourishing businesses.

Emigrants

While it is instructive to look at the Sikh diaspora in chronological order, the emergence of the Sikhs almost all over the globe shows an important facet of Sikh ethos. For the record, Sikh troops participated in the Opium Wars in the 1850s[19]. They were based in Hong Kong as well. From there, they moved through to Vancouver and then on to England for the coronation celebrations of the British King Edward

Captain Ishar Singh, VC, OBI (1895-1963), the first Sikh to win the Victoria Cross (far right), seen here with two other highly-decorated Sikhs. He won his VC for bravery on 10 April 1921 during the Waziristan campaign. He first went to England in 1929 as a VIP guest of the Prince of Wales, the future King Edward the VIII. In 1936, when this picture was taken, he was in London for five months as one of the Viceroy's Commissioned Officers selected to serve as Orderly Officer to the King.

---

19 With their tall, well-built stature, beards and turbans, the Sikhs were a familiar sight on the streets of Shanghai in the nineteenth and the early twentieth centuries. They were called 'Hongtou A San'. Hongtou was a reference to their red turbans.

Unarmed protesters during the Guru-ka-Bagh agitation. The English missionary and educationist Rev. C. F. Andrews (1871-1940) said that he saw, on 12 September 1922, 'hundreds of Christs being crucified'.

VII. By 1906, there were over 1,500 Sikh workers settled in Vancouver.

The emigrant Sikh took with him the deep-rooted beliefs and commitments to Sikh values. Wherever they went, the Sikhs earned respect for their hard work and integrity of character. Prosperity followed, and with it came the desire to know more about their roots, and a certain dogged perseverance to preserve the values that had been inculcated in them through their religious heritage and social practices.

The first Sikhs in the United States date back to 1898-99. These Sikhs found work in Washington's lumber mills and California's agricultural fields. This is where the Ghadar party[20] would eventually be conceived and nurtured. By 1906, about 600 Sikhs had emigrated from Canada to the US. Within years, laws were tightened in both the US and Canada and the immigrants faced many hardships, which were highlighted by the Komagata Maru tragedy[21].

The Sikhs also emigrated to the Far East, and by the early twentieth century we see evidence of Sikh traders in the Philippines, Burma, Indochina, Fiji and a little later, in Singapore. The participation of Sikh soldiers in World War I inevitably exposed them to foreign lands, which enticed some of them. Africa attracted them later, and it is now widely held that Sikhs are to be found all over the world. The British encouraged them to become the trading middle class, craftsmen, and security personnel in their colonies in Africa and elsewhere.

Exposure to other cultures, education and an open mind had ensured that the Sikhs were no longer content to be the fighting arm of the British—they wanted to control their own destiny back at home. The Sikh diaspora was thus responsible for feeding the flame of desire for freedom from British colonial rule.

At the time of World War II, there were two streams of opinion about participating in what was considered essentially a British war. Lack of clarity among the leaders, and the discontent of the community with the British administration, played a role in Sikh

---

20 Called Hindu Association of the Pacific Coast, the party was found in Oregon, USA, in 1913 with the objective of freeing India from the British colonial rule.
21 The Japanese passenger ship with 376 Indians, 346 of them Sikh, dropped anchor near Vancouver, but most of the potential immigrants were told to return to Hong Kong. After exhausting legal appeals and not being allowed to disembark, the ship set sail two months later, only to be refused entry to Hong Kong and Singapore. It eventually arrived at Calcutta and most of the would-be emigrants were jailed.

Gurdwara Panja Sahib, which commemorates Guru Nanak's visit to Hassan Abdal. There are many Sikh shrines in Pakistan.

soldiers fighting for both the sides. While a huge number of Sikh soldiers fought in the British army, a rebel army was also formed under the command of Captain Mohan Singh, supported by the Japanese and called the Indian National Army. Led by the newly-elevated General Mohan Singh, it comprised mainly Indian prisoners of war held by the Japanese. The initiative did not click, and the INA was eventually disbanded. The effort, though brave and symbolic, did not get proper acknowledgement by other nationalists after Independence.

Partition of India

In 1947, when India was partitioned and Pakistan was created, it was the Sikhs who suffered the most. With most of the developed and prosperous erstwhile unified state of Punjab becoming part of Pakistan, hundreds of thousands of people were displaced, and hundreds of lives were lost in the bloodbath that followed.

Prosperous Sikhs from what became Pakistan were reduced to

In the early twentieth century, exclusion laws in Canada and the United States were used to keep out immigrants of Asian origin. The picture shows potential immigrants from India who had hired the Japanese steamship, the Komagata Maru, in a vain attempt to migrate to Canada. 356 out of the 376 passengers were not allowed to enter Canada and the ship was forced to return to India, where the passengers clashed with the British police.

being destitute refugees, and families were displaced and scattered. This was a horrendous reality that marked the birth of India's freedom from British colonial rule.

Many Sikhs went abroad after Partition, other waves followed in later decades, but in the decade immediately following the Partition, a poignant situation arose. The upheaval and large-scale migration left the Sikhs in Punjab without any clear-cut direction. Decadence set in, and there was a need for new energy and fresh ideas. At the same time, diaspora Sikhs living in an environment full of curiosity about their identity and beliefs started rediscovering themselves.

Confident and resurgent, the diaspora Sikh is now a part of the modern idiom and its social relevance. The devastating happenings of the 1980s woke them up to new realities. Their inborn love and faith in their own ethos made them stand up for the cause of Sikhs. This also resulted in a fresh study of the tenets and practices, highlighting their relevance in contemporary social values. Realisation came that the way of life offered by Sikh Gurus meets the questioning mind of modern times too. The values ingrained in Sikhism are for all times.

Guru Nanak's scientific exposition of creation—'For millions and even more than millions of years, there was a haze. There was neither an earth nor sky, only the order of the Infinite was operating. Neither there was day nor night, neither there was moon nor sun, He was in a trance in void. Neither there were sources of life, nor of sound, neither there was air nor water. Neither there was creation, nor desolation, neither coming (birth) nor going (death)'[22]—given in his composition in *Raag Maru* is in consonance with the twentieth-century scientific theories of origin of the universe. Myths of miracles have no place among the Sikhs. This disarms the logic of faiths built on myths and other arguments which the rationalists hold against religion, sanctifying miracles and promises of boons hereafter.

Much of the practice of a religion is in the tradition, history and the social milieu of its origin. The teaching and ethos of Sikhi is the core of the faith that has given it a global reach, yet its history is steeped in Punjab and within the state, it is intimately connected with certain families that have been blessed by the Gurus.

What the Gurus gave to these families is a treasure infinitely worth more than mere riches for them. These families have been persuaded, many of them for the first time, to share their unique inheritance with the world through this volume. The collections that are being showcased here are those that have escaped the turbulence of times, though they have suffered from the passage of time.

We are proud to present herein rare historical relics that have never been seen side-by-side. Through the histories of the families that are the keepers of the tradition, we will look at the splendid treasures that have been passed on from one generation to another, with piety and devotion, making it a living heritage and the core of its ethos.

Sikhs performing *bhangra* on Broadway, New York, during the first Sikh Parade in New York held in 1987. The parade in Manhattan has become an annual feature.

---

22 SGGS Page 1035: *'Arbad Narbad Dhandughara…'*

Heritage

The Gurus' blessings manifested in the form of relics that they bestowed upon some families who had the honour of serving them. The family of Bhai Rup Chand at Bhai Rupa has preserved these relics well.

LOCATING
Relics

Guru Nanak Dev travelled extensively to spread the gospel of Truth within India and also outside the country. His journeys took him to places of learning and religious centres of the major faiths of the time, such as Baghdad, Banaras, Hardwar, Mecca, Medina, and Puri. In the east of India, he visited Assam and the area now in Bangladesh, and in the south he went as far as Ceylon, now Sri Lanka. There are records of his travels to Tibet and Sikkim too. Accounts of his travels are mentioned in detail in the *Janamsakhis*[1] and are found in Sikh folklore.

Guru Nanak's successors also travelled, but not to such a great extent. Wherever the Gurus went, it was customary for them to bestow some personal belongings to their hosting disciples, which have been preserved by the disciples and their families as articles of faith. This is evident from various relics which are still in existence with some families of Punjab visited by the Gurus. They have been in their continuous possession, and not only are they preserved reverentially, but are not used for material gains. References in various texts, especially Bhai Kahn Singh's redoubtable *Gur Shabad Ratnakar Mahan Kosh*, further attest to their authenticity.

Prominent among the relics are those with the family of Bhai Rup Chand, who was blessed by Guru Hargobind, the sixth Guru. He and his sons had the privilege of being associated with the Gurus since

One of the *juttis* (shoes) of Guru Amar Das, the third Guru, which has been reverentially encased in silver and preserved by a family formerly from Shekhupura, now in Pakistan.

---

1 Traditional biographical narratives on Guru Nanak. Scholars maintain they were in circulation orally before they were written down. There are a number of *Janamsakhi* traditions, the major ones being *Puratan*, *Bala*, and *Meharban*.

Deerskin chaps (over-pants) of Guru Gobind Singh. They were used while horseriding for protection and comfort.

then, and in fact, his youngest son, Bhai Dharam Singh, was with Guru Gobind Singh till the very end of his life.

The rulers of the Phulkian States are descendants of Baba Rama and Baba Taloka, sons of Baba Phul, who was introduced to the Sikh faith by Guru Hargobind, the sixth Guru. They were also recipients of the blessings of later Gurus, and thus have a significant collection of relics of Sikh heritage.

Not many relics of Guru Nanak Dev, Guru Angad Dev and Guru Ram Das are known to have survived the vicissitudes of time.

A pair of shoes of Guru Amar Das, the third Guru, is known to be with a family. Two branches of the family have divided the pair among themselves, and kept one shoe each. Before the partition of India in 1947, one branch of the family lived at village Madar in district Sheikhupura and the other in village Dhunni, district Gujranwala, both now in Pakistan. After migrating to India in 1947, these families settled in village Saide Wala of district Mansa in Punjab, and a village in district Jind in Haryana. It is an interesting tradition that these two families bring one shoe each and assemble at Pehowa (Haryana) once a year, where the pair is displayed to devotees.

There are a number of relics which can be seen in a historical Gurdwara of village Bilga in district Jalandhar, as we will see in a later chapter. Guru Arjan Dev compiled the *Adi Granth*, and the *Mool Mantra*, written by the Guru himself, can be seen in a manuscript well preserved with the Sodhi family at Kartarpur, near Jalandhar.

Dresses, shoes, weapons and contemporary paintings of Guru Hargobind, the sixth Guru, can be found at many places. *Hukamnamas* signed by him are also available. A manuscript of Sri Guru Granth Sahib with the *Mool Mantra* in his handwriting is in the collection of the Sikh Cultural Museum, Darbar Sahib, Amritsar.

There are a few contemporary paintings of Guru Har Rai, the seventh Guru in some collections, but hardly any relic of Guru Harkrishan, the eighth Guru, seems to exist, except one painting, which is said to be contemporary and is in the collection of the National Museum at New Delhi.

A contemporary painting of Guru Tegh Bahadur was in Dhaka (now in Bangladesh). It was commissioned by Balaki Dass Massand, a disciple of the Guru. This painting is now at the Victoria Memorial Museum in Calcutta, and has been mentioned by many historians. Some other relics of the ninth Guru, including a few weapons, are with families of erstwhile Sikh states.

Some of the weapons of Guru Gobind Singh from Maharaja

Ranjit Singh's collection were taken to England by Lord Dalhousie, Governor General of India, after the annexation of Punjab in 1850. He managed to keep these as his personal collection. Later, these were acquired from his family and brought to India in 1966 and are now on display at Takht Sri Keshgarh Sahib, Anandpur.

Historical weapons, dresses, shoes and *Hukamnamas* of Guru Gobind Singh are preserved in many collections. There is a contemporary painting of Guru Gobind Singh in the National Museum, New Delhi, which was with the erstwhile ruling family of Mandi state, now in Himachal Pradesh. Guru Gobind Singh stayed there for some time as guest of Raja Sidh Sen, with whom he had cordial relations. This family also had the *rabaab* of Guru Gobind Singh, which is now on display at the historic Gurdwara at Mandi.

Many historical weapons, acquired from different families, were kept with reverence at the Akal Takht, Amritsar. These included the two swords—*Miri* and *Piri*—of Guru Hargobind. Guru Gobind Singh gave his mace to his wife, Mata Sundri, who later bestowed it to Sardar Jassa Singh Ahluwalia. Two arrows of Guru Gobind Singh with gold bands were also at the Akal Takht. At the time of the attack—known as Operation Blue Star—on Akal Takht in 1984 by the Indian army, these weapons were damaged. The loss of the collective heritage was felt by the Sikhs the world over.

The Gurus' blessings manifested in the form of relics that they bestowed upon some families who had the honour of serving them. For these families, it has been a tradition to keep the sacred relics with devotion and reverence.

These relics deserve more attention, and thus we have focused on them in greater detail. This would be the first time that many of these relics have been discussed at such length and with a wide audience.

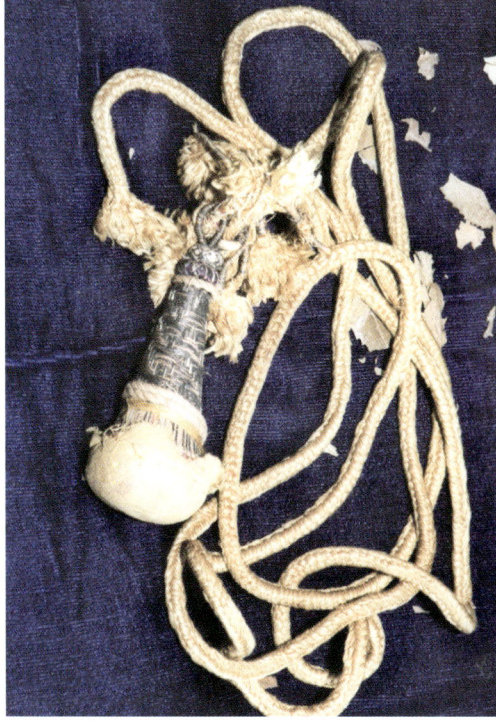

A leash used by Guru Gobind Singh for his hawk. The Guru is generally portrayed on horseback, with a hawk on his hand.

The Jand *(prosopis cinergria)* tree on which Bhai Sidhu hung the water flask. A Gurdwara near Bhai Rupa, called Jand Sahib, marks the spot where Guru Hargobind blessed Bhai Sidhu and his son Rup Chand.

BHAI RUP CHAND

Bhai Rup Chand was born to Bibi Surati and Bhai Sidhu in 1614, at Kaljharani, a village which now falls in the Bathinda district of Punjab. Surati was the daughter of Bhai Aaqal, a devoted disciple of Guru Ram Das, the fourth Guru, while Sidhu was the son of Raja Sada, whose family worshipped Sakhi Sarwar.

Sidhu came from a family of Rajputs from the Marwar area of Rajputana. He was a descendent of Raja Bhartu, who reigned during the middle of the twelfth century. He was succeeded by his son Sandher, who, in turn, was succeeded by his son Rattan Pal.

In the time of Bhadan Pal (son of Rattan Pal), Iltutmish (also spelt Altamsh), Sultan of Delhi, invaded their territory and, in a decisive victory, defeated them. Consequently, many of the Rajput tribes, rather than submitting to Mughal rule, left their homes and migrated to other parts of India. Bhadan Pal joined the coalition of Rajput tribes who opposed Altamsh.

He was slain in the fight; and his son Pun Pal, seeing that many of his allies were deserting the state, migrated with his family and a band of followers to southwest Punjab, where Mughal rule was not yet firmly established, and settled down at Kaljharani, near Bathinda. He fortified the place and, with this as his stronghold, took advantage of the weakness of the local Governor at Bathinda to appropriate the country around Kaljharani.

His son Ganesh Pal and grandson Bijai contented themselves with consolidating their power in the territory adjacent to Kaljharani

A page from Gurbilas Patshahi 6 *which narrates the story of Bhai Rup Chand. A biography of the sixth Guru, it is based on oral tradition, and was written after his demise.*

Bhai Rup Chand's ancestors were followers of Sakhi Sarwar, a Muslim seer who was much venerated in the Malwa region and in Rajasthan by both Hindus and Sikhs.

and devoted their attention to agriculture. However, by the time of their descendent, Sada, a good deal of their territory was lost.

Events with far-reaching effects occurred during the lifetime of Sidhu, son of Sada. Sidhu married Bibi Surati, a devout follower of Guru Hargobind. When Sidhu had an audience with the Guru at Darauli, he was greatly affected by the teachings. Consequently, he embraced Sikhism. His adopting of a new religion became a cause of friction in his family. With life becoming irksome in Kaljharani, Sidhu, accompanied by his wife and some of his people, migrated eastwards and settled at a place called Tuklani. When a son was born to them in 1614, the couple took him to Guru Hargobind, who was visiting his brother-in-law at village Darauli in the same area. The Guru blessed the child and named him Rup Chand.

Rup Chand became a legend in Sikh history when, in the hot month of April 1630, his father and he were harvesting their small holding in the wilderness of Malwa, near their village Tuklani. The heat of the April midday sun was intense, and, overcome by thirst, they went to drink water from a goatskin water-bottle which hung from a branch of a Jand (*prosopis cineraria*) tree nearby. The water was exceptionally cool. The father and son were moved by utter devotion to the Guru and, dedicating the water as an offering to the Guru, refrained from drinking it. The heat grew intense, their thirst aggravated, and they swooned with exhaustion, but neither father nor son touched the water. The Guru, at the time, was staying with his brother-in-law at Darauli. On learning about his devotees' pledge, despite the heat of the day, the Guru hurried to Sidhu's fields. On reaching there he took the goatskin water bottle from the tree and sprinkled the water on the faces of the father and the son, reviving them. He then drank the water, sharing it with them. To this day there stands a Jand tree on the spot. A Gurdwara called Jand Sahib has been built to commemorate this historic episode. Moved by their love and devotion, the Guru gave them his own sword, horse and robes of honour.

With deep reverence, Sidhu and Rup Chand placed the sword and robes on their heads, and led the horse to their home by a rope, for they considered these presents too sacred for their personal use. Observing this, the Guru was greatly touched and blessed them with the remark that their word would be more potent than the sword, and that they need not use the weapons[1], but should keep them in trust for the Guru's descendants to claim.

On the sixteenth day of Baisakh, in the Bikrami year 1687 (1630 AD), the Guru laid the foundation of a village at a distance of about four miles from that spot and named it Bhai Rupa honouring his devoted Sikh, and directed Bhai Sidhu and his son to shift to that place. The wooden pillar, called *mohri*[2], driven into the ground by the Guru for laying the foundation of the village, can still be seen. The site of the fireplace (*chulha*), where Rup Chand's family established the first charity kitchen (*langar*) in 1631, is less than a hundred yards from the Gurdwara where the sixth Guru had stayed at Bhai Rupa.

Like his father, Rup Chand served the Guru with utter devotion. The following year, in August 1631, Guru Hargobind, with 3,000 warriors, visited Bhai Rupa and stayed there for three months. A Gurdwara now marks the place where the Guru stayed.

It was during this stay that Bhai Rup Chand introduced a young child named Phul to the Guru, who blessed him. His two sons, Rama and Taloka, grew up to be influential chieftains called Chaudharys. Their progeny founded the Phulkian States of Patiala, Nabha and Jind. For obtaining the Guru's blessings and introducing them to the Sikh fold, these families even now hold Bhai Rup Chand's family in reverential regard.

The Guru, in recognition of his devotion, honoured Rup Chand with the title of Bhai—his own brother—and put him in charge of the spiritual welfare of the new Malwa and the area south of the Sutlej.

A ceremony anointing him as the Guru's apostle and charging him with the responsibility of propagating the Sikh faith was performed at Bhai Rupa. Ever since, the family has had the privilege of being called the Bhai-ke, or the Guru's brother's family, and the head of the family is known as Bhai Sahib.

The cot on which Rup Chand was made to sit by the Guru for his anointment has been preserved by his descendants living in the village. The Guru directed Bhai Rup Chand to maintain a *langar* to feed the needy, and gave him a long serving spoon (*karchha*) to symbolically start

Langar was started by Bhai Rup Chand on the directions of Guru Hargobind at Bhai Rupa. These present-day replica *chulhas*, or open Indian stoves, mark the historic spot.

---

1 These articles were given to Guru Gobind Singh in 1706, when he reached Dina in Kangar.
2 The *mohri* or *yupe* in Sanskrit was stuck into the earth to sanctify a selected place either for *puja* or for establishing a habitation.

Guru Hargobind (left) in a miniature preserved in the Bhai Rupa collection.

the *langar*. He was also given the responsibility of spreading Sikhi to the world, and for this, he was presented with a double-edged sword (*khanda*), as token of authority. This could very well be the first enunciation of the percept of *degh* and *tegh*, a key element in the practice of Sikhi.

Brought up as a member of the Guru's own family, Bhai Rup Chand was in Kiratpur in 1644 when Guru Hargobind passed away, and he was given the honour of being one of the four pallbearers who carried the cortege of the sixth Guru. The other three, according to *Gurbilas Patshahi 6*, were: Bhai Bhana, son of Baba Budha, on one side; and Rai Jodh, a prominent devotee from Malwa, and Baba Suraj Mal, the Guru's elder son, on the other.

Bhai Rup Chand and his youngest son, Dharam Chand, accompanied Guru Tegh Bahadur on his journey to Patna. From there, Bhai Dharam Chand accompanied the Guru on his extended mission to the east in Assam and Dhaka, while Bhai Rup Chand stayed back in Patna in service of the Guru's family. It was during this time that Guru

Gobind Singh was born.

Bhai Rup Chand's status among the Sikhs remained venerable. His service and piety were given high regard by the Gurus, and Bhai Rup Chand had the supreme privilege and honour to be chosen to conduct the nuptial ceremony (*Anand Karaj*) of Guru Gobind Singh with Mata Jito ji at Guru-ke-Lahore near Anandpur in 1677.

After leaving Anandpur in December 1705, when Guru Gobind Singh reached Kangar in Malwa in early 1706, he stayed at a place called Dina. Here, Bhai Rup Chand made him offerings of money and war material. He also presented to him the sword and vestments given to him by the sixth Guru which were to be held in trust for a later Guru. Later, the tenth Guru gave the same sword to Mata Sahib Dev at Nanded. She shifted to Delhi in 1708. The sword is now kept at Gurdwara Mata Sundri Ji in Delhi.

Bhai Rup Chand, along with his sons, Param Chand and Dharam Chand, were formally baptised (*Amrit Sanskar*) at the sacred hands of the tenth Guru. Bhai Rup Chand (Singh, actually, but still widely known by his original name, by which he will be remembered in history), then offered these sons to the personal service of the Guru. Dharam Singh was given the responsibility of disseminating the Sikh faith, and a sword of authority was given to him to induct the people of Malwa to the Sikh way of life and propagate the message of the Khalsa Panth. This sword is kept at Bagrian by his descendents. When the final recension of the Granth Sahib was completed at Damdama Sahib, Dharam Singh—referred to as 'Rupeke' in Sikh writings—had the privilege of being one of the five Sikhs to be called in attendance.

The family of Bhai Rup Chand was among the chosen Sikhs called by the Guru to accompany him on his journey to Southern India (Deccan). Consequently, Bhai Dharam Singh and Bhai Param Singh went with the Guru. At a place called Madhosinghana in Rajasthan, the Guru, pleased with their devotion and service, directed them to return home, look after their ageing father and carry on the mission of Sikhi. When the brothers reached home, their father refused to let them enter the household unless they produced some proof that they

Gurdwara at Dina Kangar, where Bhai Rup Chand met Guru Gobind Singh and, along with his sons, took *amrit* from the Guru. Bhai Rup Chand also presented the weapons given to him by Guru Hargobind to the tenth Guru. It was during his stay here that the Guru wrote the *Zafarnama*, and sent it to Aurangzeb.

had not deserted the Guru at the time of need. The brothers went back and met the Guru in the Deccan. They narrated how their father had refused to allow them to stay with him.

The Guru was touched by Bhai Rup Chand's devotion and his sons' love and attachment. He gave them a personal *gutka* (prayer book), duly autographed and a small *kirpan* (sword), and a *khanda*. These presents, along with the sixth Guru's *karchcha* (ladle) and the *khanda* (double-edged sword) are now in Bagrian.

After the demise of the Guru in November 1708, Bhai Dharam Singh returned home to Punjab[3]. Hearing the news of the passing away of the great Guru, Bhai Rup Singh (Chand), too, passed away in 1709, at the age of ninety-five, and was cremated at a village called Bhai-ki-Samadh (memorial to the Bhai).

Bhai Rup Chand's devotion and his sons' love and attachment, touched Guru Gobind Singh, who gave his personal *gutka* (prayer book), and other gifts to them.

The responsibility of carrying on the tradition of Bhai Rup Chand was handed over by his father to Bhai Dharam Singh, who continued to command great respect among the Sikhs as a religious leader. He was called upon by Banda Bahadur to join his forces to fight the oppressive ruler of Sirhind in 1714. Bhai Dharam Singh, along with his brother Bhai Karam Singh, among others, led the Sikhs of Malwa in the decisive battle that took place at Chappar Chiri near present-day Chandigarh. The Mughal Governor Wazir Khan was killed in the battle and his establishment at Sirhind was destroyed.

Most Sikh leaders of the time who participated in this conflict, carved out territories for their fiefdoms, and some became the nuclei of various Sikh states in the East of Punjab. Bhai Dharam Singh, however, took no booty whatsoever, annexed no land and went back to propagating the Guru's ways, true to his family tradition.

The descendents of Bhai Rup Chand and their families continued to play a prominent role in spreading Sikh religious traditions. The Phulkian families maintained a close and reverential relationship towards his descendants and, till recently, preferred to have all their religious ceremonies, such as successions and weddings, conducted by them.

---

3 His brother, Bhai Param Singh, had passed away at Nanded earlier.

Entrance to the original house of Bhai Rup Chand in Bhai Rupa. On the right is the wall of the Gurdwara that marks the spot where Guru Hargobind stayed in August 1631.

Before he passed away, Bhai Dharam Singh gave the responsibility of carrying out his duties to his son, Bhai Dayal Singh, who moved out of Bhai Rupa and founded the village of Dayalpura Bhaika, about four kilometres from Bhai Rupa. He took with him the Guru's relics of authority given to Bhai Rup Chand, which are now at Bagrian. We will explore these relics in greater detail, later.

However, the second son of Bhai Rup Chand, Bhai Sukhanand, and his descendants, continued to live at Bhai Rupa, engaged in their pious work. Over the years, various other family members have moved out, and are now settled in different villages of the Malwa area. Wherever they moved to, they maintained the tradition of *langar*.

A near-contemporary painting of Guru Hargobind, by a Muslim artist. Bhai Rup Chand was blessed as a child by Guru Hargobind and he served the Guru and all his descendants as a devout Sikh. The Guru even called him his own bhai, or brother. The miniature is preserved by the descendants of the family of Bhai Rup Chand at Bhai Rupa.

CUSTODIANS AT
Bhai Rupa

Bhai Rup Chand had passed on his mantle to his youngest son, Bhai Dharam Singh. On the latter's demise, his son, Bhai Dayal Singh, became the formal successor of Bhai Rup Chand's pontificate. He moved out of Bhai Rupa.

However, the second son of Bhai Rup Chand, Bhai Sukhanand, and his descendants, continued to live at Bhai Rupa, engaged in their pious work.

Bhai Sukhanand's twelfth descendant, Bhai Gurchet Singh, and his son Bhai Buta Singh, are now the keepers of the heritage at Bhai Rupa.

A *rabab* of Guru Arjan Dev, a wooden chariot (*rath*) of Guru Ram Das, a birdcage for the pet *koels* of Guru Hargobind Sahib, manuscripts and personal effects of the Gurus are preserved at Bhai Rupa by the family members and are in remarkably good condition.

Guru Hargobind founded the village of Bhai Rupa, on 28 April 1630. The *mohri,* a wooden pillar that he stuck in the earth, is reverentially preserved and can still be seen. It is here that the sixth Guru gave Bhai Rup Chand the charge of propagating Sikhism in the Malwa area, and also directed him to start a *langar,* a practice that continues till date.

Guru Hargobind sat Rup Chand down on this cot in August 1631, for the ceremony that gave him the *gaddi* and made him responsible for propagating Sikhism. *Gaddi,* in this context is a concept of authority, not any physical object. He was also given the title of Bhai, which means Brother.

The original yarn (*vaan*) stretched and woven on the frame of the historic cot shown above, is preserved at Bhai Rupa by the family.

Wooden kitchen utensils of the *langar* of Bhai Rup Chand. The *langar*, started in 1631 on the direction of Guru Hargobind, continues till date.

An old *karcha* or a brass ladle, used for serving food at the *langar* at Bhai Rupa.

Guru Hargobind was served *langar* at Bhai Rupa in these brass bowls. The two crescent-shaped brass implements are scrapers used in the *langar* for cleaning large cooking utensils.

A pair of wooden *kharawans* or toe-knob sandals that belonged to Guru Arjan Dev.

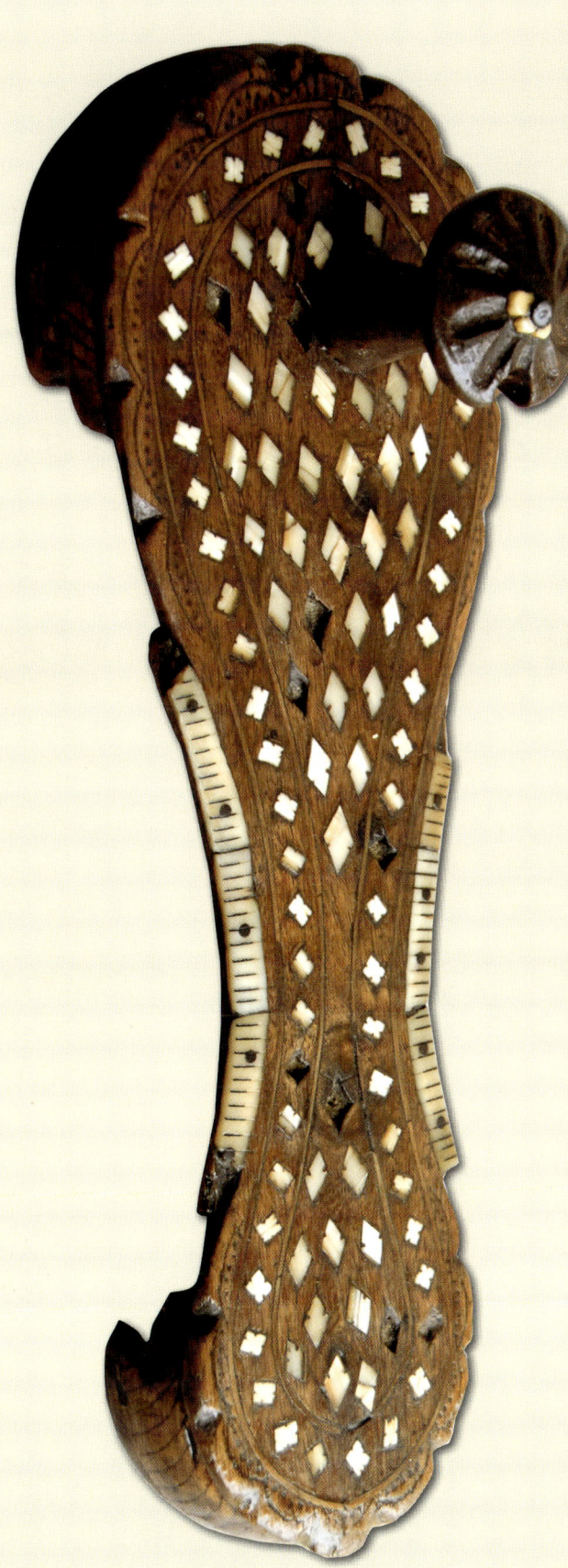

Detail of the *kharawan*, showing the ivory inlay and delicate carving.

A wooden *kharawan* or toe-knob sandal of Mata Ganga, wife of Guru Arjan Dev. The ivory inlay on wood is typical of the time and lends a feminine touch to an essentially utilitarian object.

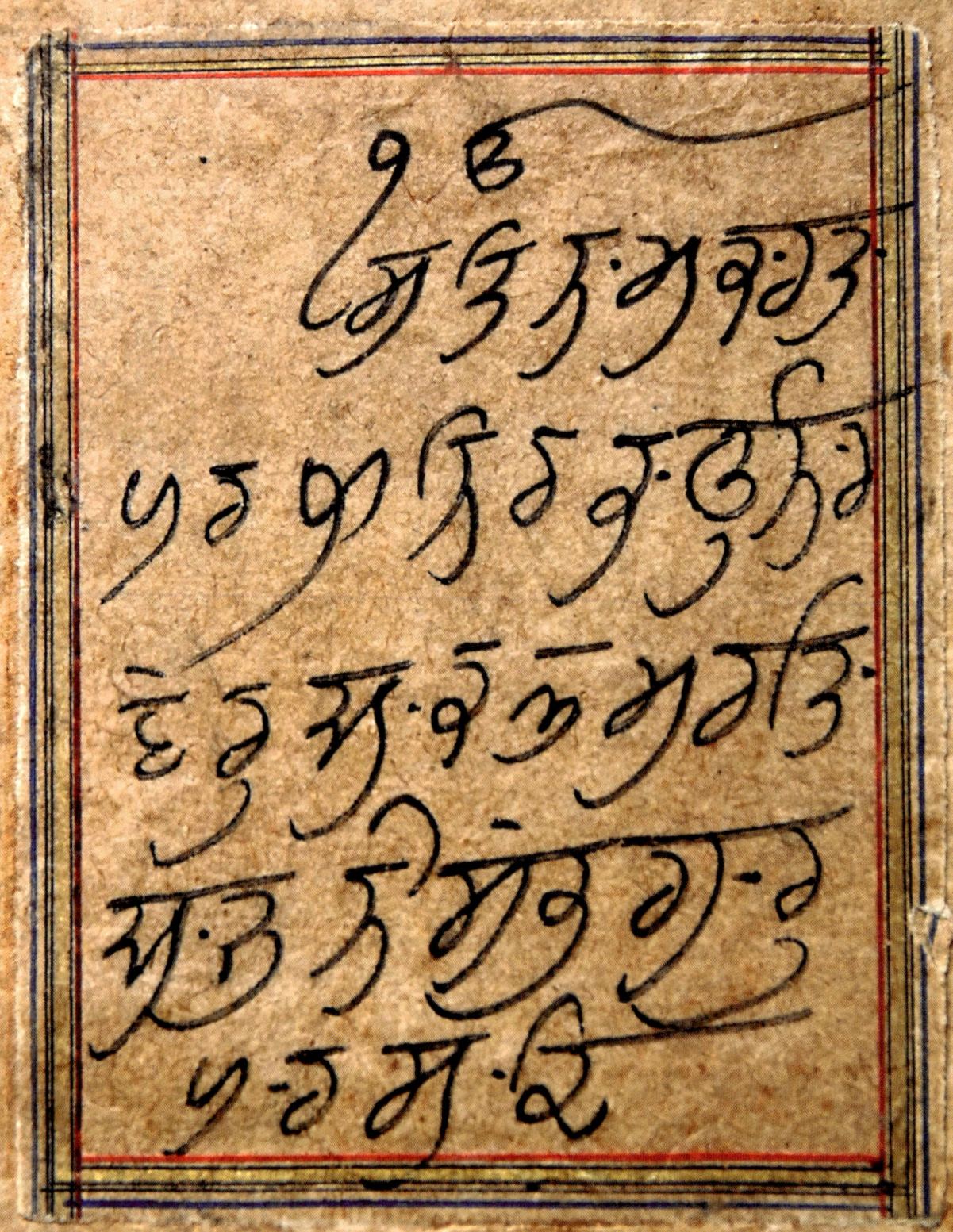

Mool Mantra in the handwriting of Guru Hargobind, as seen in a section of the *Adi Granth*, at Bhai Rupa. It is interesting that another section of the same manuscript is with the descendants of Bhai Bidhi Chand in the Sursinghwala village, near Amritsar.

Guru Hargobind with a hawk. The painting was commissioned by Bhai Bidhi Chand, according to *Gurbilas Patshahi 6*. A similar painting is at Sursinghwala. Please turn to page 188 to see it.

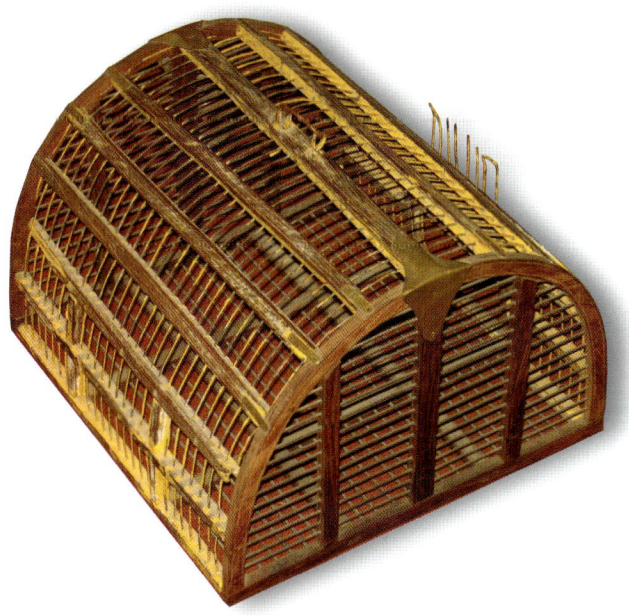

A cage for the pet birds of Guru Hargobind. The Guru was fond of *koels* (cuckoos) and in one of his *Hukumnamas* to the *sangat* of Patna, we find a reference, where he asks them to send him a pair of healthy *koels*.

Detail of the craftsmanship of the *rabab* of Guru Arjan Dev, which shows fine carving.

A *rabab* of Guru Arjan Dev, who was an accomplished musician. When he compiled the *Bani* of his predecessors, he arranged it in *ragas*, and gave Sri Guru Granth Sahib its unique format in which the compositions are arranged under the headings of the *ragas*.

A portrait of Guru Har Rai. The Guru was fond of flowers and gardens, and thus often depicted with a flower in his hand. His dress, too, is often embellished with horticultural motifs by artists.

Bairagan or *aasa*, armrest of Guru Har Rai, the seventh Guru. Such *bairagans* were often used for resting while meditating.

CUSTODIANS AT BHAI RUPA 117

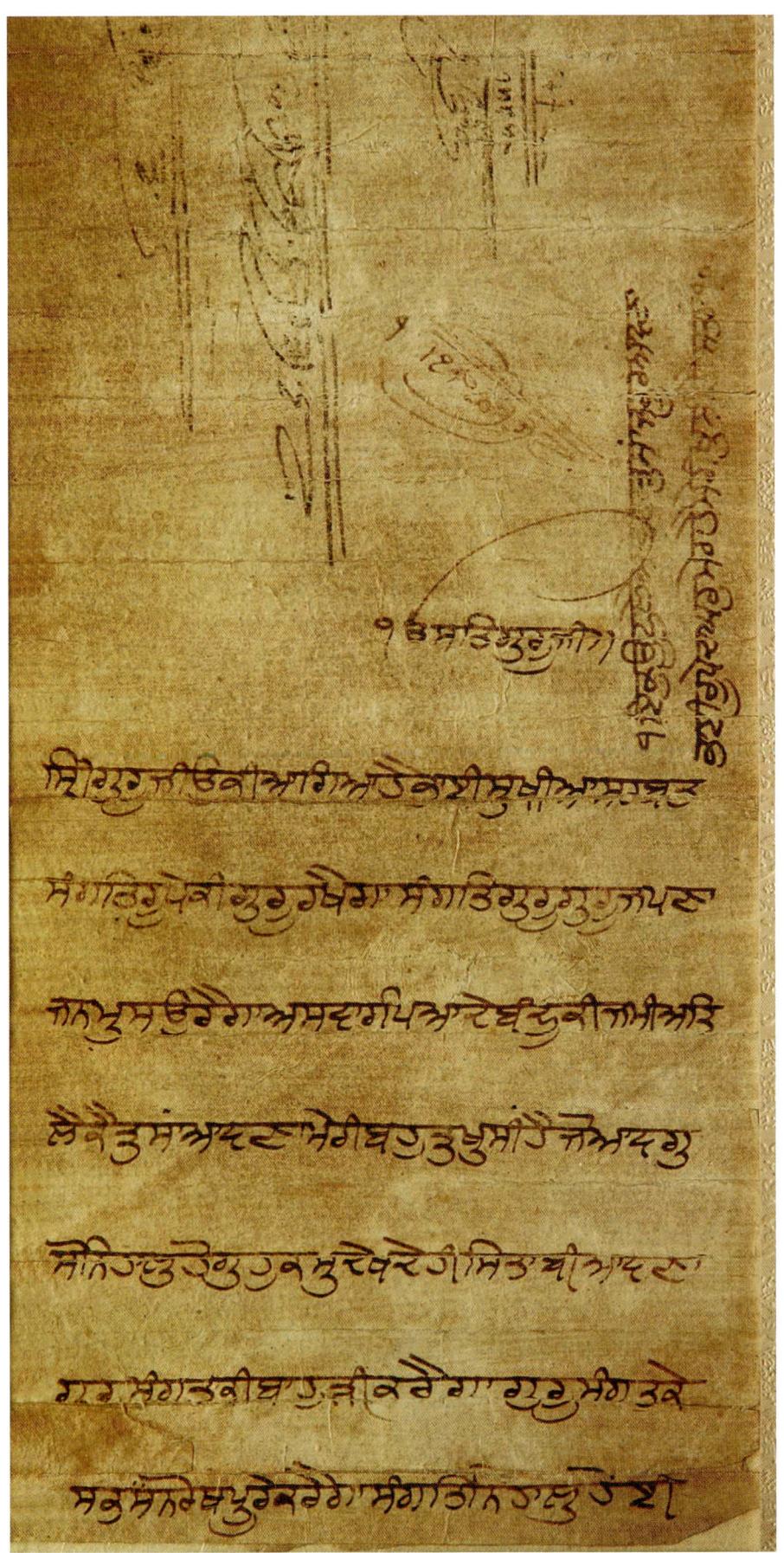

Guru Gobind Singh's signature (*nishaan*) and endorsement in his own handwriting on a *Hukamnama*, dated 2 August 1696, addressed to Bhai Sukhia and the *sangat* of Bhai Rupa, ordering them to bring infantry, cavalry and war material to Anandpur stating, '*Bhai Rupa da Ghar Mera Hai*'. On the same day, the Guru sent a similar *Hukamnama* to Bhai Rama and Bhai Taloka, sons of Baba Phul.

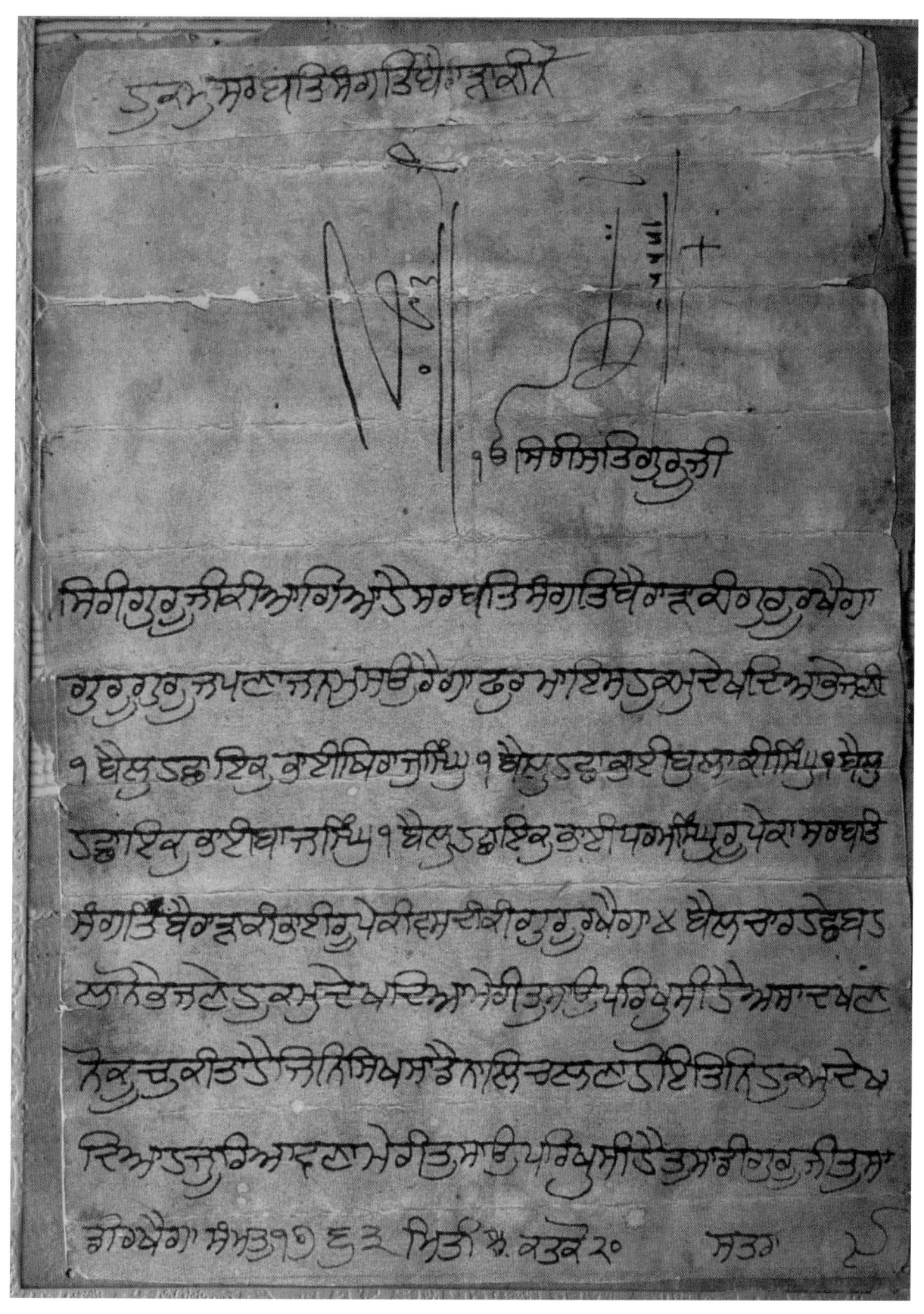

Hukamnama of Guru Gobind Singh, dated Katak 20 Samvat 1763 (October 1706) addressed to the Sangat of Brar, which was under the charge of Bhai Rup Chand, asking Bhai Dharam Singh Rupeka to accompany him to the Deccan.

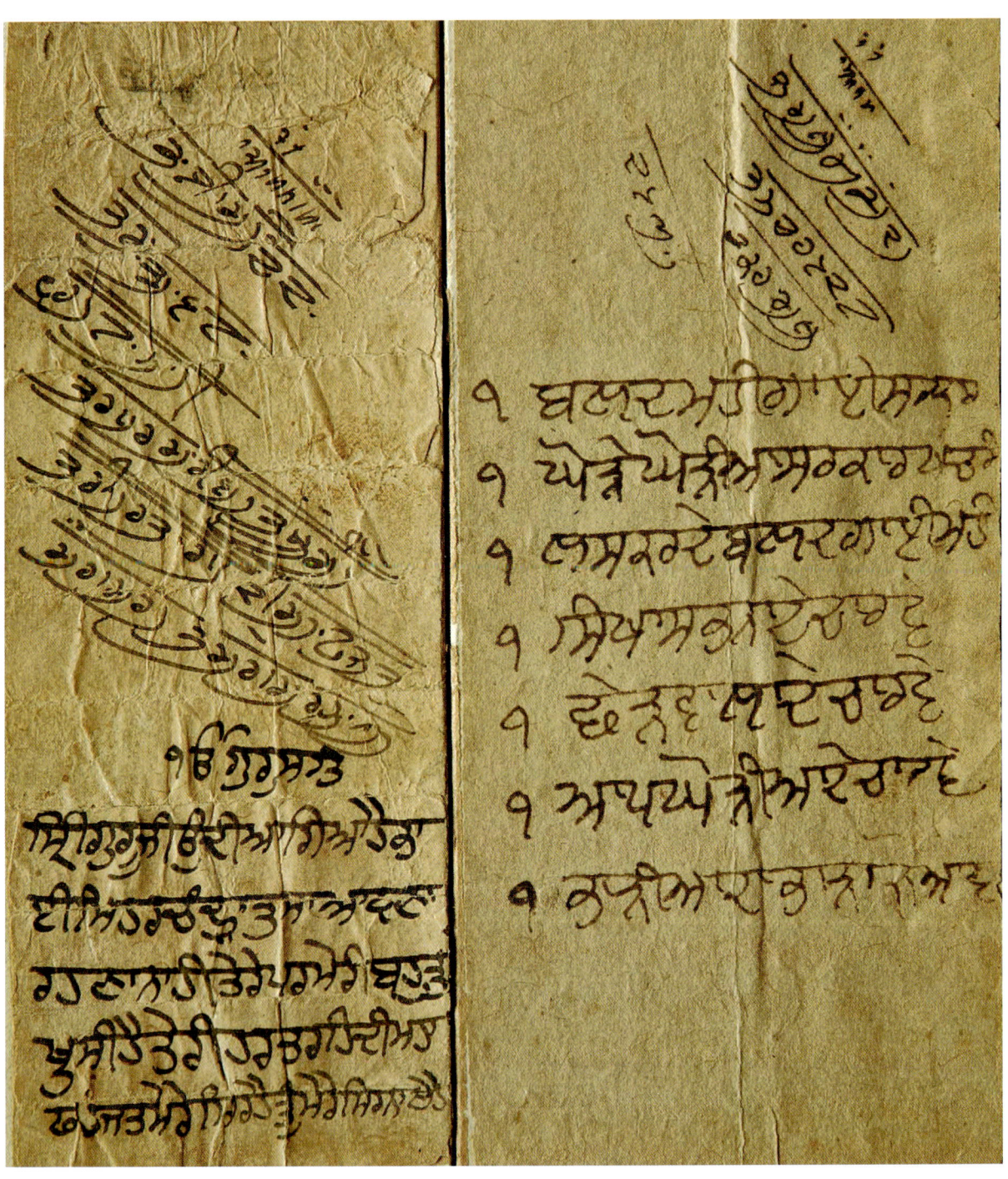

Two notes from Guru Gobind Singh. The note on the left was sent to Bhai Mehar Chand, summoning him to Anandpur and assuring him of the Guru's patronage. On the right is a note, which authorises the grazing of various categories of animals. Family tradition holds that Bhai Rup Chand's family used to look after the Guru's livestock.

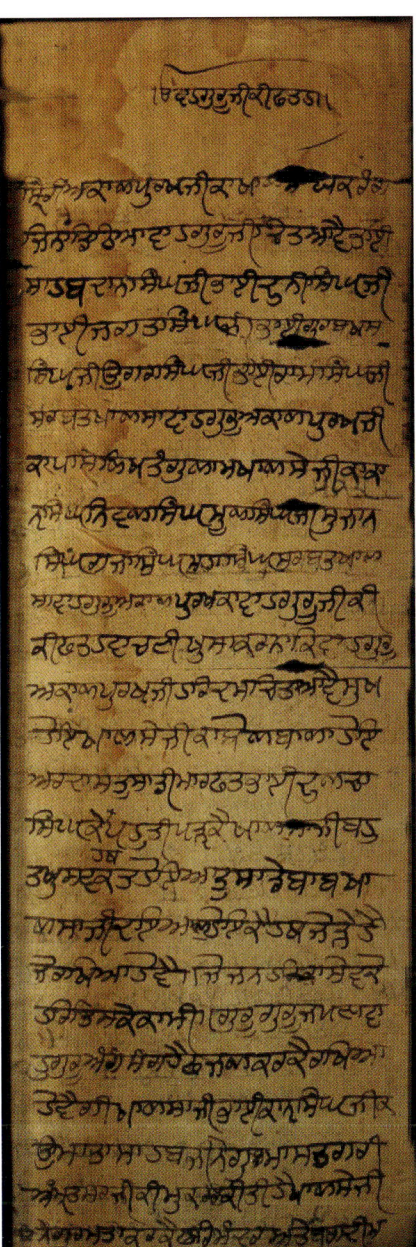

Hukumnama of Banda Bahadur, addressed to Bhai Dharam Singh, Param Singh and others, calling upon them to join him in the campaign against Sirhind. (Banda had left Nanded before Guru Gobind Singh's demise and, perhaps, was not aware of Bhai Param Singh having passed away). Dharam Singh, with his elder brother Bhai Karam Singh, led the Malwa Sikhs and joined Banda's forces to fight in the battle of Chappar Chiri on 7 May 1710. In the battle, which the Sikh forces won decisively, the Governor of Sirhind, Wazir Khan, was killed, shaking the foundation of the Mughal rule in North India.

After Guru Gobind Singh's demise, his widow, Mata Sundri, guided the community. She also issued *Hukumnamas* on important matters. In the *Hukamnama* shown above, addressed to the family of Bhai Rup Chand, she reiterates that the Khalsa must not recognise anybody other than the *Akalpurakh* as Supreme, and revere no Guru in human form other than the ten Gurus. Further, it says that he who considers any other person as Guru in human form shall be committing an unpardonable offence.

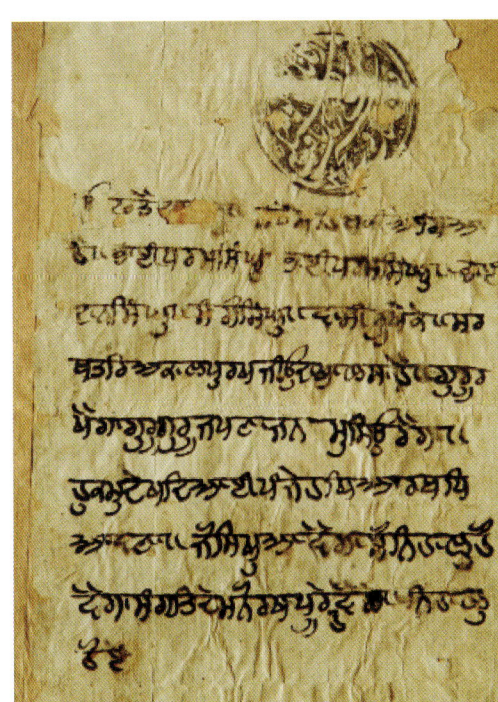

CUSTODIANS AT BHAI RUPA   121

Below: This wooden chariot (*rath*), crafted by Khuda Bakhsh, a Kashmiri artisan, was presented to Guru Ram Das in Amritsar. It was used by Mata Ganga Ji, wife of Guru Arjan Dev. Later, Guru Hargobind's grandson, Baba Ram Rai, travelled in it from Kiratpur Sahib to Delhi. After his father disowned him because of Baba Ram Rai changing the text of *Gurbani*, he took the *rath* to Dehradun. Bhai Gian Chand, grandson of Bhai Rup Chand, brought the *rath* to Bhai Rupa in 1717.

Details showing the craftsmanship of the *rath*.

122 Sikh Heritage: Ethos and Relics

A letter written by Baba Aala Singh of Patiala addressed to Bhai Gian Chand and *sangat* of Bhai Rupa in response to a communication sent to him earlier. The correspondence ends with greeting '*Wahe Guru Ji ki Fateh Bulai, Matha Tekeya*' showing his deep respect towards the family of Bhai Rup Chand.

A small prayer book with visible water stains, said to have been carried by a Sikh accompanying Guru Gobind Singh. The Sirsa rivulet was in spate when Guru Gobind Singh and his Sikhs crossed it in December 1705, after evacuating Anandpur Sahib.

The opening folio of the illuminated manuscript of Sri Guru Granth Sahib at Bagrian. The rich golden illumination work on the manuscript was done by late nineteenth-century Kashmiri artists.

CUSTODIANS AT Bagrian

In 1717, Bhai Dharam Singh's son, Bhai Dayal Singh, moved out of Bhai Rupa village and founded a new village at a distance of about four kilometres, and called it Dayalpura Bhaika. He took the sacred relics given by the Gurus to Bhai Rup Chand with him and started another *langar* at Dayalpura, thus continuing the family tradition as per the directions of the sixth Guru. This *langar* is still being run by his descendants.

Bhai Dayal Singh's son, Bhai Guddar Singh, is particularly remembered for his piety and charitable disposition. He was earnestly devoted to the propagation of Sikhism, and his activities were not confined to Malwa alone, for he travelled far and wide to preach the gospel of Guru Nanak. There used to be a Gurdwara in Peshawar commemorating his visit. In his absence, the service of the *langar* was looked after by his wife Mai Rajji, which consequently came to be known as Mai Rajji da Langar, both at Bagrian and Dayalpura.

In 1754, the Mughal Governor of Jalandhar, Adina Begh Khan, and Punjab Commander-in-Chief, Sadiq Begh Khan, while passing through Dayalpura, were impressed by Bhai Guddar Singh's piety and influence in the area, and gifted the village of Bagrian (now in Sangrur district of Punjab) to his *langar*.

Raja Gajpat Singh, the ancestor of the rulers of Nabha and Jind, held Bhai Guddar Singh in high esteem. When Bhai Guddar Singh came to know that a girl was born to Raja Gajpat Singh's wife and that the child, according to the evil custom of those days, was being buried alive, he went straight to the couple at their fort in Badrukhan and reprimanded them for their reprehensible act. He took them to the place where the child was buried in a *gharha*, or an earthen

Mai Rajji da Langar, Bagrian. A plaque at the entrance of the *langar*, which narrates how the traditions started by Guru Hargobind in 1631 at Bhai Rupa, has been by faithfully adhered to by the descendants of Bhai Rup Chand. This *langar* was established by Bhai Guddar Singh and his wife Mai Rajji in 1765.

pot commonly used for storing water. The infant was still alive. The Bhai Sahib blessed the baby, who was named Raj Kaur. She was later married to Sardar Mahan Singh Sukarchakia and bore a son, named Ranjit Singh, who established the Sikh State and became the greatest ruler in the history of Punjab.

After Bhai Guddar Singh died in 1766, his adopted son, Bhai Mohar Singh, shifted his headquarters from Dayalpura to Bagrian. In 1808, when Maharaja Ranjit Singh swooped down the Cis-Sutlej territory, levying exactions on the chiefs and rulers, it was Bhai Mohar Singh who dissuaded him from harassing rulers of the Phulkian States. Through the efforts of the Bhai Sahib, the Maharaja of Patiala agreed to enter into a symbolic brotherhood with Maharaja Ranjit Singh. This facilitated Bedi Sahib Singh's endeavour to negotiate a compromise between them. Similarly, Nawab Attaullah Khan of Malerkotla had only to pay a tribute and he was not troubled by Maharaja Ranjit Singh, after the Maharaja was reminded, by the Bhai Sahib, of the protests made by his ancestor at the time of execution of the tenth Guru's younger sons, following which the Nawab's family was blessed to rule by the tenth Guru. During this visit, Maharaja Ranjit Singh called on the Bhai Sahib at Bagrian and donated some villages to the *langar*.

By then the family had grown into an influential and powerful independent state, and came to be regarded as one of the two most important houses in Malwa. One was Aaleka, that is, Patiala, the house of the descendants of Maharaja Aala Singh; and the other Dayaleka, i.e. the house of the descendants of Bhai Dayal Singh. Bhai Mohar Singh's wife, Mai Gohar, too, became famous for her charity in Bagrian, just as had been the case of Mai Rajji before her.

Bhai Bahadur Singh, son of Mohar Singh, out of sentiment for his faith and his people, took no part in the campaign of the East India Company against the Sikh State. After the defeat of the army of Sarkar Khalsa, and the occupation of Lahore by the British, the Bhai Sahib lost his status as an independent chieftain; most of his property was confiscated by the British and he was reduced to a position of virtual penury. He was so shocked by the fall of the Lahore Darbar that he confined himself to his fort and did not leave it till his death.

Bhai Bahadur Singh was especially known for his piety and missionary work among the socio-economic backward classes. He brought thousands of them into the Sikh fold, giving them equal status. It was during the time of Bhai Sampuran Singh, his son, that the government of the day restored a small portion of the confiscated estate of his ancestors. It was then consolidated by his son Bhai Narain

One of the four legs of the cot (*peedha*) of Bhai Guddar Singh, upon which he sat while meditating. Bhai Guddar Singh started the *langar* at Bagrian in 1765.

126   Sikh Heritage: Ethos and Relics

Singh and the status of the family was restored after ten years.

Bhai Arjan Singh, who succeeded Bhai Narain Singh in 1885, was highly respected as a Sikh leader of his times. He enjoyed a de facto prominence as the religious head of the Sikhs. During the Delhi Darbar, held in December 1911 to commemorate the coronation of King George V and Queen Mary as Emperor and Empress of India, he was asked to sit in attendance of the Guru Granth Sahib, which was taken out in a procession on an elephant from the Red Fort in Delhi and was scheduled to go to the site of the Darbar. However, on reaching Gurdwara Sis Ganj Sahib en route, he stopped the elephant, saying that the Guru's destination is the Gurdwara and it would not go to the Darbar of a mere human, be it the Emperor of India or the King of England. He played an active role in the Sikh reform movements, especially the Singh Sabha Movement and Gurdwara reforms. One of the earliest Singh Sabhas was formed at Bagrian. He was chosen as the first president of the Chief Khalsa Diwan in 1902, a position he held for 15 years. Bhai Arjan Singh passed away in 1946.

The historic *loh*, or iron griddle, on which *chapatis* (unleavened flat bread) are baked. This is the first *tawa* installed at the time of starting the *langar* in 1765 at Bagrian, and the tradition continues to this day.

Thereafter his son Bhayee Ardaman Singh (1899-1976) inherited the responsibility of maintaining the family traditions. He would regularly tour the villages of Malwa propagating Sikhi, and conducting *Amrit Sanchar*. Educated at Khalsa College, Amritsar, and by traditional religious teachers at home, he was a pragmatic interpreter of Sikhi. The influence of the likes of Professor Teja Singh, his teacher, and association with the great Bhai Kahn Singh of Nabha, a close family friend, along with the influence and company of his saintly father, Bhai Arjan Singh, helped him become a true Gursikh. Besides, he had a deep grounding in *kirtan* tradition acquired from his father and from the great *kirtania* Mahant Gajja Singh, and the in-house *rababi kirtania*, Bhai Ghasita. A firm believer in preserving the rich tradition of Sikh religious music, he persistently promoted and spoke about the preservation of old *reets* (compositions associated with the Gurus and their period).

He was widely known as an upright scholar who provided direction to Sikh thought during the trying period the *Panth* underwent when it was trying to establish its role and identity in newly-independent India. He provided an apolitical leadership in the spiritual tradition of his illustrious forefathers. A dominating persona on the Sikh theological scene for thirty years, he was looked up to by the community to provide a pragmatic exposition of Sikh ethos and direction. Bhayee Ardaman Singh passed away in 1976 leaving behind three sons, Bhai Haridhan Singh, Bhai Ashok Singh and Bhayee Sikandar Singh, and two daughters, Bibi Harinder Kaur and Bibi Manoranjan Kaur.

Bhai Sahib Ardaman Singh of Bagrian performing the *Ardaas* at the coronation of Maharaja Rajbir Singh of Jind in March 1948. He is holding the Sri Sahib given to Bhai Dharam Singh by Guru Gobind Singh.

In acordance with family practice, the eldest son, Bhai Haridhan Singh, took over the responsibility of maintaining the *langar* tradition. After a prolonged illness, he passed away in 1996. During his earlier days, he was involved in the freedom struggle. He had received traditional instructions in Gurbani and Sikh literature at home, and held an MA in History and an LLB from Lucknow University.

Bhai Ashok Singh is a well-known figure among the Sikh intelligentsia, and a sombre enunciator of Sikh thought. He has been active in Sikh political and religious matters, and was president of the Institute of Sikh Studies, Chandigarh.

Bhayee Sikandar Singh, an MBA from the University of Western Ontario, Canada, and MA English from University of Delhi, is deeply involved in Sikhi and its propagation, and is on the editorial board of the *Nishaan*, a quarterly publication dedicated to the cause of the Sikh community, well accepted all over the world. His special interest is the inherited love for the traditional Sikh *kirtan lores* and he has written about its importance in Sikh practices.

The present keeper of the tradition at Bagrian is Bhai Jujhar Singh, son of Bhai Haridhan Singh. The tradition of *langar*, which started under the directions of Sri Guru Hargobind Sahib in 1631 at Bhai Rupa, is still maintained at Bagrian and Dayalpura Bhaika by Bhai Rup Chand's progeny.

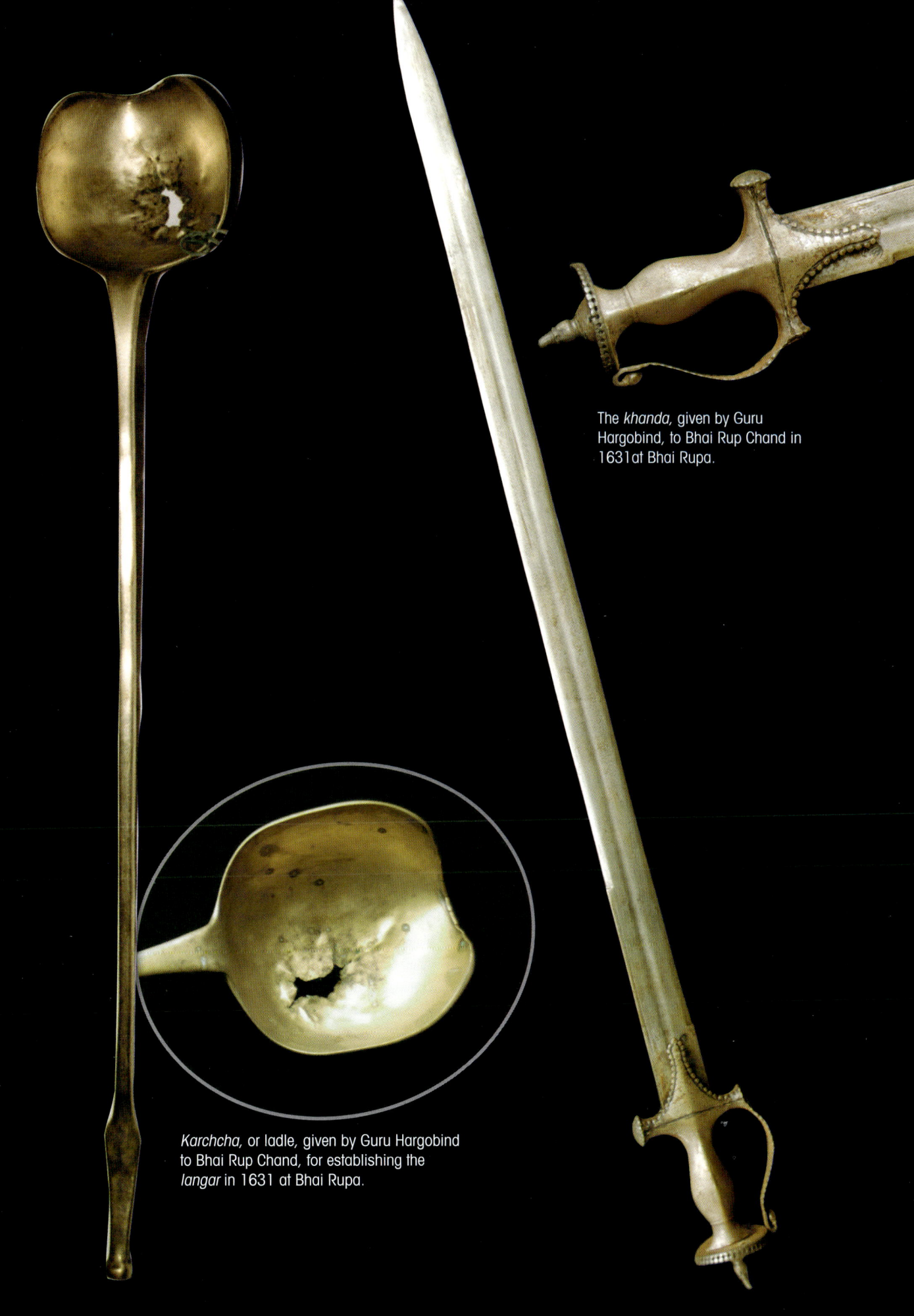

Karchcha, or ladle, given by Guru Hargobind to Bhai Rup Chand, for establishing the *langar* in 1631 at Bhai Rupa.

The *khanda*, given by Guru Hargobind, to Bhai Rup Chand in 1631 at Bhai Rupa.

Guru Gobind Singh's turban adornments—two miniature *kirpans* and a *khanda*. The weapons have been placed on an original Dhaka muslin cloth that dates back to the Guru's time, and in which the personal *gutka* (prayer book) of the Guru was originally wrapped.

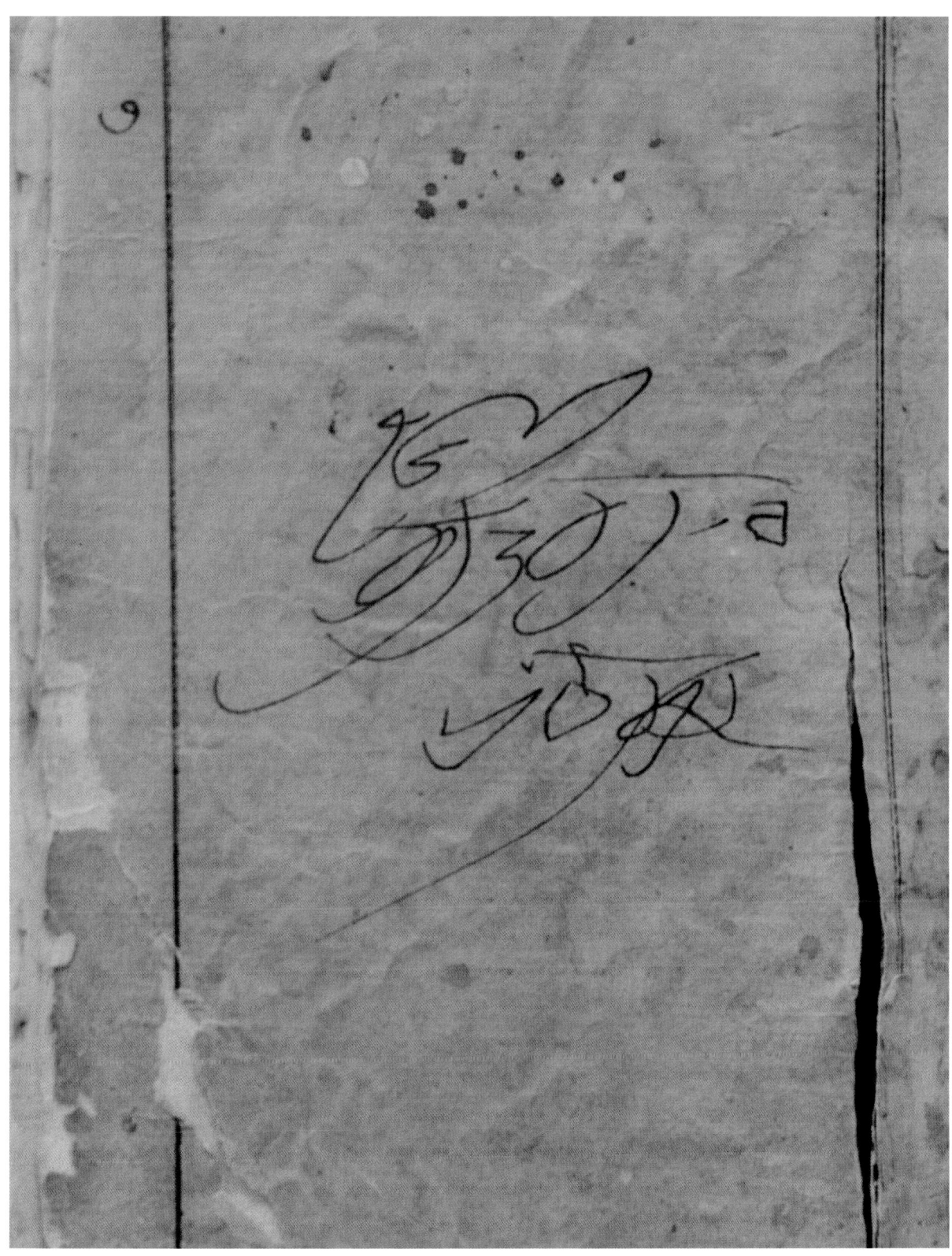

Guru Gobind Singh's *gutka*, given to Bhai Dharam Singh at Nanded at the time of parting, as a token of his pleasure. According to family tradition, the inscription, which reads, *Ek Onkar Satgur Parsad,* was done by the Guru with an arrowhead, while on horseback.

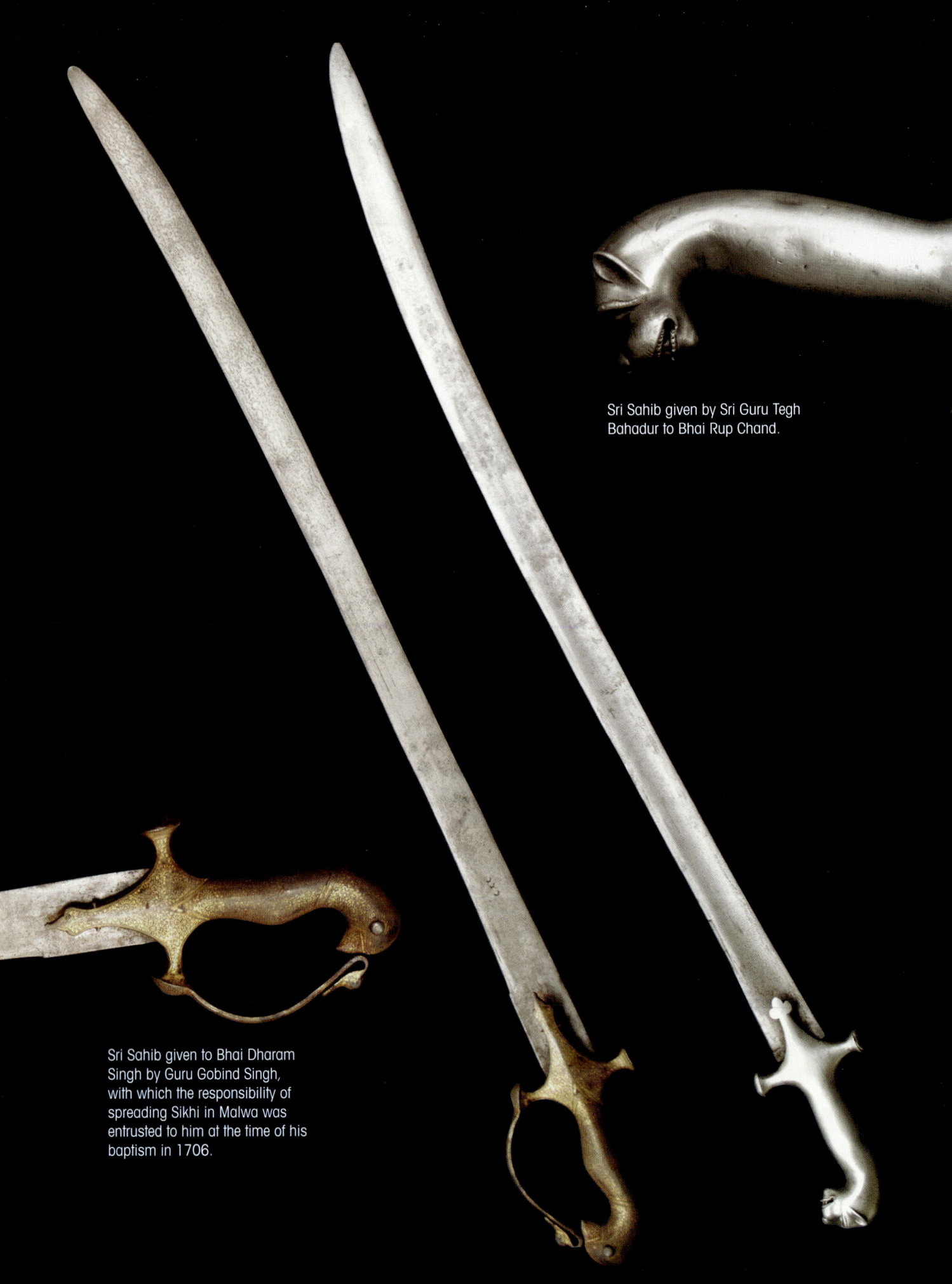

Sri Sahib given by Sri Guru Tegh Bahadur to Bhai Rup Chand.

Sri Sahib given to Bhai Dharam Singh by Guru Gobind Singh, with which the responsibility of spreading Sikhi in Malwa was entrusted to him at the time of his baptism in 1706.

Three *katars* given to Bhai Dharam Singh by Guru Gobind Singh at the time of the former's baptism (administering of *amrit*) in 1706 at Talwandi Sabu at Damdama Sahib. Bhai Dharam Singh, referred to as Rupeka, was one of the five Sikhs who were present at the time of the completion of the final version of the *Adi Granth* and later anointed the Sri Guru Granth Sahib at Nanded in October AD 1707.

The *langar* building at Bagrian. The tradition of providing food to all continues there.

CUSTODIANS AT BAGRIAN

A painting depicting Baba Phul with an ascetic, captioned 'Bava Samerpuri ji'. From the collection of the Maharaja of Nabha.

THE
Phulkian States

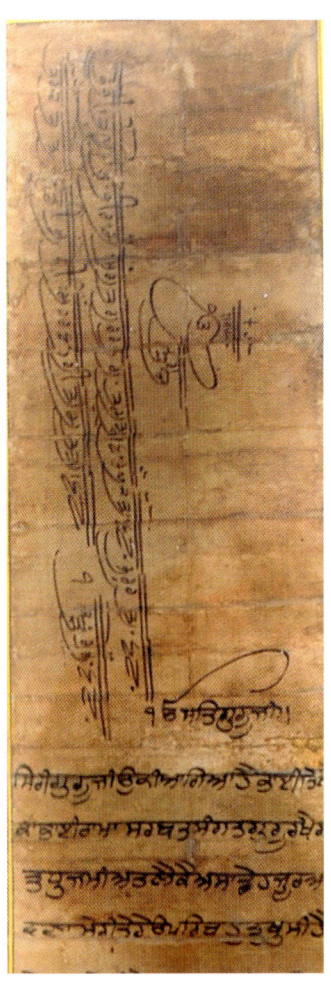

Guru Gobind Singh's signatures and endorsement in his own handwriting on a *Hukamnama* addressed to Bhai Rama and Bhai Taloka, sons of Baba Phul, dated 2 August 1696, calling upon them to come to Anandpur with men and material. It is significant that the writing in the Guru's hand went beyond the usual inscription, *'Ek Onkar, Sat Guru Prasad'*. In this case, the summons are reiterated in his own hand as the blessings, and a mention of the robe that he is sending as a token of his affection. On the same day, the Guru sent a similar *Hukamnama* to Bhai Sukhia at Bhai Rupa.

The rulers of the three prominent, erstwhile Sikh Princely States of India—Patiala, Nabha and Jind—draw their lineage from Baba Phul (1627-1690). His uncle, Kala, had taken him to seek the blessings of Guru Hargobind. The Guru blessed the four-year-old with prosperity and wealth.

The ancestors of Baba Phul link their heritage with Jaisal, the Bhatti Rajput Prince who founded the town of Jaisalmer in 1156. It was during the incursions of the Muslim rulers of Delhi into the Rajputana, that his descendant moved into southwest Punjab, to the area around what is now Bathinda.

With the blessings of the Guru, Baba Phul and his brother Sandali settled in the village of Mehraj. In 1657, when Guru Har Rai honoured Bhai Rup Chand with a visit, it meant Baba Phul was once again blessed by the Guru. Phul's sons Rama and Taloka grew up to be men of means and power, and were known as Choudharys. They rendered great service to the cause of the Gurus and later to the community during the turbulent times of Banda Bahadur, in early eighteenth century.

During the days of hardship and conflict in Anandpur, between 1690 and 1705, they provided men and material to the tenth Guru[1]. The two brothers with their men also reached Chamkaur in December 1705.

Both Rama and Taloka were formally baptised by the tenth Guru in Anandpur in 1702. From time to time, these brothers were called upon by the Gurus for help and support. The Guru bestowed gifts of weapons and royal edicts upon them, which they preserved with great care and devotion.

The two brothers, along with their forces, joined Banda Bahadur at Chappar Chiri in May 1710, after the battle of Sirhind. Rama's

---

1 A *Hukamnama* to this effect, dated 1696, has been preserved at New Moti Bagh Palace, Patiala.

Phulkian States and Their Founders

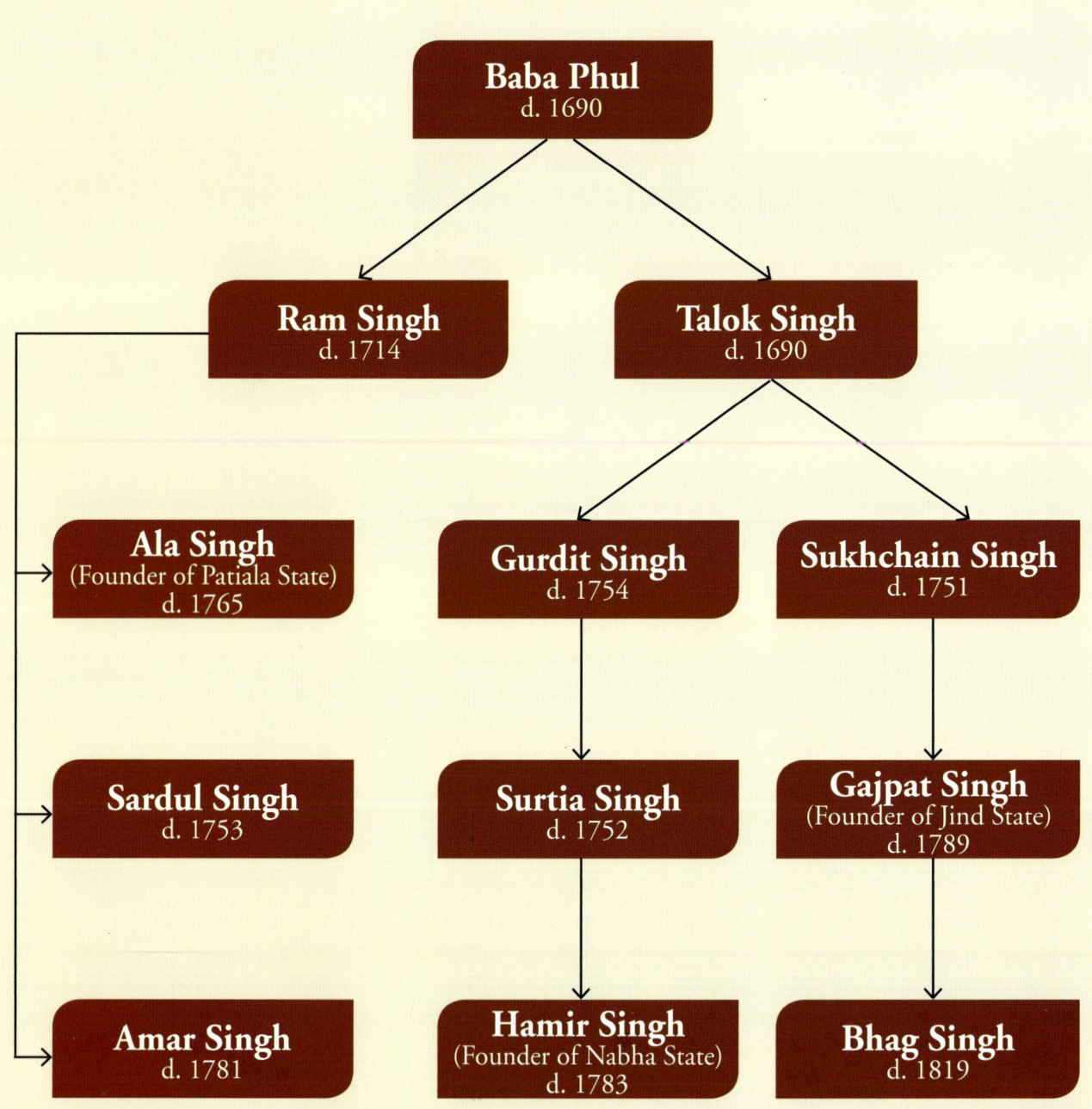

Source: *Gur Shabad Ratnakar Mahan Kosh* by Bhai Kahan Singh

descendants established the state of Patiala, and Taloka's descendants founded Nabha and Jind.

The descendants of the royal families of Patiala and Nabha have been meticulous in keeping their heritage alive. We will deal with these two families in separate sections.

Jind was founded in 1763 by Raja Gajpat Singh, who ruled until 1789. Raja Gajpat Singh's daughter, Raj Kaur, became the wife of Sardar Mahan Singh Sukarchakia. She was the mother of Maharaja Ranjit Singh.

Raja Gajpat Singh was succeeded by his son, Raja Bhag Singh, who shrewdly sought an alliance with the British. They recognised in him a friend, and showered upon him many marks of favour and regard.

Raja Bhag Singh died in 1819, and Fateh Singh succeeded him. He ruled only for a short time, and died merely three years later, in 1822. Raja Sangat Singh, who was eleven years old at the time, succeeded him, but also passed away prematurely on 2 November 1834.

Since there was no other male heir, Sarup Singh, his cousin, succeeded him. He was very friendly and loyal to the British, and assisted them in 1857. Raja Sarup Singh died in 1864. He was succeeded by his son, Raghbir Singh, who was so helpful to the British that they conferred the title of Raja-i-Rajgan on him.

Raja-i-Rajgan Raghbir Singh died in 1887. His only son, Balbir Singh, had predeceased him and therefore his minor grandson, Ranbir Singh, was named the Raja. A council of regency administered the state during his minority. He was invested with full ruling powers in November 1899. He ruled the state till it was merged with PEPSU[2] and later, with the Union of India on 15 July 1948.

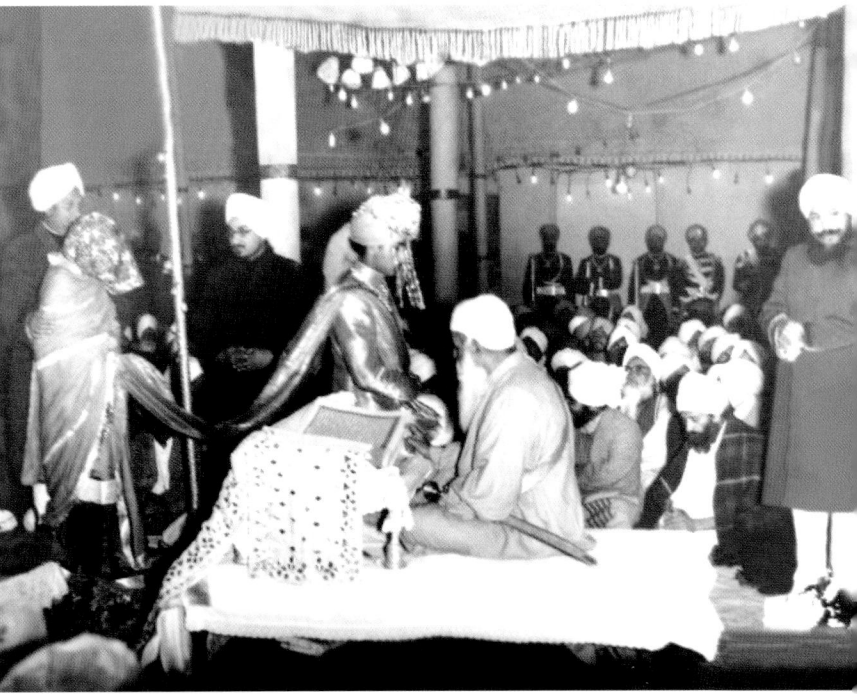

Bhai Sahib Arjan Singh of Bagrian performing the *Anand Karaj* (marriage ceremony) of Kanwar Rajbir Singh of Jind in 1939.

---

2 The Patiala and East Punjab States Union (PEPSU) was one of the states of India from 1948-56, with its capital in Patiala. It was created by amalgamating eight Princely States of Punjab: Patiala, Jind, Nabha, Kapurthala, Faridkot, Kalsia, Malerkotla and Nalagarh.

Baba Aala Singh (1691-1765), the founder of Patiala State, as shown in a painting at the New Moti Bagh Palace in Patiala.

CUSTODIANS AT
Patiala

Baba Aala Singh (1691-1765), the founder of the former state of Patiala, was the grandson of Phul, who had been blessed by the sixth and the seventh Gurus. Phul and his son Rama had taken *amrit* from the hands of Guru Gobind Singh at Talwandi Sabo in 1706. Rama, the elder son of Phul, had established a separate estate from his brother Taloka. He also captured numerous villages. This way, Rama had grown in influence and power over the course of time.

Aala Singh was Rama's son. He expanded his possessions and consolidated his position in the Malwa region. In 1714, he took over a few villages in present-day Bathinda district. He gathered around him a band of dashing and daring young men, and, by inspiring them with his courage and leadership he further increased the area under his influence. Aala Singh established his headquarters in Barnala in 1722. By 1723, he had increased his holding to thirty villages. Emboldened by his series of conquests, he ravaged the territory of Rai Kalha of Raikot and Jagraon, which left the Muslim chiefs of the area threatened. Due to all his bold forays, he is regarded as the real founder of the house of Patiala.

He defeated Zain Khan, the Governor of Sirhind, and captured it in 1765. He was known for his political correctness and as an astute ruler, who, even while supporting the Khalsa, stayed on the right side of the Afghans and Durranis. So much so, he even received the title of Raja from Ahmad Shah Abdali, though only after paying a heavy fine and committing to an annual tribute.

He was succeeded by his grandson, Raja Amar Singh, in 1765, whose father Sardul Singh had pre-deceased him. The Mughal Empire was floundering, and Raja Amar Singh took advantage of the situation to capture vast territories and enlarge his estate, which now included all of Bathinda. He died at the age of thirty-three in 1781 and was succeeded by his son Sahib Singh, a minor of six years.

During Sahib Singh's minority, and later in his lifetime, because

Detail from a mural in Quila Mubarak, Patiala, showing Raja Karam Singh (1798-1845).

A long-bladed sword that belonged to Baba Aala Singh, the founder of Patiala.

Baba Aala Singh's five-pronged lance.

of his lack of acumen, the affairs of state were managed by his grandmother Mai Hukaman and Dewan Nanoo Mal. After her demise, it was Raja Amar Singh's aunt, Bibi Rajinder Kaur, who helped Nanoo Mal manage the state till her own demise in 1791.

Thereafter Raja Sahib Singh's older sister, Bibi Sahib Kaur, took over the role of the regent and guide. In 1794, she led the Patiala forces in a decisive battle against the Marathas, Anand Rao and Lachman Rao, at Mardanpur.

After her demise in 1799, Raja Sahib Singh's wife Aas Kaur took over the affairs of the state. It was during this period of Raja Sahib Singh that Patiala became a protectorate of the East India Company. Raja Sahib Singh was succeeded by Raja Karam Singh on 30 June 1813, who, at the age of fifteen, was very supportive of the British, and helped them during the Sikh Wars of 1845 against Lahore Durbar.

After his father's death in December 1845, Maharaja Narinder Singh took over the State in 1846, and continued to help the East India Company in their wars against the now crumbling Khalsa Darbar of Lahore. Later, during the Mutiny of 1857, he, along with his collaterals of Jind State, rendered much support to the British by sending their troops to Delhi. Consequently they were rewarded with new territories, honours and titles.

Maharaja Mahindra Singh succeeded his father in 1862. During his rule, the State of Patiala underwent great development in the socio-economic fields. He was the first ruler to have studied in the English medium, and as such, he was a votary of modern education. He contributed liberally to the newly-formed Punjab University, Lahore, and also founded Mohindra College, Patiala, in 1873, where higher education was free to all. He died in 1876 and was succeeded by his son, Maharaja Rajendra Singh, in January 1877. Infrastructure development by way of the extension of the rail road to distant places like Bathinda took place during his period. Like his predecessor, he lent his bit to the expansion and consolidation of the British rule in the Northwest, for which he was duly rewarded.

Maharaja Bhupinder Singh, son of Maharaja Rajendra Singh, was the most well-known ruler of Patiala in the first half of the twentieth century. He was educated at the Aitcheson College, Lahore, which was a school for the elite in pre-Partition India. A good sportsman and administrator, he lived life to the fullest.

The Patiala army fought alongside the British army during the first half of the twentieth century, on various fronts. It won laurels for having the finest soldiers in keeping with the best tradition of the Sikhs. For the British government, the Maharaja was a popular face of

Sikh leadership. He became the Chancellor of the Chamber of Princes in 1926, and died in 1938 after having led an eventful rule.

His son, Yadavindra Singh, succeeded him as the Maharaja of Patiala. A good administrator, he ran the State efficiently during the short span of ten years that he was at the helm, promoting education as well as sports. He played a major role in welcoming thousands of refugees who fled from, what had been earmarked as, Pakistani territory in early 1947 and then rehabilitating them after the Partition.

He led the Indian Princes who relinquished their power and wealth for an integrated, unified India in 1948. Captain Amarinder Singh then came to head the house of Aala Singh, and is highly respected among his community as the titular Maharaja of Patiala. He is active in politics, and became a Member of Parliament from Patiala in 1980 on an Indian National Congress ticket. However, he resigned from Parliament in 1984, as a protest against the Indian army's entry into the Harmandar Sahib during Operation Blue Star. Later, he was minister for agriculture, forests, development and panchayats in an Akali Dal government in Punjab, but had a falling out with them and eventually rejoined the Congress.

Capt. Amarinder Singh was chief minister of Punjab from 2002 to 2007, and is now the most prominent leader of the Congress party in the state. He has also written books on Sikh history and important wars, including *Lest We Forget*, about the battles fought in the 1965 War, *A Ridge Too Far,* on the Kargil conflict and *The Last Sunset: Rise and Fall of the Lahore Durbar*, on Maharaja Ranjit Singh and his kingdom. He has preserved his community's heritage immaculately.

Capt. Amarinder Singh's wife, Maharani Praneet Kaur, has served as minister of state for external affairs with the government of India.

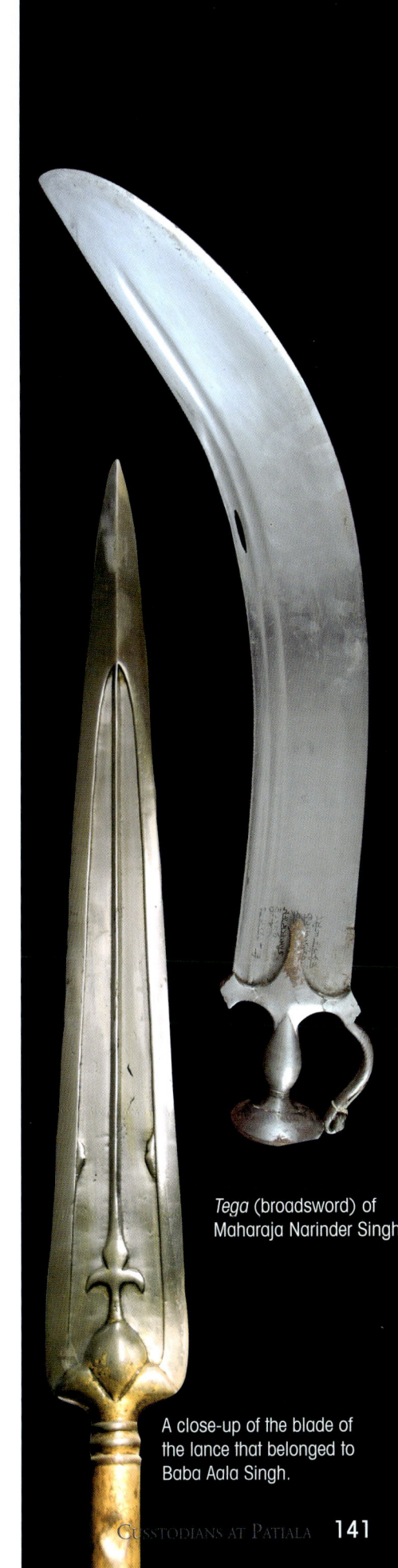

Tega (broadsword) of Maharaja Narinder Singh

A close-up of the blade of the lance that belonged to Baba Aala Singh.

Char Aäinä, this metal armour mounted on a leather belt, was worn by Guru Gobind Singh during the battle of Bhangani in which Bhim Chand of Kahlur and Fateh Singh of Srinagar (Garhwal) plotted with other Hill chieftains and attacked the Guru. The Sikhs met them seven miles east of Paonta on 18th Baisakh 1746. The following pages show the four panels of the armour, each inscribed with *Gurbani*:

The following is the translation of the text of the first *chhand* (opening stanza) of *Akaal Ustat* of Guru Gobind Singh, inscribed on the armour seen above.

One. Omnipotent. Realised though the Grace of the True Preceptor; Blessed am I with the protection of *Akaal*; Available to me is the defence of *Sarabloh* (All Steel); blessed am I with the shield of *Sarabkal* (Eternal); Available ever is the protection of *Sarabloh*.

The following is the translation of the text of the first *chhand of Jaap Sahib* of Guru Gobind Singh, inscribed on the armour seen above.

One. Omnipotent. Realised though the Grace of the True Preceptor. That which hath neither physical features nor peculiarities, nor contours, colours or caste, nor genealogy. There is not to say for anyone what Its form, what Its complexion, what Its physiognomy, and what Its uniform. Stable entity, the Light *sui generis*, without measure, so it may be stated. Count countless god kings of gods, earthly kings and their emperors, (and the Lords of all three worlds) the gods the mortals and the titans, all these (together): (still) every blade of grass beareth witness that, Not that, 'Not that'. Who can make all-true propositions, *Sarvanaam* about Thee, the wise thus utter adjectival statements (to refer to Thee).

The following is the translation of the text of the opening creedal statement from *Japji Sahib,* inscribed on the armour seen above.

One. Omnipotent, Truth, Name, Creator, All-pervading, Without Fear, Without Malafides, Timeless Being, Without Birth, Self-Created Light, Realised through Grace
True at the commencement of time, True within the flux of time, True shall it be,
May the Wondrous Lord be with me.

The following is the translation of the text of the *Sahskriti Slok* of Guru Arjan Dev, starting with the words *Sirmastak Rakhia*, enshrined on page 1358 of Guru Granth Sahib. The *shloka* is inscribed on the armour seen above.

Supreme Being hath placed His hand on my head, He has saved my body.
I am gratified that He has stepped into my home and thus saved my being.
Merciful Guru has given me protection and removed my fears and sorrows.
O Akalpurkh, Father of Orphans, Protector of the Faithful, and Refuge of the Helpless, imperishable, all-pervading Being; Nanak is in your protection.

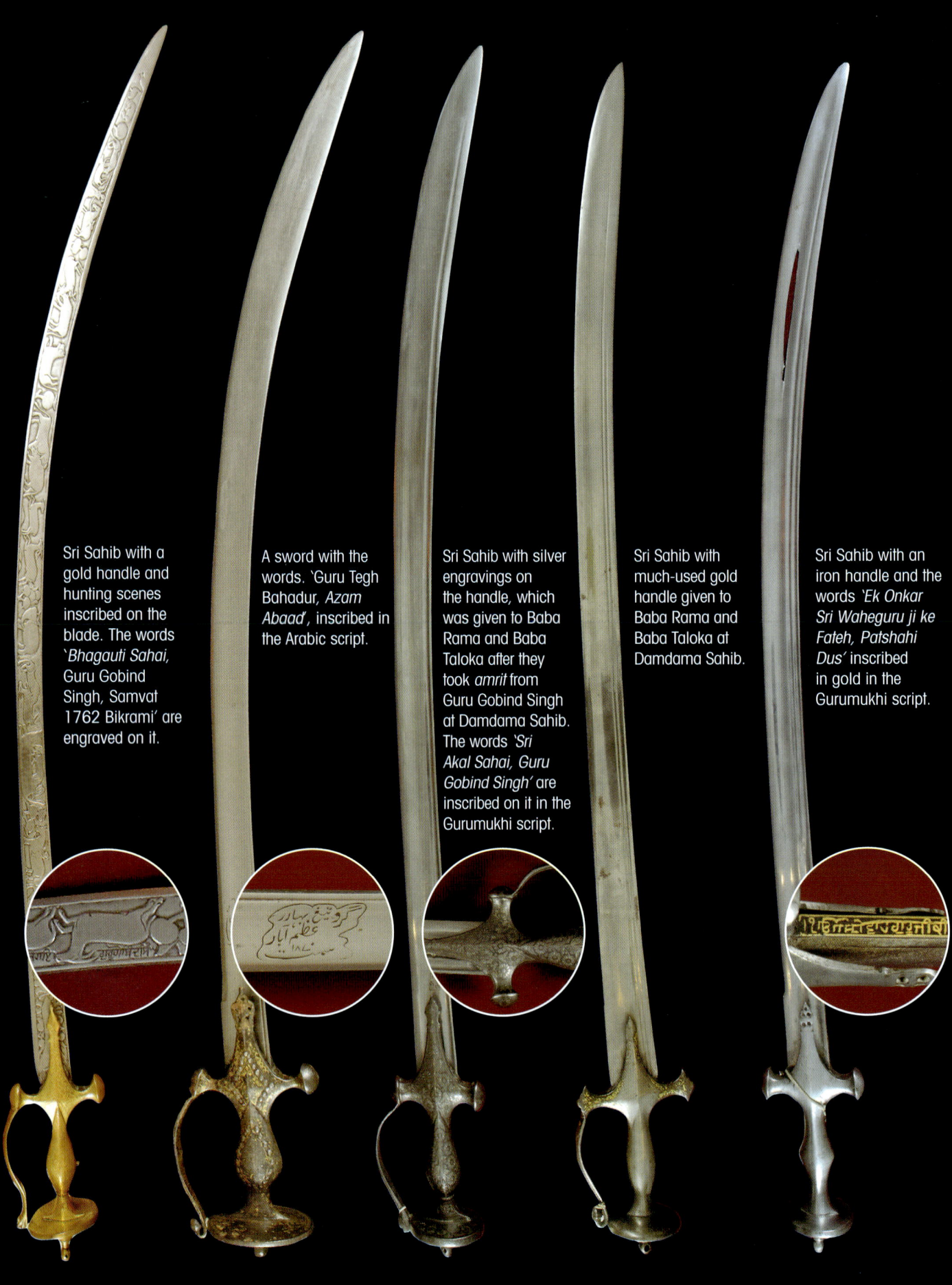

The *gutka* with the *Mool Mantra* inscribed by Guru Gobind Singh on the right page. This *gutka* contains a selection of *baani* composed by his father, Guru Tegh Bahadur.

An illuminated page from the *gutka*.

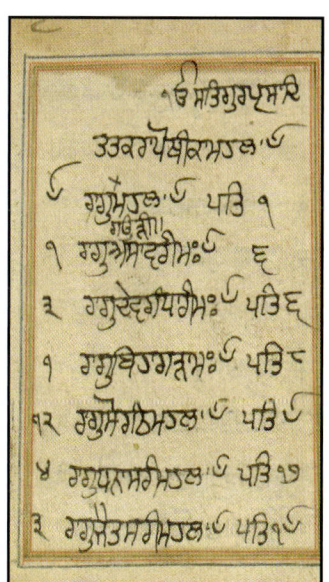

Selections of *Raag Gauri, Raag Asawari, Raag Devgandhari, Raag Bihagarha, Raag Sorath, Raag Dhanasri* and *Raag Jaitsri*, which are enumerated on the first page of the table of contents.

Custodians at Patiala 147

Close-up of one of the Nishan Sahibs, preserved at the New Moti Bagh Palace, Patiala. They were given by Guru Gobind Singh at the time of administering *amrit* at Anandpur in 1702 to Babas Rama and Taloka. The cloth is frayed and in a very fragile state.

A *khanda* with an all-steel handle, which was given by Guru Gobind Singh to Babas Rama and Taloka at Damdama Sahib.

A *khanda* with a wire handle, which was given by Guru Gobind Singh to Babas Rama and Taloka at Damdama Sahib.

Guru Gobind Singh's forked and serrated *khanda* with inscriptions in Gurmukhi and Devnagari scripts. The Gurmukhi inscription reads: '*Ek Onkar, Sat Guru Prasad, Degh Togh Fatoh, Nusrat Bedrang, Yafat Az Nanak Guru Gobind Singh*'. The Devnagari script is faded.

Katar (punch dagger) of Guru Gobind Singh, with hunting scenes in gold inlay.

A sword, shaped like a Gurkha *khukhri*, which was given by Guru Gobind Singh to Babas Rama and Taloka at Damdama Sahib.

A pair of carved wooden *kharawan* or the toe-knob sandals of Guru Gobind Singh given to Maharaja Bhupinder Singh by a Seth or big businessman of village Gheb.

A close-up of an arrow given by Guru Gobind Singh to Babas Rama and Taloka at Anandpur Sahib in 1696. The arrow has three bands of gold on it.

A *kirpan* that belonged to Guru Gobind Singh, which he gave at Talwandi Sabo to Babas Rama and Taloka, before leaving for the Deccan in 1706.

Six arrows, given by Guru Gobind Singh to Babas Rama and Taloka at Damdama Sahib in 1706.

Custodians at Patiala

Detail of a Sri Sahib of Guru Gobind Singh. The handle shows gold work with pearl inlay. Along with the sword is a small knife with an ivory handle, which is nestled in the scabbard of the sword.

Safajang, or a battleaxe given to Babas Rama and Taloka by Guru Gobind Singh at Damdama Sahib in 1706.

Sri Sahib of Guru Gobind Singh, given to Babas Rama and Taloka in Anandpur Sahib in 1696. Engraved in Gurmukhi script are the words: '*Guru Gobind Singh Akal Sahai Degh Tegh Fateh. Darshan Karega Nihal*'.

An old *khanda* with faded gold inscriptions presented by Langar ji at Bagrian to Maharaja Patiala.

Sword given by Jassa Singh Ahluwalia to Maharaja Amar Singh on the occasion of administering *amrit* to him in 1763.

A close-up of the inscription in Persian script that reads 'Sarkar Ahluwalia', on the sword given by Jassa Singh Ahluwalia to Maharaja Amar Singh.

Maharaja Hamir Singh (1783), the founder of Nabha State.

CUSTODIANS AT
Nabha

Hamir Singh, great-grandson of Baba Taloka, the elder son of Baba Phul, founded the city of Nabha in 1755. During the struggle of the Sikhs against the Mughal governor Zain Khan in 1763, Hamir Singh stood shoulder to shoulder with his co-religionists. He took possession of all the territories he had freed from Mughal power during this period. By establishing what amounted to an almost completely independent suzerainty, he succeeded in creating the State of Nabha, named after the city he founded. The ruling house of Nabha shares its ancestry with the Phulkian families from Patiala and Jind.

Jaswant Singh, his son, succeeded Hamir Singh in 1784, assuming the title of Raja. He, along with his Phulkian kinsmen, later entered into treaty relations with the British, becoming their protectorate. He maintained cordial relations with the Mughal Emperor in Delhi, secured recognition of his father's conquests and was bestowed with high titles of honour. His younger son and successor, Raja Devendra Singh, chose not to take sides during the Anglo-Sikh Wars. After annexing Maharaja Ranjit Singh's empire, the British charged him with intriguing with the enemy and abrogating his treaty obligations, and large tracts of his territory were confiscated. The Raja abdicated in favour of his eldest son, Bharpur Singh, then a minor.

Raja Bharpur Singh accepted the changed political scenario pragmatically, and at the age of 17, he led his troops in support of the British during the Indian Mutiny. The Nabha contingent held Ludhiana against the mutineers for a continuous period of six months. His services were rewarded with a guarantee of his possessions, and high honours and titles were bestowed upon him. Additional territories and a seat on the Viceroy's Council were granted. His early death in 1863, deprived the state of a promising ruler. Raja Bhagwan Singh, his younger brother, then succeeded him. But, tragically, he died young, eight years later, and without an heir.

Maharaja Ripudaman Singh of Nabha, who played an important role in securing legal sanction to *Anand Karaj* marriages for the Sikhs, through the Anand Marriage Act. His defiance of the British colonial authority, however, led to his exile from his state.

Maharaja Ripudaman Singh chose to be anointed as ruler of Nabha in accordance with Sikh practices, much to the chagrin of the British. The picture shows him in the presence of Sri Guru Granth Sahib at the Gurdwara at the Nabha Fort, when Bhai Sahib Arjan Singh Bagrian (to his left) performed the *Ardaas* to seek Divine blessings. On the bottom left of the photograph is seated the much-venerated Sant Attar Singh of Mastuana.

The British appointed a commission to search for a successor to the vacant throne. The unanimous choice was Hira Singh, the son of Kunwar Sukha Singh, of Badrukhan, Jind, who was then declared the new Raja of Nabha. The choice proved to be a fortuitous one. His long and prosperous reign saw his little patchwork State transformed. Buildings and monuments sprang up everywhere, roads and railways were constructed, and agriculture expanded. The State gained a great deal from the construction of the Sirhind irrigation canal in Punjab. Land revenue income grew rapidly, and this was ploughed back to improving agriculture, infrastructure, schools and hospitals. A small but efficient army was trained in modern ways. He sent a contingent

Close-up of a string of beads, with the words 'Sri Wahe Guru Ji Sahai' engraved in the Devanagari script on each bead.

of soldiers to participate in the Second Afghan War in 1878, and in the Tirah expedition of 1897. Maharaja Hira Singh lived long enough to attend all the Imperial Darbars, but in his later days, he increasingly entrusted affairs of State to the hands of his promising son Tikka Ripudaman Singh.

After Maharaja Hira Singh's death, his son decided to get anointed by a descendant of Bhai Rup Chand, Bhai Arjan Singh Bagrian, in accordance with Sikh rites. By doing so, he flouted the convention of being crowned by a representative of the British monarch.

Maharaja Ripudaman Singh succeeded his father in 1911, having already served under him as virtual administrator for some years. His abilities were noticed by the British authorities, who appointed him to the Central Legislature. There he took up the Sikhs' cause, supporting and pioneering reformist legislation for the benefit of his religion and the country, a significant effort being the passage of the Anand Marriage Act. However, soon after his succession, relations with his larger and more powerful kin in Patiala deteriorated. Schemes and feuds abounded on both sides, sometimes resulting in dangerous and reckless actions.

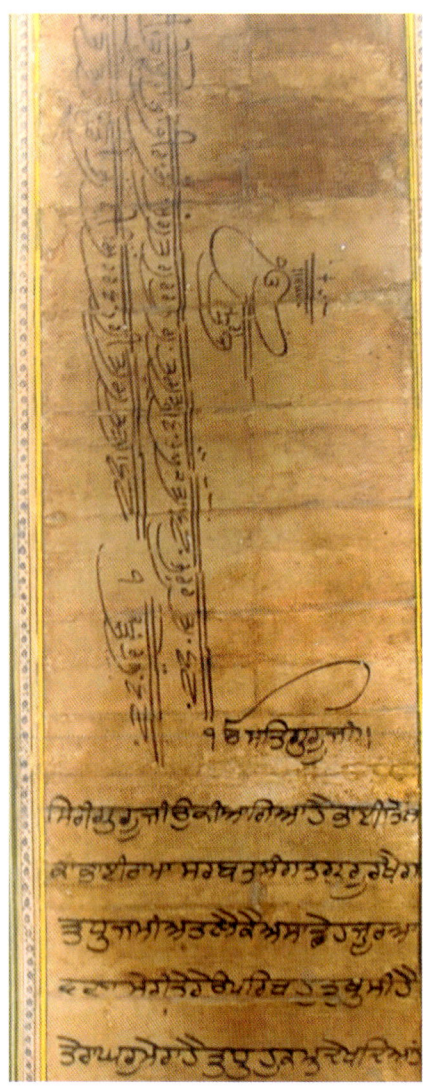

A copy of the *Hukamnama* of Guru Gobind Singh, dated 2 August 1696, addressed to Baba Taloka and Baba Rama, sons of Phul, asking them to come with a force of cavalry to Anandpur. The original *Hukamnama* is in Patiala. It also states 'Your house is my own and I am sending you a dress to keep.'

Unfortunately for Ripudaman Singh, his State was small and less important in comparison to Patiala, which was a favourite of the British. Ripudaman Singh had publicly opposed the British over the Jallianwala massacre at Amritsar in 1919. Peeved by his nationalistic inclination, the British forced him to relinquish administrative powers and exiled him from his State. A small allowance was given to him, and he settled in Dehradun. However, he continued his religious and nationalistic activities, much to the consternation of the colonial rulers. Accused of breaching the terms of exile, he was deposed, stripped of his titles and exiled to Kodaikanal, in South India, where he died during the Second World War.

In 1928, the British appointed as his successor, his son Maharaja Pratap Singh, who was then a minor. He received a modern Western education, but his interests were more traditionally Sikh. As such, he took much interest in military affairs, joined the army and served with distinction during the Second World War. He ended his service at the rank of Colonel.

In independent India, Nabha, with fellow Phulkian rulers of Patiala and Jind, was made to relinquish its independent statehood and the Patiala and East Punjab States Union (PEPSU) was created in 1948. This was a natural outcome of their acceptance of the post-Independence political realities in India.

Being a grouping of erstwhile Sikh states, the newfound nationalism in Indian polity was in no mood to tolerate such a centre of power, even by name. The Union was dissolved in 1956, and the government merged the States with greater Punjab. Nevertheless, Maharaja Pratap Singh continued to serve India in a military capacity, acting as ADC to the president, and serving as colonel of the Sikh Regiment for many years. He saw the momentous changes wrought by Indira Gandhi's policy of derecognising the rulers in 1971[1]. On his passing away at the age of 76 in 1995, his son, Maharaja Hanuwant Singh, inherited the rich heritage of the house of Nabha, which he continues to look after with care and devotion.

---

1 Royal families in India were allotted Privy Purse payments as part of their agreements to first integrate with India in 1947, and later to merge their States, after which they lost the right to rule. The 26th Amendment to the Indian Constitution cut off their privileges and allowances.

Chola, a gown of Guru Gobind Singh sent to Bcba Taloka and Baba Rama. It is mentioned in a *Hukumnama* dated 2 August 1696.

Detail from the *chola*. It is stitched on the saffron fabric as backing.

Syed Badr-ud-din, popularly called Pir Budhu Shah, was a Muslim saint who belonged to Sadhaura village in Ambala district of Punjab. His quiet disposition led others to call him *budhu* or dim-witted. Pir Budhu Shah became a great admirer of the tenth Guru, and called on him at Paonta.

Pir Budhu Shah recommended a group of Pathan soldiers to the Guru, who gave employment to them.

A few months later, some hill chiefs mounted an attack on the Guru. Before the battle took place, the Pathans deserted the Guru. When the Pir came to know about it, he hurried along with his sons and 700 disciples, joined the Battle of Bhangani, in which the tenth Guru's forces were victorious.

Sixteen years after the battle, Usman Khan, the Darogha of Sadhaura, killed the Pir and his family in cold blood on 21 March 1705. Henceforth, the Pir's tomb became a place of pilgrimage for Hindus, Muslims and Sikhs alike.

Dastar (turban) of Guru Gobind Singh, given to Pir Budhu Shah of Sadaura after the battle of Bhangani at Paonta Sahib, in frayed condition. The Guru's *kangha*, along with his hair, is also seen in the picture.

A close-up of Guru Gobind Singh's *kangha,* the Sikh's obligatory comb, along with the turban shown earlier, given as tokens of appreciation to Pir Budhu Shah after the battle of Bhangani. Raja Bharpur Singh of Nabha (1840-1860) rehabilitated the Pir's descendants and acquired these sacred relics from them. Since the *kangha* and *kesh* (uncut hair) are the sacrosanct elements of the Sikh identity, being two of the five inalienable symbols of the Khalsa, this relic is of special significance.

Detail of the Sri Sahib given by Guru Gobind Singh to Baba Taloka. The Gurmukhi inscription says *'Sri Bhahaguti Sahai, Guru Gobind Singh, Patshahi Dus'*. The detail can be seen above.

Sri Sahib of Guru Tegh Bahadur, with the words *'Sat Sri Akal Guru Tegh Bahadur'* inscribed in Gurmukhi script. The date 1713 Samvat (1656) is inscribed on the blade.

An idealized portrait of Guru Tegh Bahadur, in the Late Mughal style.

Right: *Tega* (broadsword) of Guru Hargobind. The picture above shows the leather-padded hilt.

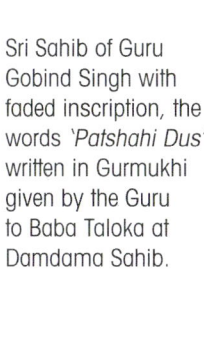

Sri Sahib of Guru Gobind Singh with faded inscription, the words 'Patshahi Dus' written in Gurmukhi given by the Guru to Baba Taloka at Damdama Sahib.

Bhayee Sikandar Singh performing *Ardaas* at the wedding of Maharaja Hanuwant Singh's son, Yudhistar Singh, with the sword of the tenth Guru.

Detail of Sri Sahib of Guru Gobind Singh with 'Patshahi Dus' inscribed in Gurmukhi.

CUSTODIANS AT NABHA

Above: The opening page of the illuminated *Dasam Granth*. Detail of the illumination on the right.

166 Sikh Heritage: Ethos and Relics

Guru Gobind Singh and his Khalsa army, executed in the Kashmiri style, as seen in the illuminated folio of the *Dasam Granth*.

Sikh History and Ethos
as Envisioned by Artists in the Late Nineteenth Century

Episodes from the life of Guru Nanak. The painting depicts the scene at Saidpur where Guru Nanak was first imprisoned by the Mughal invader, Babur. He was later released because of his obvious divinity. The picture shows, on the right, the grinding stones rotating by themselves to the divine songs of the Guru. On the left is Babur having a dialogue with Guru Nanak. This painting is signed by Mohammad Sharif.

Emperor Akbar met Guru Amar Das in 1567 at Goindwal. The panel shows the digging of the *baoli* or a stepped well to provide water for residents, and a *langar* in progress.

CUSTODIANS AT NABHA 169

Guru Tegh Bahadur receiving the news of the birth of his son, Gobind Rai, and sweets being distributed among his followers in Dhaka (left). On the right is Mata Gujri with the child, receiving greetings from common people and distributing gifts in Patna.

Guru Tegh Bahadur holding a Darbar at Anandpur. The young Gobind Rai is seated on the right. The painting is signed by Basahathullah.

Martyrdom of Guru Tegh Bahadur in Chandni Chowk, Delhi (top right). On the right, the Guru's companions, Bhai Sati Das and Bhai Mati Das, are shown being tortured. On the left, Aurangzeb receives the news.

Gobind Rai being anointed the tenth Guru at Anandpur Sahib, after receiving the news of the martyrdom of his father, Guru Tegh Bahadur. The painting is signed by Basahathullah.

CUSTODIANS AT NABHA 173

Massa Ranghar, a Mughal satrap, invaded Amritsar and desecrated the Golden Temple. He turned it from a place of worship to a centre for his debauchery. Two Sikhs, Bhai Mehtab Singh and Bhai Sukha Singh, avenged the desecration by killing Massa Ranghar in August 1740. On the left, they are shown arriving, tying their horses under the *beri* tree (extreme right) and then walking into the Harmandar Sahib to kill Massa Ranghar.

Sikhs battle Mughal forces. The painting by Basathullah shows various scenes of clashes between Sikh and Mughal forces.

Bilga, a small village near Phagwara, proudly preserves personal items of Guru Arjan Dev. The picture shows the Guru as envisaged by an artist who painted this mural at Baba Atal tower in the Harmandar Sahib complex.

CUSTODIANS AT
Bilga

Bilga was a small settlement of only a few huts, with no real distinguishing feature when Guru Arjan Dev visited it. He was on his way to a village called Mau where Krishan Chand, his father-in-law-to-be, lived. Krishan Chand's daughter, Ganga Devi, popularly known as Mata Ganga in Sikh lore, was engaged to the Guru.

According to local tradition, it was at Bilga, a village fourteen kms west of Phillaur, that Guru Arjan Dev changed his apparel.

The Guru left the clothes he was wearing and some personal articles with the local people, who had provided him with whatever hospitality they could, given their modest circumstances.

After the Guru left for Mau, the villagers kept the gifts of the Guru as sacred relics and have preserved them till now. The relics are now kept in Gurdwara Panjvin Patshahi, administered indirectly by the Shiromani Gurdwara Parbandhak Committee.

At this Gurdwara, which is located inside the village, we get to see a pair of pajamas, a scarf, a handkerchief, a shawl, a purse and a low stool, now covered with a brass sheet.

The Gurdwara itself is built on high ground. It houses a divan hall, with the sanctum sanctorum at the far end where Sri Guru Granth Sahib is placed.

Besides the relics, a large number of paintings depicting scenes from Sikh history are also on display.

The Gurdwara, and indeed, the entire village, draws in large crowds when a fair is held from 18 to 20 of Har (early July) to commemorate Guru Arjan Dev's visit.

A *pajama* of Guru Arjan Dev with red stripes.

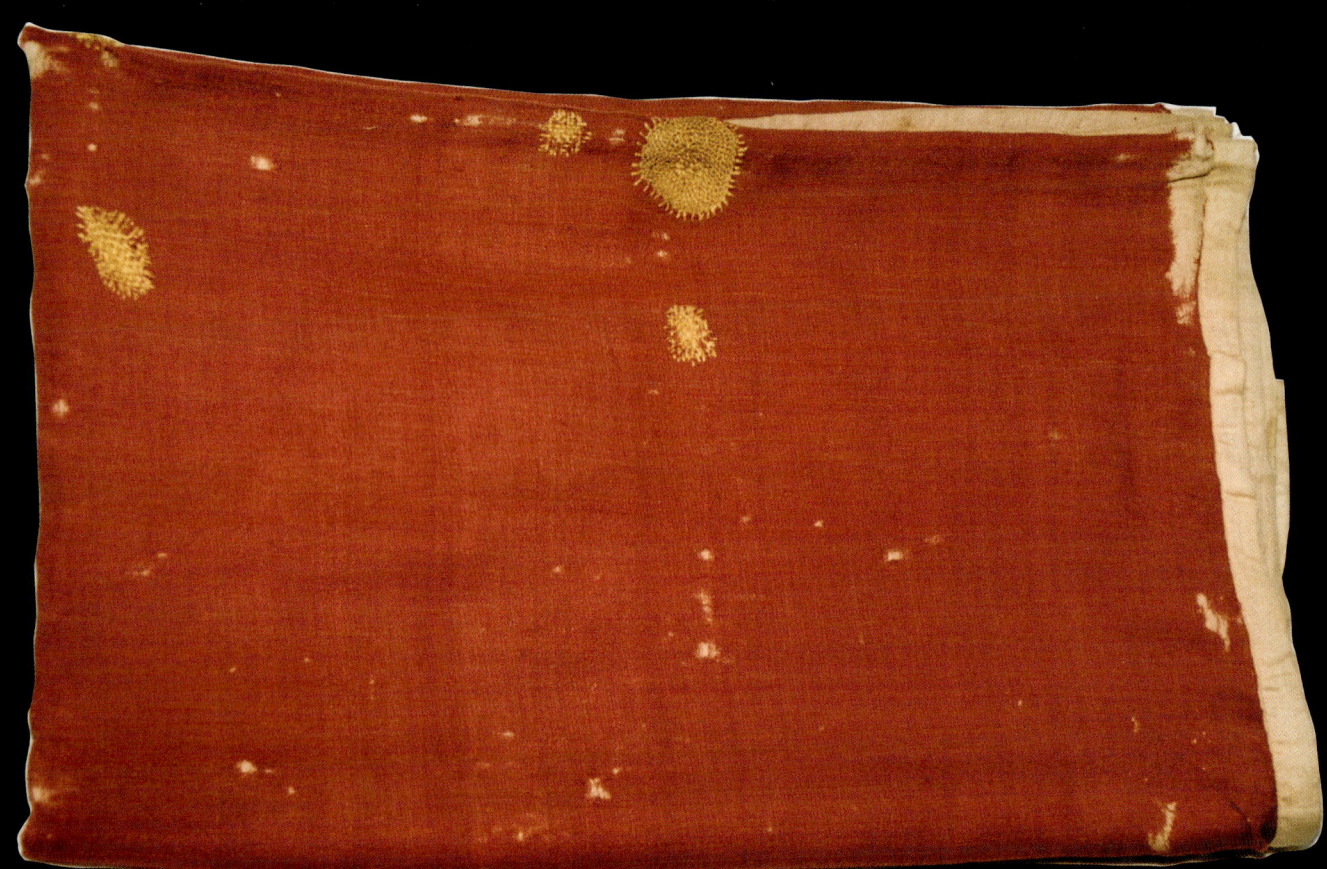

A shawl that belonged to Guru Arjan Dev.

A stool, covered with a copper sheet, used by Guru Arjan Dev for bathing during his stay at Bilga.

An embroidered *hazuria*, scarf, of Guru Arjan Dev.

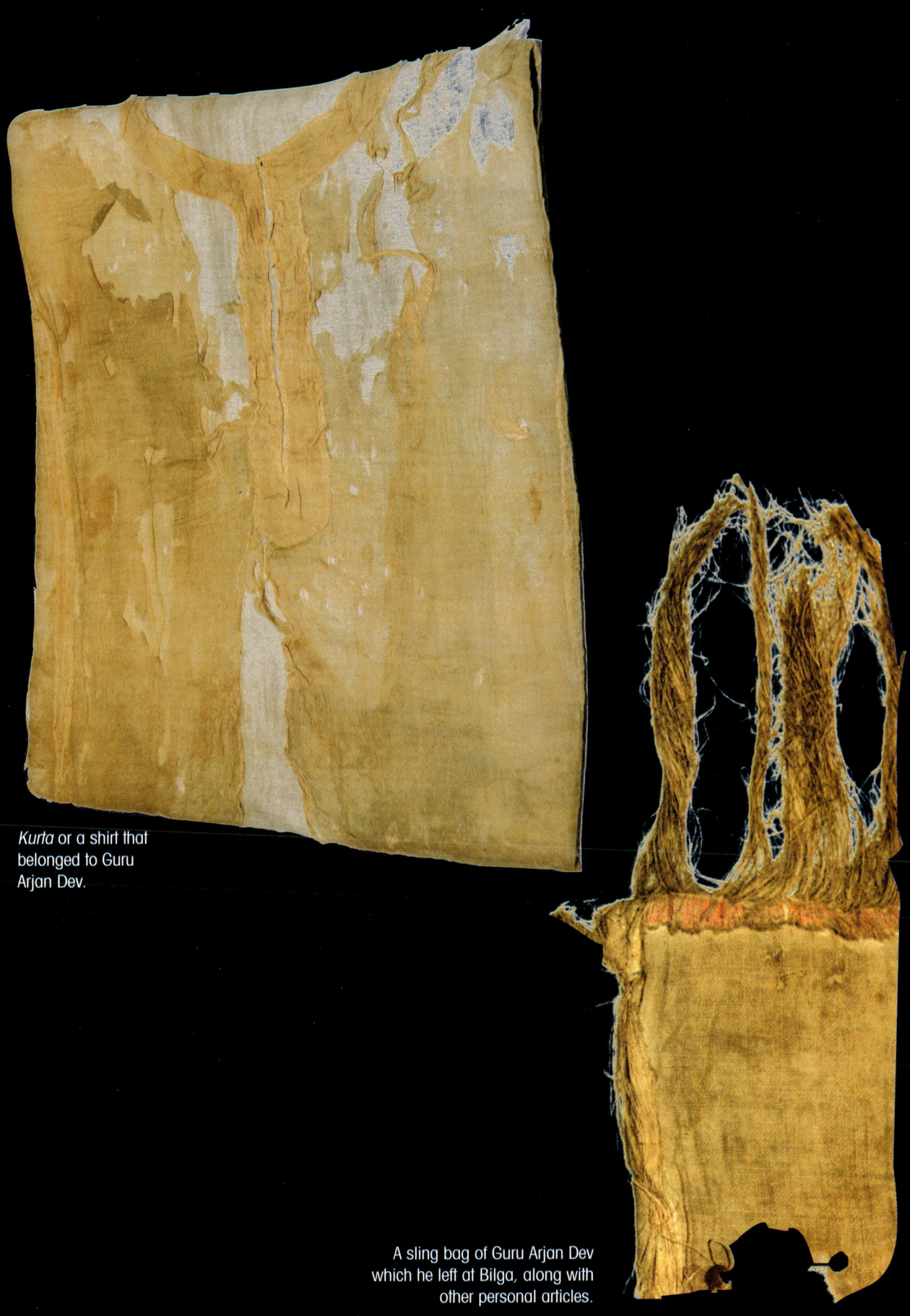

Kurta or a shirt that belonged to Guru Arjan Dev.

A sling bag of Guru Arjan Dev which he left at Bilga, along with other personal articles.

Guru Hargobind established the Akal Takht in Amritsar. It is situated right across the Harmandar Sahib in Amritsar, and from this seat of Sikh sovereignty, the temporal affairs of the community were managed. During his travels in Malwa, he often stayed with his brother-in-law, Bhai Sain Das, at Darauli.

CUSTODIANS AT Darauli

The village of Darauli, in present-day Faridkot district in Punjab, owes much of its importance to the fact that Bhai Sain Das lived there. He was related to Guru Hargobind's wife, Mata Damodri, since her sister, Mai Ramo, was married to him. Guru Hargobind was fond of Bhai Sain Das and Mai Ramo, and would often stay with them for extended periods.

They were also devoted followers of the Guru. Local tradition and old accounts attest to their devotion. It is maintained that when Bhai Sain Das built a new house for his family, he refused to live in it until the Guru came and stayed in it first.

Bhai Sain Das' desire was fulfilled when Guru Hargobind visited the village with his family and stayed in the newly-constructed house in 1613. Guru Hargobind's eldest son, Baba Gurditta, was born here on 15 November 1613. Baba Gurditta was to play a major role in shaping the Sikh spiritual canon. A Gurdwara at the village marks his birthplace.

During his first visit to the village that was home to his brother-in-law in 1613, the Guru blessed Bhai Sidhu and Bibi Surti, parents of Bhai Rup Chand. Another long stay of the Guru in Darauli was in 1631, when he went to drink water in Bhai Rup Chand's fields, and founded the village of Bhai Rupa.

Mata Damodri, the Guru's wife, passed away at Darauli. Gurdwara Kirtan Sohila was built in her memory. Her parents, Bhai Narain Das and Mata Daya Kaur, died within a few days of each other. After performing their last rites, Guru Hargobind Sahib sent his family to Kartarpur with Baba Gurditta.

The descendants of Bhai Sain Das have reverently preserved articles associated with the Guru from the days of his stay there. We have here a *chola*, or dress, that belonged to the Guru; a brass *jhawan*, or foot-scraper, used by the Guru; *Ganga Sagar*, a copper jug, and a *thaal*, a copper tray, used in his service and other items of personal use, including a shawl that belonged to Mata Damodri.

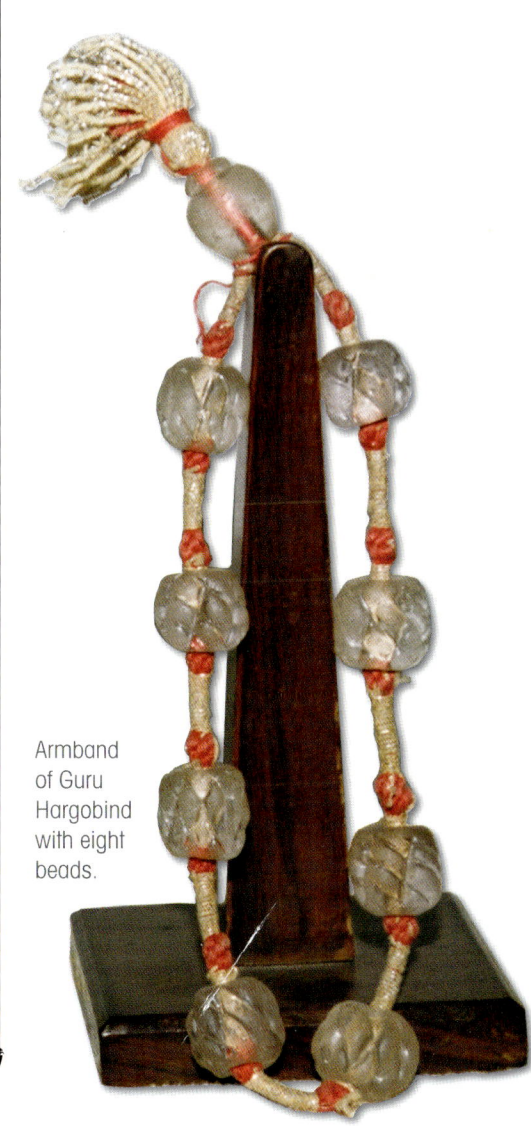

Armband of Guru Hargobind with eight beads.

Ganga Sagar, a copper jug, and a plate (*thaal*) used for serving water to Guru Hargobind.

Thaal, a copper tray used for serving meals to Guru Hargobind during his visit to Darauli.

Brass *jhawan* or foot-scraper used by Guru Hargobind.

A carved wooden *kharawan* or toe-knob sandal of Guru Hargobind, reverentially preserved at Darauli.

A painting of Bhai Bidhi Chand on horseback, gouache on paper, in the Mughal style.

CUSTODIANS AT
Sursinghwala

Bhai Bidhi Chand was a devoted Sikh. He had been a bandit in the earlier part of his life, but everything changed for him when one day, he came in contact with a follower of Guru Arjan Dev. Impressed by his piety, Bidhi Chand felt the need to meet the Guru who could inspire ordinary people to live a noble and pious life. He went to meet Guru Arjan Dev and on meeting the Guru, he underwent a metamorphosis.

He became one of the main people that Guru Arjan Dev depended on to spread his teachings. As a good organiser, Bhai Bidhi Chand also proved useful in providing leadership and training to Sikhs as they started to take up arms. Once, two prized horses were being brought for Guru Hargobind, but they were intercepted by the Subedar of Lahore, who impounded them. Bhai Bidhi Chand infiltrated the fort of Lahore and escaped with the two horses, which he subsequently presented to the Guru at Bhai Rupa.

He was a great warrior and was one of the five Sikhs chosen by Guru Arjan Dev to accompany him on his journey to Lahore, where the Guru was martyred in 1606. Bhai Bidhi Chand died in 1638 at Deonagar, near Ayodhya in present-day Uttar Pradesh. He was cremated there and his ashes were brought to his ancestral village of Sur-singhwala by members of his brother's family.

Baba Daya Singh, from his lineage, is now the keeper of the family heritage in Sursinghwala. *Gurbilas Patshahi 6* records the details of Bidhi Chand's association with the Guru. It also mentions how Bhai Bidhi Chand accompanied Guru Hargobind when the latter stayed at Bhai Rupa. According to *Gurbilas Patshahi 6*, a Muslim artist was commissioned at that time to paint portraits of the Guru, which the family has preserved. Bhai Rup Chand's family at Bhai Rupa also has similar paintings, attributed to the same artist.

Guru Har Rai on horseback. A stylized portrait in the Pahari style.

A sword of Guru Hargobind with his name engraved in the Persian script. The inset shows the engraving in detail.

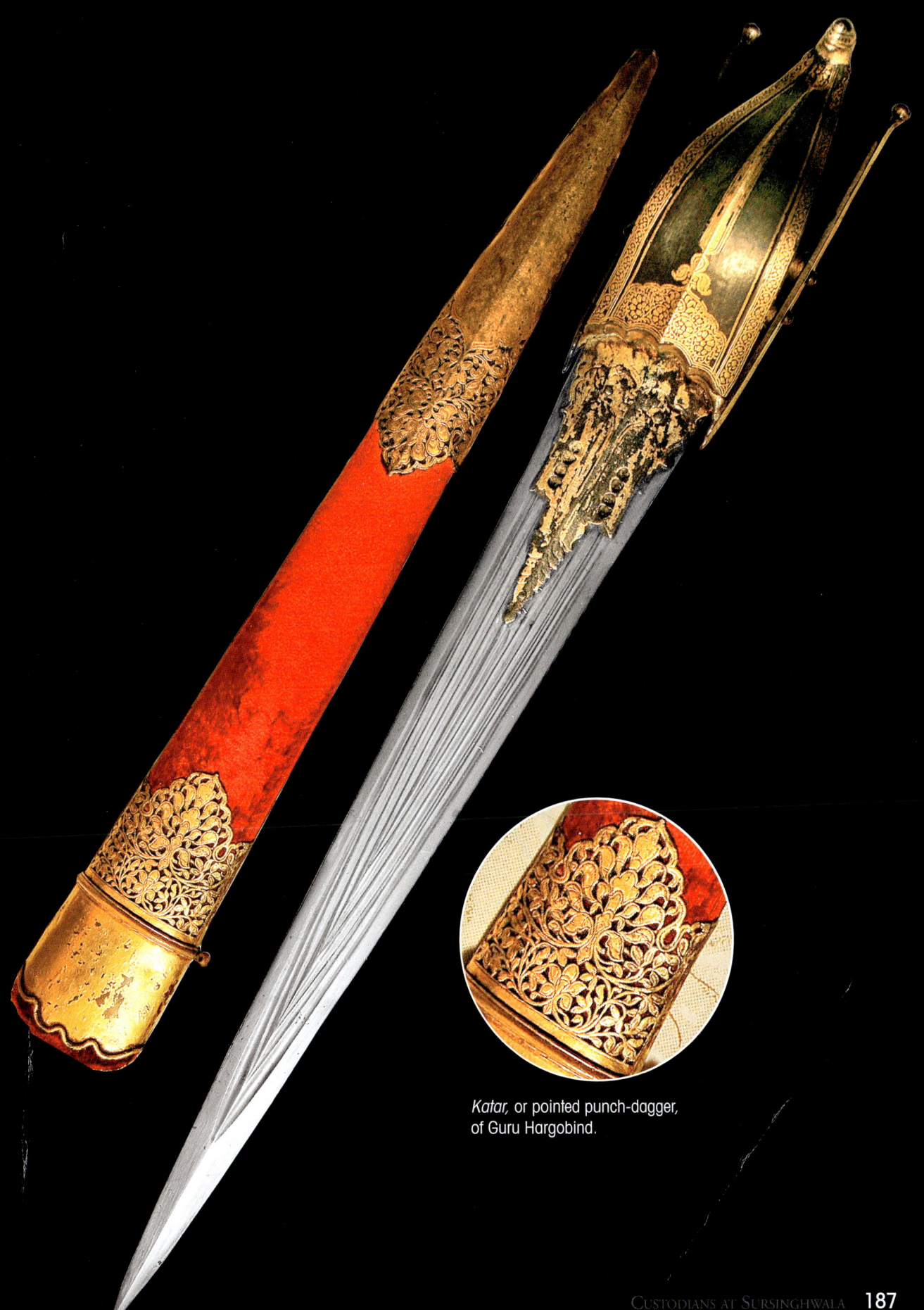

Katar, or pointed punch-dagger, of Guru Hargobind.

Guru Hargobind, a painting in the collection of the family, which has been referred to in the *Gurbilas Patshahi 6*. The similarity between this painting and the one in the collection of Bhai Rup Chand's descendants at Bhai Rupa is striking. Both families maintain that these paintings have been done by the same artist, who was a contemporary of the Guru. Please turn to page 115 to see the other painting.

Guru Har Rai is shown wearing plain apparel in this Pahari-style painting. He is also often depicted holding a flower in his hand.

CUSTODIANS AT SURSINGHWALA

Guru Hargobind was a great musician and a warrior, who was also fond of wrestling. The Pahari-style painting shows him on horseback. Please turn to page 188 to see another painting by the same artist.

Guru Har Rai is remembered for this deep knowledge and love of plants and medicinal herbs. Paintings that depict him invariably make use of horticultural motifs, as this Pahari-style painting shows.

Selected Bibliography

Punjabi

Ganda Singh, ed. *Hukamname*. Patiala: Punjabi University. 2nd Edition. 1999.
Gian Singh Giani. *Itihas Riyasat Bagrian*. Patiala. 1917.
Gurdit Singh Giani. *Bhai Roop Chand Ate Unhan di Vansh*. Bhai Rupa: Bhai Roop Chand Yadgari Committee. 1999.
Gurdit Singh Giani. *Ithias Sri Guru Granth Sahib*. Chandigarh: Sikh Sahit Parkashan. 1990.
Kahan Singh Bhai. *Guru Shabad Ratnakar Mahan Kosh*. Patiala: Bhasha Vibhag. 2nd Edition. 1960.
Kahn Singh Bhai. *Gurmat Martand*. Amritsar: Shiromani Gurdwara Prabhandak Committee.
Santokh Singh. *Sri Gur Pratap Suraj (Prakash) Granth*. Lahore: Caxton Press. 1843.

English

Ashok Singh Bhai, ed. *Thoughts of Bhai Ardaman Singh*. Chandigarh: Institute of Sikh Studies.
B. N. Goswamy. *Piety and Splendour: Sikh Heritage in Art*. New Delhi: National Museum. 2000.
Dharam Pal Ashta. *The Poetry of the Dasam Granth*. New Delhi: Arun Parkashan. 1959.
Dharam Singh. *Dynamics of the Social Thought of Guru Gobind Singh*. Patiala: Punjabi University. 1998.
Gurinder Singh Mann. *Religions of the World: Sikhism*. Upper Saddle River, New Jersey: Prentice Hall Inc. 2004.
Harbans Singh, ed. *Perspectives on Guru Nanak*. Patiala: Punjabi University. 1975.
Harbans Singh. *The Heritage of the Sikhs*. New Delhi: Manohar. 1994.
Hari Ram Gupta. *History of the Sikhs*. New Delhi: Asian Publications. 1994.
Harish Dhillon. *The Lives and Teachings of the Sikh Gurus*. New Delhi: UPSBD. 1977.
Himadri Banerjee. *The Other Sikhs: A View from Eastern India*. New Delhi: Manohar. 2002.
Irvine William. *Later Mughals*. London: Luzac & Co. 1922.
J.D. Cunningham. *A History of the Sikhs*. New Delhi: S Chand & Co. 1981.
J.C. Dua. *Misl, Sikh State and the Institution of Khalsa*. Delhi: Low Price Publication. 2006.
Kharak Singh. *Guru Nanak A Prophet with a Difference*. Amritsar: Guru Nanak Dev University. 2007.
Max Arthur Macauliffe. *The Sikh Religion: Its Gurus, Sacred Writings and Authors*. London: Oxford University Press. 1909.
Nikky-Guninder Kaur Singh. *Sikhism: An Introduction*. New York: NY. I.B. Tauris. 2011.
S. S. Gandhi. *Sikhs in the Eighteenth Century*. Amritsar: Singh Brothers. 2008.
Sangat Singh. *The Sikhs in History*. New Delhi: Uncommon Books. 1999.
Sirdar Kapur Singh. *Prasharprasna (Baisakhi of Guru Gobind Singh)*. Amritsar: Guru Nanak Dev University. 1998.
Sunita Puri. *Advent of Sikh Religion: A Socio-Political Perspective*. New Delhi: Munshiram Manoharlal. 1993.
Surinder Singh. *Sikh Coinage: Symbol of Sikh Sovereignty*. New Delhi: Manohar. 2004.
Teja Singh and Ganda Singh. *A Short History of the Sikhs*. Rev. Edition. Patiala: Punjabi University. 1989.
W. Owen Cole and Piara Singh Sambhi. *The Sikhs: Their Religious Beliefs and Practices*. New Delhi: Vikas Publishing House. 1978.

Appendix

Sikh Heritage Foundation

The Sikh Heritage Foundation was established in 2000 by a group of American Sikhs concerned with preserving Sikh Heritage. The foundation maintains its commitments to promoting Sikh identity and heritage through various activities in America and around the world. It is a charitable tax-free organization registered in the state of West Virginia, USA.

Objectives
1. To present and promote Sikh heritage to Sikhs and non-Sikh Americans through collaborative projects with American museums, libraries, and other institutions.
2. Promote Sikh art and culture through exhibitions.
3. Document and record material items of Sikh heritage wherever they maybe.
4. Make information available to public through publication, digital, and electronic media.
5. To provide technical need in preserving endangered heritage objects in India.
6. To enable American institutions to increase their collection of Sikh heritage material available in the world markets.

Activities
The various activities done by Sikh Heritage foundations are:
1. Sponsoring exhibition (the Sikhs Legacy of the Punjab and National History Museum of Smithsonian Institution Washington, DC from 2004 to 2008).
2. CDs of lectures delivered by various prominent Sikhs at Michigan, Long island in New York as well as Washington, DC.
3. A scientific delegation from Smithsonian visited Punjab to educate about the preservation of Sikh art.
4. Poster presentation in Holland on Sikh soldiers in the First World War.
5. *Sikhs: The Legacy of the Punjab* exhibition at Natural History Museum of Santa Barbara, California.

List of Members

Drs. Amrik S. & Jaswinder K. Chattha
Grewal Family & Singh Development, LLC

Narinder K. & Rajinder K. Keith
Sohan S. & Kamaljit K. Chaudhary
Dr. Brijinder S. & Manorma K. Kochhar
Gurdip S. & Nirmaljeet K. Malik
Dr. Charan S. & Surinder K. Nandra
Dr. Harvinder S. & Asha K. Sahota
Drs. Harvinder S. & Sonia K. Sandhu

Dr. Ajit S. & Rita Arora
Kuldip S. & Pinderpal K. Bains
Dr. Kamaljit S. & Kavelle K. Bajaj
Drs. Surinder S. & Jagdeep K. Bajwa
Mrs. Manjit K. Bansal & Grandchildren
Balbir S. & Kuldeep K. Basi
Guriqbal S. & Jagdish K. Basi
Dr. Raghbir S. & Barjinder K. Basi
Dr. Manraj S. Bath
Drs. Smir M. & Amita K. Bhatt
Sardar & Sardarni Ishar S. & Kuljit K. Bindra
Balbir S. & Raminder K. Brar
Drs. Rakesh S. & Joceliza G. Chaudhary
Drs. Sandeep S. & Kulreet K. Chaudhary
Ashok S. & Subina Chawla
Satpal S. & Komal Kiron K. Dang
Mohinder S. & Pawan K. Datta
Dr. Prabhjot S. & Sheena Deol
Dr. Eldan B. Eichbaum & Dr. Geetinder K Chattha
Dr. Narrinder S. & Jasbir K. Gahunia

Dr. Inderjit S. & Nautan K. Gill
Narinder S. & Pritpal K. Grewal
Dr. Sachinder S. & Bijaya A. Hans
Dr. Ranjeet S. Singh & Justine Overtruf Singh
Daljit S. & Rajinder K Khara
Manjit S. & Kirandeep K. Khara
Surendra Pal S. & Harjit B. Mac
Baljeet S. & Reena K. Mahaj
Dr. Jasbir S. & Vickie C. Makar
Dr. Jasbir S. & Satinder K. Mann
NirmaJ S. & Balbir K. Nilvi
Dr. Gurnam S. & Khushwant K. Purewal
Dr. Kulbir S. Pannu
Dr. Sardul S. & Surinderjit G. Pannu
Ajit S. & Kanwaljit K. Randhawa
Harbhajan S. & Saranjit K. Samra
Drs. Rajbir S. & Satwant K. Samra
Sukhminder S. & Ranjit K. Sandhu
Dr. Unal S. & Sukhbinder K Sandhu

Jagjits S., Parkash K. & Pauljeet S. Sehdeva
Drs. Baljit S. & Jatinder K. Sidhu
Drs. Navtej & Rekha K. Singh
Drs. Piara & Kamal K. Singh
Ajit S. & Darshan K. Thiara
Dr. Steven & Barjesh Bath Walters

Photo Credits

Anuragh Singh: 21, 48, 61, 87
Archival pictures collected from various sources: 38, 73, 78, 79, 81, 84, 85, 88, 92, 95, 96, 97, 126, 150, 151, 172, 173-175, 176-179
Asian Cultural History Program, Smithsonian Institution: VIII, IX, XI
Baljit Singh: 50
Balwinder Singh: 176-179
Chandigarh Museum and Art Gallery: 9, 10, 13, 19, 25, 33, 35, 37, 47, 49, 57, 75, 77, 100, 101
Cultural Resource Conservation Initiative, New Delhi: 41
Jansher Singh 136
Kamaljit Singh: 39, 40, 42, 43, 102, 106, 108, 113 (top), 115 (top), 119 (left), 121 (top)
Kanwar Sumer Singh: 53
Major A.P. Singh: 86,
Malkiat Singh: 26, 55, 58, 60, 62, 64, 68, 70, 98, 103, 116, 117, 119 (right), 180-187
Naninder Singh Dhillon: 56, 91
National Museum, New Delhi: 43, 52
Nishaan Collection: 66, 69, 89
Punjab Digital Library, Chandigarh: 5, 74, 90
Ramkrishan Singh: 23, 53, 54, 59
Roopinder Singh: 4, 6, 7, 8, 11, 12, 14, 17, 18, 20, 22, 24, 27, 28, 30, 31, 32, 44, 46, 65, 71, 72, 80 , 82, 83, 93, 99, 104, 105, 107, 109, 110, 111, 112, 113 (bottom), 114, 115 (right), 120, 121 (bottom), 122, 123, 124, 125, 127, 128, 129, 130-133, 138-149, 152-171
Santa Barbara Museum of Natural History: X
Sarabjit Singh Lali: 137
Surinder Singh: 63
Victoria Memorial Museum, Calcutta: 45

The authors have tried to ensure that proper credit has been given to each photographer. In case some name has been inadvertently missed, or if there is any other error, it will be duly corrected in the next edition of the book.

Index

A

Aala Singh, Baba 75, 139
Abdali, Ahmad Shah 75–76, 139
Abdul Samad Khan 71
Adi Granth 16, 35–38, 114, 133
Adina Beg Khan 73, 125
Afghans 4, 75, 77, 139
Ahluwalia, Jassa Singh 73, 75–76, 99, 153
Ahmed Mujaddid Alif Sani, Sheikh 66
Ajit Singh, Sahibzada 53–55
Ajmer Chand Raja, 53
Akal Takht 39, 99, 180, *see also* Harmandar Sahib
Akalpurakh 20, 23, 25, 48, 51, 60, 73, 121
Akbar, Jalal-ud-Din Muhammad, Emperor 34–35, 38
Amar Das, Guru 33–35, 97–98, 168-169
    Adi Granth 35
    banned practice of sati 34
    emphasised the rejection of renunciation 34
    meeting with Emperor Akbar (1567) 168–169
    pair of shoes of 97
Adi Granth 37, 39, 98
Amar Singh, Raja 139–140
Amarinder Singh, Capt. 141
Amir Khusrau 15
Amritsar 29, 33, 35–37, 39–41, 46, 50, 71–73, 75–78, 84–86, 88, 98, 114, 122, 127, 174, 180
Anand Marriage Act 155, 157
Anandgarh Fort 53
Anandpur, siege of 54–56
Andrews, Rev. C. F. 88, 90
Angad Dev, Guru 32–33, 98
Anglo-Sikh Wars 80–81, 155
Ardaas 50, 79, 128, 156, 165
Ardaman Singh, Bhai 127, 128
Arjan Dev, Guru 16, 22, 27, 35–39, 45, 51, 56, 98, 112–113, 116, 122, 145, 176–179, 185
Arjan Singh, Bhai 85, 88, 127, 157
Ashok Singh, Bhai 127–128
Attariwala, Sham Singh 80
Attaullah Khan, Nawab 126
Aurangzeb 38, 42–44, 46, 52–54, 56–58, 63, 105, 172
    death of, 58, 63
Aziz-ud-Din, Faqir 78

B

Babur, Zahir-ud-din Mohammad 4–6, 30–31
Bachitar Natak 26, 48–49
Badhera, Mir 41
Badrud Din, Shah 64
Baghel Singh 76
Bagrian, custodians at 125–134
    gutka given by Guru Gobind Singh 131
    illuminated manuscript of Sri Guru Granth Sahib 124
    karchcha, or ladle, given by Guru Hargobind 129
    katars given by Sri Guru Gobind Singh 133
    khanda, given by Guru Hargobind 129
    loh, or iron griddle, for langar installed in 1765 at Bagrian 127
    Sri Guru Granth Sahib, illuminated manuscript of 124
    Sri Sahib given by Sri Guru Gobind Singh 132
    Sri Sahib given by Sri Guru Tegh Bahadur 132
    turban adornments of Guru Gobind Singh 130
Bahadur Shah 58–60, 66–67, 68, 70
    death (18 February 1712), 67
    edict of, 69
Baisakhi 23, 36, 44, 50, 71, 76–77
Banda Bahadur 40, 56–57, 59, 61–71, 74, 106, 121, 135
Battle of Panipat 5–6, 8
Battle of Sabhraon 80
Behlol, 28

Bhagwan Singh, Raja 155
Bhai Rupa, custodians at 109–124
    Bairagan or *aasa*, armrest of Guru Har Rai 117
    brass bowls 111
    cage for the pet birds of Guru Hargobind 109, 115
    Guru Hargobind with a hawk (painting) 115
    Hukamnama of Guru Gobind Singh 119
    Hukumnama of Banda Bahadur 121
    karcha or a brass ladle 111
    kharawan or wooden toe-knob sandal of Guru Arjan Dev 112
    kharawan or wooden toe-knob sandal of Mata Ganga 113
    letter written by Baba Aala Singh of Patiala 123
    Mool Mantra in the handwriting of Guru Hargobind, 114
    notes from Guru Gobind Singh 120
    portrait of Guru Har Rai 117
    rabaab of Guru Arjan Dev 109, 116
    rath (wooden chariot) of Guru Ram Das 109
    wooden kitchen utensils of the langar 111
Bhai-ki-Samadh 106
Bharpur Singh, Raja 155, 155, 161
Bhupinder Singh, Maharaja 140, 150
Bidhi Chand, Bhai 39, 114–115, 184–185
Bilga, custodians at 177–179
    hazuria, scarf of Guru Arjan Dev 178
    kurta of Guru Arjan Dev 179
    pajama of Guru Arjan Dev with red stripes 177
    shawl of Guru Arjan Dev 178
    sling bag of Guru Arjan Dev 179
    stool, used by Guru Arjan Dev for bathing 178
British colonial rule 82–83, 90, 92
Buddhism 3, 11
Budha, Baba 39, 44, 104
Budhu Shah, Pir 64, 160–161

C
Chappar-Chiri 65
Chatardwaj Singh 44
Chief Khalsa Diwan 85
Chuhar Singh 63
Clive, Robert 80
Cunningham, J. D. 80

D
Dalhousie, Lord James Broun-Ramsay 99
Damdama Sahib 57, 76, 105, 133, 146, 149–152, 165
Damodri, Mata 181
Darauli, custodians at 181–184
    armband of Guru Hargobind 181
    Ganga Sagar, a copper jug, and a *thaal* (plate) 182
    jhawan or brass foot-scraper used by Guru Hargobind 183
    kharawan or toe-knob sandal of Guru Hargobind 183
    thaal, a copper tray used for serving meals to Guru Hargobind 183
Darbar Sahib 37, 98
Darshani Deodi, *see* Harmandar Sahib
Dasam Granth 17–18, 42, 51, 166–167
Delhi Darbar (1911), 127
Devendra Singh, Raja 155
Dhar, Ganga Ram 54
Dharam Singh, Bhai 62–64, 98, 105–107, 109, 119, 121, 125, 128, 131–133
Dina Nath, Diwan 78
Ditt Singh, Giani 85
Divine Will (*Bhana*) 51, 80
Durrani, Ahmed Shah, invasion of Afghanistan 73
Dyer, R. E. H. Gen. *see also* Jallianwala Bagh massacre, 87

E
East India Company, The 68, 78, 80, 82, 126, 140
    regency of 81
    treaties with 79
Emigrant Sikhs 89–91
Exclusion laws in Canada and the United States 92

F
Farrukh Siyar 54, 69–70

Fateh Singh, Bhai 63–64
Fateh Singh, Sahibzada 54
Fatehgarh Sahib, Gurdwara 54, 76

G

Gajpat Singh, Raja 77, 125, 137
Ganga, Mata 113, 122, 177
Ghadar party 90
Gobind Rai 46–47, 170–171, 173
Gobind Singh, Guru 17–21, 23, 26–27, 29, 38, 40, 46–65, 67, 71, 98–99, 103, 105–106, 118–121, 123, 128, 130–133, 135, 139, 142–143, 146–152, 158–162, 165, 167
    abolished Guruship in human form 71
    arrows of 99
    dresses 99
    historical weapons 99
    hukamnamas of 99
    katar (punch-dagger) of 53
    khanda of 23
    kirpan of 20
    Mata Sundari (widow of) 60
    nishaan (signature) 118
    nuptial ceremony (Anand Karaj) 105
    pahari miniature painting, detail of 19
    painting in the National Museum 99
    received baptism from the five Sikhs 23
    shoes of 99
Golden Temple, *see* Harmandar Sahib
Guddar Singh, Bhai 125–126
Gurbani, 35, 122, 128
Gurchet Singh, Bhai 39, 60, 109
Gurdas, Bhai 36–37, 42, 44
Gurditta, Baba 181
Gurdwara Reform Movement, 87
Gurdwara reforms, 127
Gurmukhi, 6, 24, 33, 149, 152, 162, 165
Guru *Panth*, 21, 23
Guru, 25–27, 29–61
    Amar Das, Guru 33–35
    Angad Dev, Guru 32–33
    Arjan Dev, Guru 36–37
    Gobind Singh, Guru 46–50
    Har Rai, Guru 42–43
    Hargobind, Guru 39
    Harkrishan, Guru 43
    Nanak Dev, Guru 30–32
    Ram Das, Guru 35–36
    Teg Bahadur, Guru 43–45
Guru's Word (*Bani*) 35
Guru-ka-Bagh 88, 90
Guru-ka-Bazaar 35
Guru-Ki-Masit 40
Guru-Shabad, Supremacy Sovereignty and Dignity of 61
Gyan Singh, Giani 86

H

Hamir Singh, Raja 136, 154–155
Har Rai, Guru 42–43, 117, 135, 185, 189, 191
    portrait of 98, 117, 185, 189
Hargobind, Guru 27, 36, 39–44, 49, 52, 60, 71, 97–100, 102–105, 107–111, 114–115, 122, 125, 128–129, 135, 180–188, 190
    cage for the pet birds of 115
    contemporary painting of Guru Hargobind 108
    establishes Akal Takht 39–40, 180
    Guru-ki-Maseet 41
    hukumnamas 98
    katar, or pointed punch-dagger of 187
    khanda, 52
    Kiratpur (new centre of Sikh faith) 42
    Mata Damodri (wife) 181
    Mool Mantra handwritten 114
    Pahari-style painting 190
    release from Gwalior fort 71
    sword of 186
    Tega (broadsword) of 164
    with a hawk (painting), 115
'Hymns of Blood' 31
Hargobindpur 37, 66
Haridhan Singh, Bhai 127–128

Harkrishan, Guru, 43–45, 98
Harmandar Sahib, 22, 29, 35–40, 45, 71–72, 76, 79, 81, 141, 174, 176, 180
Hinduism, 3, 9–11, 14, 29, 33, 50, 83
Hira Singh 156–157
Hola Mahalla festival 24
Holy Quran 54, 57
Hussain, Madho Lal 10

I

Ilahi Baksh, General 78
Iltutmish, Shams-ud-din, Emperor 7
Indian National Army 91
Iradat Khan, 67–68
Islam
    and Hinduism, clash between 3
    brotherhood of 12
    qazis and *maulanas* (priests) 12
    religious-cultural forces of 9

J

Jahangir, Emperor 38, 40, 46
Jainism 3, 11
Jajau, battle of 58
Jalal Khan 68
Jala-ud-Din 64
Jallianwala Bagh massacre (1919) 82, 87, 158
Jamshed Khan 59
Jan Muhammad of Buriya 68
Janamsakhi 6–8, 17, 31–32, 97
Jand Sahib Gurdwara 102
Jaziya (special protection tax) 7
Jihad 67
Jodh Singh, Bhai 87
Jujhar Singh, Bhai 128
Jujhar Singh, Sahibzada 54

K

Kahan Singh, Bhai 86–88, 97, 127, 136
Kalimah 12
Kam Bakhsh 59

Karam Singh, Bhai 63–64, 106, 121
Karam Singh, Raja 139–140
Kartarpur 16, 32, 37, 41, 98, 181
Kashmiri Pandits 45, 47, 52
Khalsa, 8, 21, 23–24, 26–27, 32–33, 48–51, 56, 59, 61, 64–65, 70–72, 75, 77–80, 82, 84–86, 105, 121, 127, 139–140, 161, 167
    concept and dynamics of the, 49
    creation of the, 51–52
    ranks of, 23, 78
    women's rights, 23
Khalsa College Establishment Committee 86
Khalsa Darbar, betrayal of 79
Khalsa Diwan 84–85, 127
Khan, Genghis 6
Khanda (double-edged sword) 52
Khilji dynasty 4
King George V 127
Kirpan 20
Kirtan tradition 17, 127
Ks (five symbols) 24

L

Lahore Singh Sabha 85
Lal Beg 41
Lalo, Bhai 11
Langar (community kitchen) 32–34, 103–104, 109, 111, 125–129, 133, 168–169
Lehna *see* Angad Dev, Guru 14, 22, 32
Lodhi dynasty 4, 8
Lodhi, Ibrahim 6
Hukaman, Mai 140

M

Macauliffe, Max Arthur 86–87
Madho Das 59
Mahan Singh 77, 126, 137
Mahmud Ghazni 4
Mai Rajji da Langar, 125
Malwain, Mai 77, 126, 137, 140
Mani Singh, Bhai 71

Majithia, Sundar Singh 85
Manjis, 34
Massa Ranghar, 72, 174
Massands, authorised representatives, 22–23
Mati Das, Bhai 45–46, 172
Medini Parkash, Raja 48
Mehta Kalu (father of Guru Nanak Dev), 30
Mehtab Singh, 72, 174
Mian Mir, Sain 37
Mir Manu, Lahore Governor, 73, 75
Mir Musalul Khan, *see* Massa Ranghar
Mirza Raja Jai Singh, 43
Mohammad Ghauri, 4
Mohan Singh, Capt. 91
Mohar Singh, Bhai 126
Mohindra College, Patiala 140
Mool Mantra 16, 22, 98, 114, 147
Muktsar, battle of, 64
Mullahs, 9

N
Nabha, custodians at 155–175
    chola, gown of Guru Gobind Singh 159
    dastar (turban) of Guru Gobind Singh 160
    hukamnama of Guru Gobind Singh, (1696) 158
    illuminated folio of the *Dasam Granth* 167
    kangha of Guru Gobind Singh 161
    Mughal style portrait of Guru Tegh Bahadur 163
    opening page of the illuminated *Dasam Granth* 166
    Sri Sahib given by Guru Gobind Singh 162
    Sri Sahib of Guru Gobind Singh 165
    Sri Sahib of Guru Tegh Bahadur, 162
    tega (broadsword) of Guru Hargobind 164
Nadir Shah 72
Namdhari movement, 83
Nanak Dev, Guru 3, 30–32, 97–98
    advent of 8
    and his teachings 17
    beliefs and practices of contemporary Muslims 12
    believed in the organic fusion of spiritual and worldly life 14
    concepts of Nirankar and absolutism 83
    edict of sewa 54
    invasion of Babur 30–31
    Japji Sahib 14
    message of universal love 14
    scientific exposition of creation 93
    Sikhi of 46
    socio-religious implications of revolutionary programme 14
    spiritual experience of God 14
    teachings 10
    travel to Mecca, 12, 28
Nankana Sahib 30, 87
Nanoo Mal, Dewan 140
Narain Singh, Bhai 127
Narinder Singh, Maharaja 140–141
Nasir Khan 53
Nath Yogis 3, 10, 14
Nirankari movement 83
Nizam-ud-Din of Kasur 77
Nur-ud-din Mubarak Ghaznavi 7

O
Occupation of Lahore by the British 126
Operation Blue Star 99, 141

P
Pahul, double-edged sword 56
Painde Khan, 53
Paindha Khan, 41
Pandits 11
Panja Sahib Gurdwara 91
Panjvin Patshahi Gurdwara 177
Panth Prakash 72, 86
Paonta 40, 47–49, 142, 160
Parbandhak Committee 85
Partition of India (1947) 82, 89, 91–93
Pashtun Ghilzai 4
Patiala 14, 20, 44, 135, 137, 139–145, 148, 153, 158–159
    custodians at, 139–153

arrows, given by Guru Gobind Singh 151
char aaina (armour) 142-145
gutka with the *Mool Mantra* inscribed by Guru Gobind Singh, 147
 gutka, illuminated page from 147
 katar (punch dagger) of Guru Gobind Singh, 150
 khanda (forked and serrated) of Guru Gobind Singh 149
 khanda with a wire handle 149
 khanda with an all-steel handle 149
 khanda with faded gold inscriptions 153
 kharawan or the wooden toe-knob sandals of Guru Gobind Singh 150
 kirpan of Guru Gobind Singh 151
 Nishan Sahibs 148
 Safajang (battleaxe) of Guru Gobind Singh 152
 Sri Sahib with a gold handle and hunting scenes 146
 Sri Sahib with an iron handle 146
 Sri Sahib with much-used gold handle 146
 Sri Sahib with silver engravings on the handle 146
 sword given by Jassa Singh Ahluwalia 153
 sword of Guru Tegh Bahadur 146
 sword, shaped like a Gurkha *khukhri* 150
PEPSU (Patiala and East Punjab States Union) 137, 158
Phula Singh, Akali 80
Phulkian States 98, 103, 126, 135–137
 Aala Singh, Baba (1691–1765), 138
 Founders 136
 Gajpat Singh, Raja 137
 Phul, Baba (1627–1690), 135
Prithvi Raj, 7
Prophet Mohammad, 12
Pushpa Devi, Rani 44

Q
Queen Mary 127

Qutb-ud-din Aybak 4, 7

R
Rabaabi kirtania 127
Raghbir Singh, Raja 137
Rai Bhoe-ki-Talwandi, *see* Nankana Sahib
Rai Kalha 55, 139
Raj Kaur, Bibi *see* Mai Malwain
Rakabganj Gurdwara 47
Ram Das, Guru 35–36, 60, 98, 101, 109, 122
 excavation of a *sarovar* 35
 Guru-ka-Bazaar 35
Ram Singh 44, 63, 84, 136
Ram Singh, Baba 64
Ramdaspur 35–36
Ramo, Mai 181
Ranjit Singh 37–38, 73, 77–79, 80–82, 85–86, 99, 126, 137, 141, 155
 Anglo-Sikh Wars, The 80–81
 death of 80–81
 emphasis on educating the girl child 85
Red Fort, The 76, 127
Refugees 89, 92, 141
Ripudaman Singh, Maharaja 86, 88, 155–157
Rup Chand, Bhai 42, 62–64, 96, 101–109, 111, 119–123, 125, 128–129, 132, 135, 157, 181, 185, 188
Rustam Khan 53

S
Sabhraon, battle of 80
Sadiq Begh Khan 125
Sahib Dev, Mata, Nanded 105
Saifuddin Mohammad, Nawab 44
Sain Das, Bhai 180–181
Salehi Chand, Raja 53
Sampuran Singh, Bhai 126
Sandhanwalia, Thakur Singh 84
Sangat 14, 21–23, 42, 59–60, 115, 118, 123
Sant-sipahi, Sikh ethos of 40
Sardar Khan of Chundla 68

Sarkar Khalsa 78, 123
Sati Das, Bhai 45–46, 172
Sepoy Mutiny, The (1857) 82
Sewa, practice of 22
Shabad 18, 20, 22–23, 25–26, 37–38, 51, 61, 86, 97
Shah Jahan 41
Shahab-ud-din, King of Ghazni 7
Shahadat, Islamic concept of 46
Shaikh Ahmad Sirhindi Mujaddid-i-alif-sani 40
Sharia (Islamic religious law) 6
Shia-Sunni division 3
Shiromani Gurdwara Parbandhak Committee 88, 177
Siddhas 8, 10
Sikandar Lodhi 4
Sikh commonwealth 77, 84
Sikh Cultural Museum 98
Sikh History and Ethos 168
Sikh Panth 34, 38
Sikh sangat, 14, 34, 42, 44
Sikh soldiers participation in World War I, 90
Sikh theology, thoughts of 56
Sikh Wars of 1840s 80, 140
Sikhi, spirit of 29–61, 93
Sikhism 3, 8–9, 14–15, 17, 19, 22–23, 25–26, 29, 37–38, 42, 73, 78, 80, 83–84, 87, 93, 102, 109–110, 125
    acceptance of the plurality of faiths, 37
    essentially a religion of *Naam* (Name), 38
    Guru is the central concept and theme in, 26
    insisted upon disciplined spirituality, 15
    law of karma, 19
    self-realisation, 17
Singh Sabha movement 83–87, 127
    objectives identified by the Singh Sabha, 84
    purity of Sikh precept and practice, 83
    reform of Sikh ceremonial observances, 83
    reformation of Sikh shrines, 84
Sirhind, conquest of 64–65
Sis Ganj Gurdwara 46, 127

Siyar, Farrukh 68, 70
Socio-religious environment 8–15
    Bhakti movement 8–9
    Buddhism 11
    Hatha Yoga 10
    Jainism 11
    Naths *yogis* 10
    Siddha tradition 8–9
    Sufism 8–9
Sri Guru Granth Sahib 4, 6, 17–18, 20, 22–23, 26–27, 29, 37, 45, 60–61, 71, 79, 98, 116, 124, 127, 133, 145, 156, 177
Sukarchakia, Charhat Singh 76
Sukha Singh 21, 72, 156, 174
Sundri, Mata 71, 99, 121
Supreme Will 20
Surati, Bibi 101–102
Sursinghwala, custodians at 185–191
    Katar, of Guru Hargobind 187
    Mughal-style painting of Bhai Bidhi Chand 184
    Pahari-style portrait of Guru Hargobind 190
    Pahari-style painting of Guru Har Rai 189
    Pahari-style portrait of Guru Har Rai 185
    Portrait of Guru Hargobind 188
Syed Badr-ud-din, *see* Pir Budhu Shah

T

Takht Sri Keshgarh Sahib 50, 54, 58, 99
Talok Singh, Baba 64
Tarn Taran 37
Tegh Bahadur, Guru 43–47, 52, 56, 60, 64, 67, 104, 132, 146–147, 162–163, 170–171, 173
    contemporary painting from Dhaka 98
    Darbar at Anandpur Sahib 171
    martyrdom of 172
    receiving the news of the birth of his son 170
Teja Singh, Professor 87, 127
Temple of God, *see* Golden Temple
Timur-e-lang 4, 6
Tirah expedition (1897), 157
Tripta, Mata (mother of Guru Nank Dev), 30s

U
Udasi, Sundar Das 88

V
Victoria Memorial Museum, Calcutta 98
Vir Singh, Bhai 86–87
Vivekananda, Swami 50

W
Wada Ghalughara 75
Wahdat-ul-wujud (unity of being) 13
Wasil Beg 59
Wazir Khan 53, 59, 64–65, 67, 106, 121
World War II 82, 90

Y
Yadavindra Singh, Maharaja 141
Yahiya Khan 73
Yogic mysticism 19

Z
Zafarnama 49, 56–58, 105
Zain Khan 76, 139, 155
Zakariya Khan 70, 72–73
Zamindari system, abolition of 66
Zorawar Singh (Sahibzada) 54